WOODCARVING TOOLS, MATERIALS & EQUIPMENT

VOLUME 1

WOODCARVING TOOLS, MATERIALS & EQUIPMENT

NEW EDITION

VOLUME 1

CHRIS PYE

GUILD OF MASTER CRAFTSMAN PUBLICATIONS LTD

First edition published 1994 by
Guild of Master Craftsman Publications Ltd
Castle Place, 166 High Street,
Lewes, East Sussex BN7 1XU

Reprinted 1996, 1997, 2000

This new edition in two volumes 2002

Reprinted 2003, 2007

Text © Christopher J. Pye 1994, 2002
© in the Work GMC Publications 2002
Principal photography by Chris Skarbon,
© GMC Publications 2002;
other photography as listed on page 234
Line drawings © Christopher J. Pye 1994, 2002,
except where otherwise stated

ISBN-13: 978-1-86108-201-5 (Volume 1)
ISBN-10: 1-86108-201-0 (Volume 1)
ISBN 1-86108-202-9 (Volume 2)
(ISBN 0-946819-49-1 first edition)

A catalogue record for this book is available from the British Library.

Edited by Stephen Haynes
Designed by Ian Hunt Design
Cover design by Danny McBride
Cover photograph by Anthony Bailey, © GMC Publications 2002
Set in Goudy and Trajan

Colour origination by Viscan Graphics (Singapore)
Printed and bound by Kyodo Printing (Singapore)

For
GINO MASERO
Master Woodcarver

Gino Masero's hands

CONTENTS OF VOLUME 1

OUTLINE OF VOLUME 2

MEASUREMENTS

Although care has been taken to ensure that the metric measurements are true and accurate, they are only conversions from imperial; they have been rounded up or down to the nearest whole millimetre, or to the nearest convenient equivalent in cases where the imperial measurements themselves are only approximate.

HEALTH AND SAFETY

Notes on safety are found throughout this book. They are gathered together here for reference, with no apology for repetition. No claim is made for completeness, as full, or particular, circumstances cannot be accounted for.

The best safeguard against accidents is mindfulness. It is lack of concentration and forethought that causes most accidents. For example, putting your hand on the edge of a projecting gouge: what actually caused the accident was not the gouge, but the attitude that placed it dangerously in the first place. Lack of experience is also important. An effort should be made to understand and familiarize yourself with all tools and equipment before using them in earnest.

Safety lies in:

- being in control

- being aware of the dangers

- not being distracted

- not being over-confident

- gaining experience.

GENERAL SAFETY PRECAUTIONS

IN THE WORKSHOP

- Stand at the entrance to the workplace with a notepad and challenge yourself to think of all the ways you could be hurt in the space in front of you, including the tools and equipment.

- Keep a fully stocked first aid box easily accessible.

- Remember that there are even more possibilities for accidents when children and visitors enter the workplace.

- All electric wires should be installed, earthed and covered properly.

- Store and arrange tools and equipment safely, securely and conveniently.

- A fire alarm and extinguisher should always be installed.

- The carver's environment tends to be dry and contain inflammable wood chips, finishing agents, etc. Never leave a naked flame unattended. No smoking is the best advice. If you need to use a source of heat, first make sure it is safe.

- Bag up and remove dust and debris regularly, especially any rags used for finishing.

- Use and store solvents, glues, turpentine, spirit- and oil-based stains, as well as all other finishes, in well-ventilated areas. Keep containers closed when not in use, and keep them away from children, heat and naked flames.

- Make sure that where you walk is free from the danger of sharp edges and corners, things to bump into and wires to trip over. See that you can easily and safely work around your bench, and that wood chips and dust on the floor do not make it slippery.

- Sharp tools left clamped in vices with their tangs or edges exposed, or projecting in the air over the bench, are dangerous.

- Long hair, etc. should be tied back, and loose clothing (cuffs and ties) and jewellery (necklaces and rings) should be kept away from the moving parts of machines, and in general out of the sphere of activity.

ELECTRIC TOOLS AND EQUIPMENT

- Always follow the manufacturer's instructions and recommendations.

- Familiarize yourself with any tool or piece of equipment before using it.

- Safety guards, rests, etc. should be properly adjusted and used.

- Keep hands and fingers well clear of moving parts – remember that accidents happen quickly, sometimes before you have noticed anything wrong. Never reach over or across machines.

- Double-check everything, including the locking of chucks, the table, or any fence before starting the machine.

- Face or eye protection is always advisable. Grit and sparks are quite capable of penetrating the eyeball; chips of wood can fly off; and it is possible for a cutter or burr to break.

- Keep face masks and eye and ear protection easily to hand – and put them on before using the equipment.

- Fix work securely before drilling, power-shaping, and so on.

- Keep wiring from machines and electrical hand tools neatly out of the way, not trailing over the floor or work surfaces.

- Always sharpen, or change, a blade or cutter with the machine isolated – that is, with the plug pulled out.

- Do not drip water from the cooling jar over motors, electrical connections or plugs.

- Use a cutter or other accessories for a high-speed shaft at or below its maximum rated speed. Used above the speed for which it is designed, the cutter could fly apart, bend or otherwise be damaged.

- Never use a bent or damaged cutter or burr, or one that vibrates or chatters, in a high-speed flexible shaft – throw these away. Never force or pressure these accessories.

SAFETY PRECAUTIONS FOR WOODCARVERS

Again, many of these points occur in context in this book and should be studied there.

- Always hold work securely to a stable bench or surface.

- Do not lay carving tools down with their edges projecting, or close to where your hands are working.

- Keep your tools sharp and clean. Blunt tools require more force – sharp ones are less dangerous.

- Keep both hands, and all fingers, behind the cutting edge at all times.

- Never cut, or exert pressure, towards any part of the body.

- A tough glove is recommended when rasps are being used. A fingerless glove will protect the heels of the hands when working on wood with rough or sharp edges.

- Take particular care when using the benchstrop, especially on the forward stroke.

- Both hands should be on the carving tool, with the blade hand resting on the wood. The only exceptions to this are during mallet work and when using specific one-handed carving techniques.

- If using one hand to hold the work and the other to manipulate the chisel, use the thumb of the work-holding hand as a pivot or guide to control the cutting – never cut towards the work-holding hand.

- In vigorous mallet work, especially with very hard, brittle or old and dry woods, eye protection is advisable.

- Never try to catch a falling carving tool. Carve in footwear strong enough to protect the feet from such an event.

- When sanding, use a dust mask; never blow; and protect your eyes.

There are two other conditions which can affect carvers, besides the obvious family of accidents:

HAND AND WRIST DAMAGE

Hand and wrist damage caused by thumping tool handles with the palm of the hand is mentioned in the section on using mallets (Volume 2, Chapter 1). The damage can be permanent, so it is sensible to avoid the risk by using a mallet instead.

REPETITIVE STRAIN INJURY

RSI is felt as a burning sensation in the wrist or elbow joints of those prone to it, possibly accompanied by redness and swelling. It is commonly known as 'tennis elbow' or condylitis. The condition is caused by mechanical stress on a tendon attachment, especially through holding or repeating the same tense position of the joint for long periods of time. Seek medical advice early; this is important for reasons of health insurance.

It can be a slow condition to clear up, and may be incapacitating in the long term. On the other hand, there are forearm straps which can remove strain from the elbow and help full recovery. Do not imagine that the problem has gone, just because you have taken painkillers. Besides removing the strain from the joint, you will need to find new techniques of working which eliminate, or at least reduce, strain. Fortunately there is plenty of scope for this in woodcarving.

FOREWORD TO THE FIRST EDITION

I first met Chris Pye in 1974, shortly after I had moved from London to Sussex. In my newly acquired rural workshop, sited among blossoming apple trees, we took stock of one another across a carving bench, and became friends. I was on the verge of possible retirement, while Chris was in the early stages of his career, but it has always seemed remarkable how a common interest in woodcarving can quickly bridge any age gap.

Although having an irrepressible sense of humour, he struck me as being a thoughtful and studious person, an adept carver and with the ability to express himself well on craft matters – a rare combination.

Since those days in the early 1970s he has taught carving and developed into a designer-craftsman of some stature. This has been borne out by the creation of a very successful carving and woodturning business in the south-west of England, which thrived despite the recession.

As a woodcarving instructor myself, over the years I have made a point of reading through many craft books and periodicals on the subject, but only at intervals did I find something of major interest that I could pass on to students. There seemed to be a certain lack of vital information published, and to some degree it troubled me.

To be taught by a caring expert is the best possible way of learning a craft, and Chris Pye is foremost in this, being blessed with friendliness as well as approachability, and a genuine interest in his students, talented and otherwise. For the amateur, who for one good reason or another has to go it alone, it can be conceded that with some ability, carving is not too onerous in the initial stage (after all, our palaeolithic ancestors did not do too badly carving bone and ivory figurines). But major and minor problems can soon arise, often leading to frustration and despair. Setbacks tend to occur when the student, naturally, wants to progress towards more ambitious work. Apart from the inevitable problems that stem from lack of technique, the most serious difficulties, I have found, arise from trying to carve with blunt tools, or even damaged ones. So it was a most welcome and splendid surprise when Chris sent to me the outline of his book on carving tools, materials and a whole range of equipment that traditional and modern carvers require for their work.

Even at the initial stage I was happily aware of a very closely researched and comprehensive source book, packed with information, and with sketches and photos galore. I believe that it is a most useful work, and can only anticipate that it will be widely read, so increasing student potential, as well as obtaining for them the maximum enjoyment that a truly great craft can offer.

Gino Masero
December 1993

FOREWORD TO THE
NEW EDITION

By the middle of the twentieth century the craft of woodcarving in the English-speaking world had dwindled, largely because the use of traditional ornament and the making of accurate figure sculpture had fallen out of fashion. It was continued in a handful of workshops satisfying a limited market for architectural and furniture ornament, and in those involved in the restoration of cathedrals and other historic buildings. People like Gino Masero, who guided Chris Pye, and William Wheeler, who taught me, were among the few who were willing and able to pass on their skills to outsiders. For the most part, woodcarving became the preserve of the amateur and the folk carver. Most of the amateurs were self-taught, or were instructed by the self-taught. In many cases in their teaching and writing they passed on bad habits and were ignorant of the methods and standards of the earlier master carvers. In a book by one such, I once read that oak was too hard to carve; the writer thereby dismissed most of the woodcarving done in medieval Europe, including great works of ornament and sculpture. Most recommended the use of sandpaper as a remedy for a rough finish, even on carvings where the effect would be to reduce the forms to lifelessness while consuming inordinate time and effort.

Since first encountering the writings of Chris Pye about carving and the carver's tools, I have valued and respected his ideas. Like me, he sets the greatest store by the old and well-tried ways using hand tools, but when some new development arises he is willing to employ it, provided it produces the desired result and saves time.

We all know people who collect gadgets, every time hoping that the new acquisition will prove the carver's panacea, the one magic tool that will effortlessly turn them into brilliant carvers. In the real world this does not happen. There is no substitute for study through drawing and a sequence of planned exercises supervised by good teachers – in other words, for hard work. However, down the centuries carving tools have evolved, each new shape being a solution to a carver's problem. Mostly the carvers were aiming to save time, to produce clean work and to be able to carve more sophisticated shapes. By now, the number and variety of tools and ancillary equipment is so bewildering that a book such as this is invaluable both for the novice wondering what is needed to start and for the experienced carver wishing to extend his or her range.

This new edition is an enlarged and up-to-date version of a book that has already become a most useful reference work. It is all-embracing and accurate in its content, and full of intelligence and good sense. It may not be a magic gadget but, used intelligently, it will set you on the way to carving well.

Dick Onians
September 2001

ACKNOWLEDGEMENTS

When I cast my mind, like a net, over all the people who have, in whatever way, contributed to this book, I soon realized that my gratitude must extend more widely than I have room to record. In fact there seems no end to those who have influenced me.

For example, I would include the makers of every carving I have ever gazed at, their patrons and toolmakers. Then there are those who have taught me, whose workshops I have visited, and who have shared their experience with me. And the authors of books and articles I have read, some long dead but whose thoughts I have taken as my own. And the carvers whose names appear as watery shadows on the handles of many of my tools, but of whom I know little or nothing at all. And students, whose names I have forgotten, who made me think about what I was telling them and why – and who caused me to write the original sheets on which this book is based. I want to acknowledge my debt to all these.

Foremost among them all must come the indefatigable Gino Masero, who oversaw my initial attempts at sharpening, and witnessed the first time I laid a cutting edge into a piece of limewood. His spirited friendship was a source of great joy, and I dedicate this book to him – an inadequate gesture of appreciation.

In the genesis of the book itself I am particularly grateful to my editor, Liz Inman, whose encouragement and enthusiasm really made the book possible.

In its preparation I took up the time of many people who freely gave me information, ideas and advice, and sometimes the tools and equipment themselves to try out: Tony Walker of Robert Sorby Ltd; Bill Tilbrook of Tilgear; John Tiranti of Alec Tiranti Ltd; Barry Martin of Henry Taylor Tools Ltd; Tony Iles of Ashley Iles (Edge Tools) Ltd; Charles Stirling of Bristol Design; Peter Peck of Record Tools; and Glynn Bilson of HTF Tools. I also thank Ray Gonzalez for the idea of numbering gouge handles to indicate particular circle arcs.

Coming closer to home, I would catch, as it were in a quick gather of the net, some of the many people who so generously gave their time to read through different parts and made helpful corrections and suggestions: Stephen Parr, Tony Walker, Candy Harrison and Ken Day. I would very much like to thank Gino Masero again for his efforts in this respect, as well as for the use of his drawings of the tilting portable bench. As for my good friend Phil Hutchins who, having no interest in carving whatsoever, took the role of an objective reader – his effort on my behalf can only be described as heroic. I am also very grateful to Phyllis van de Hoek who made life a lot easier by tirelessly photocopying the drawings.

And in my net, saving the loveliest catch till last, my wife Karin Vogel, who has put up with such a lot as I wrestled with several learning curves and has given me unstinting support in the background. I sincerely wish to thank her for her help and patience.

Since the first edition appeared, my mentor and friend Gino Masero has died, leaving only flashes of scaly lights in the mesh. It's a real pleasure to improve on what he started, and I am sorry he didn't have a chance to see this book in colour – he'd have loved it.

Many firms have given generous help in updating this book, both by making tools and equipment available and by freely giving advice and information. In particular I thank: Barry and Tony Iles of Ashley Iles (Edge Tools) Ltd; Alan Styles of Axminster Power Tool Centre; Geoff and Martin Brown of BriMarc Associates; Douglas Ballantyne of Carroll Tools Ltd; Nick Davidson of Craft Supplies Ltd; Clair Brewer of Bosch Ltd; Brenda Keely of Dremel UK; David Bennet of Falls Run Tools; Hegner UK; Rod Naylor; Dennis Abdy of Henry Taylor Tools Ltd; Richard Starkie of Starkie & Starkie; Mike Hancock of The Toolshop; and Wally Wilson of Veritas Tools Inc.

Special thanks to Stephen Haynes for his sharp eye and sedulous, but caring, editing; Chris Skarbon for his sympathetic photography; and Ian Hunt and Danny McBride, the book and cover designers.

That loveliest catch just grows more so.

INTRODUCTION

In the 1980s I wrote a set of handouts on carving tools and sharpening for students in the adult education evening class which I was teaching. I wrote them to fill in a shortcoming I found in woodcarving books at the time. Years later, I still felt students were inadequately supplied with basic information on tools and sharpening, and that was why I enlarged these notes into book form. I was very pleased to find that this book was well received and proved useful to many carvers, both beginners and those with more experience. And now, a few more years on, I have had a chance to revise and refresh all this material and bring it up to date. I feel that the majority of what I wrote remains as true, pertinent and valuable as before, but there have been changes in some specific areas – different sharpening stones and methods, and new power tools, for example – which I have taken the opportunity to include in this new edition.

Most carvers today (in Britain at least) are individuals carving in their leisure time, and most will have learned about carving and carving tools from books – the apprentice system having long been unavailable. On the whole, books about carving tend to treat the subjects of sharpening and handling carving tools in a rather perfunctory way, as a chapter to be got through before you begin carving something – anything – quickly.

A medieval Green Man from southern Germany. Fewer tools, and of less variety, were in use at this time; perhaps this in itself gives the design its robustness and energy

There seems to be an assumption that competence in sharpening and handling tools grows naturally with experience of carving, but this is far from the case with the majority of beginners. Often they are only able to spend intermittent hours at their craft, and a great deal of frustration – if not despair – arises in students as a result of their inability to care for, sharpen and use their tools properly, and to work comfortably with their chosen material. This frustration affects the way they carve, as well as the final carving itself.

There are other consequences too, including the greatly increased use of sandpaper as an expedient (rather than for its legitimate use of abstractly bringing out the grain). Then there is the growth in sales of pre-sharpened tools and the increased marketing of electrical sharpening systems, which, to be used properly, still rely on experience.

Some of the carvers who have learned from the type of books referred to above end up writing books themselves, and repeat a pattern that downgrades and minimizes carving-tool skills, which are in fact an essential foundation for good carving. It is not that this kind of information *cannot* be written down, or that there is no information to be had. If the scanty bits about carving tools, equipment and sharpening – in books, magazines and manufacturers' leaflets – are added up, there seems to be plenty to read. But the information is superficial, incomplete and without due emphasis on the basics. Students continually appear with badly sharpened tools, and are frustrated with their work and progress, even though they have lots of carving books. There is something missing: an attitude or approach.

This book is my attempt to describe, as completely as possible, what tools and equipment are available to the woodcarver – particularly those specific to carving – together with the fundamental skills of caring for them, sharpening them, and using them to a high standard. By concentrating on tools first, I am acknowledging a fundamental truth about woodcarving: the tools and the carving are inseparable – as inseparable as the hands and mind.

These techniques and approaches to sharpening woodcarving tools represent a long tradition, but have been around for a long time only because they work. If they did not, they would have been dropped long ago. This does not mean that they cannot be bettered, but I feel it is a mistake to drop them for something less effective.

I have presented several sorts of information in these two volumes: some practical information and advice which is vitally and immediately useful, especially for beginners; some reference information

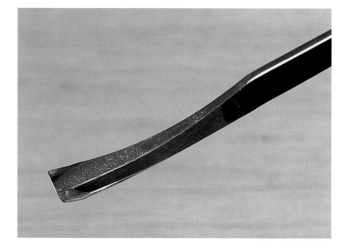

Carving tools have been called 'extensions of the carver's hands'. They transmit the carver's vision into the wood

which will be lying in wait for a particular need, filling gaps as experience increases; and some information that is simply intended to be interesting, enlarging the general pool of knowledge for all levels of carvers. Volume 1 deals with the selection and sharpening of woodcarving chisels and gouges – what I think of as 'woodcarving tools' proper. Volume 2 is concerned with the other tools used in woodcarving, and with other matters of fundamental importance to the carver: modifying tools for specific purposes; the workplace and its accessories; wood itself; wood finishing; and how to approach the design aspect of woodcarving.

It must be pointed out that in this book there is an element of personal opinion – descriptions of *my* way of doing or seeing things. I make no apologies for this. Carvers do vary in their approach and about what they think is important; they have their own habits, which work for them, and ultimately each individual must arrive at his or her own conclusions. For example, I have had to make some decisions about what to call things – I might call a spade a spade, but others have different names. I have tried to set down clearly what is meant by a particular technical term, and, where there are common alternatives, to make

Finely made carving tools have an elegance and purposeful beauty all of their own

sure these are mentioned. Terms in bold type are explained in the Glossary of woodcarving terms at the end of Volume 2.

These two volumes will complement and support your carving, but they do not contain carving projects as such. Carving itself, in its various aspects, is the subject of my other books. My aim here is to present enough concrete information on how, when and where woodcarving tools are used, on qualities of wood, and on how these factors relate, to enable someone either to start or to improve their carving.

As more and more people are taking up wood-carving – and for many of these being in a workshop, or handling any tools, is a new experience – I have felt it necessary to emphasize safety as an important aspect of carving. Please pay attention to such details.

Each part starts with a set of 'aims' for that part. Besides outlining what I hope to communicate, these sections also serve as an introduction to more general concepts, ideas and attitudes. I believe that the attitudes and mental states which underlie what we do are as important as the actions themselves, and it is guidance on attitudes that I wish to put across, as much as technical, practical information. As a consequence, I sincerely hope for nothing more than that this book results in a more satisfying experience of woodcarving for the reader – and ultimately, of course, more satisfying carvings.

A detail of The Banquet at Simon's *(1490–2) by Tilman Riemenschneider. Uncomplicated but effective tool cuts to the edge of Mary's hood are typical of this carver. The hair is carved with fluidity, and falls like liquid*

PART I

UNDERSTANDING WOODCARVING TOOLS

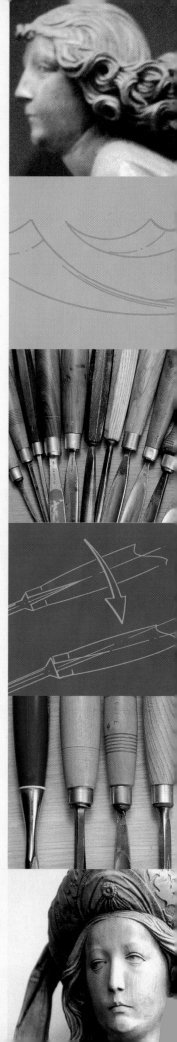

AIMS OF PART I

- To help sort out the wide variety of shapes that are found among woodcarving tools, and describe their purposes

- To describe what a woodcarving tool consists of, and how it 'works'

- To show how to assess the quality of a carving tool in order to know exactly what is being bought

- To show how the shapes of carving tools relate to their function

- To consider some recent innovations in carving tools

- To advise on the care of woodcarving tools

- To promote, through understanding, a degree of confidence in the use of woodcarving tools

I will begin by considering in a little more detail each of these aims in turn.

The wide variety of shapes found among woodcarving tools, and their purposes

By **woodcarving tools** I mean specifically the many different kinds of chisels and gouges which are designed expressly for woodcarving; other tools which are commonly used by carvers are considered separately in Part III. The vast choice of chisels and gouges is often one of the first things to bewilder a newcomer to carving – indeed, one manufacturer has the ability to make over 2,000 different shapes and sizes – and even this range is not complete. A degree of confusion may also arise in some woodcarvers who, although they have been carving for some time, started with a few randomly bought tools, and in beginners who have been given a boxed set of tools and are looking to expand their range. All of these people, and others, may be unsure as to whether the specific tools they need are available, or whether a particular tool might meet their requirements. Fortunately there is a system for finding what you need (Chapter 1).

What a woodcarving tool consists of, and how it 'works'

It is a cliché that, when someone joins the army, before they can even think of firing their brand-new rifle, they are made to take it apart – then 'politely' asked to put it back together again. Then to take it apart… This is not as meaningless as it might at first appear; it establishes a deep familiarity with the weapon at an early stage, a confidence which may prove life-saving. The key points here are that if you have an intimate knowledge of the tools on which your skill is based, are thoroughly familiar with them, unafraid of them, and even feel free to alter their shape if you want (see Volume 2, Chapter 3) – all this adds enormously to your confidence as a carver. And through confidence comes competence (Chapters 2 and 3).

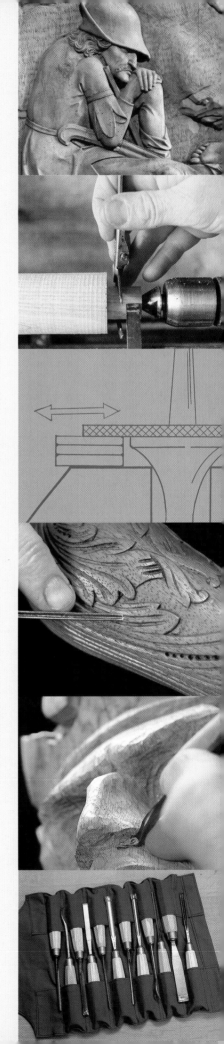

Assessing the quality of a carving tool, and knowing exactly what is being bought

It is very important to appreciate a good carving tool when you see one, and just as important to avoid one of inferior quality. There are some tools on the market which are so badly made as to be worse than useless. There are others of excellent steel but badly shaped; these, with a little attention, can be greatly improved – both in how they feel and how they work. There are also perfect tools which a carver will almost venerate. We will look at factors which decide this (Chapter 4).

How the shapes of carving tools relate to their function

You may only need one or two tools for a certain job, or you may need a small range to start woodcarving seriously. You may be tempted by sets, special offers or old woodcarving gouges in shops. Knowing what a particular tool can do will help you buy only those that you need, and so avoid ending up with tools that are rarely, or never, used (Chapter 5).

Innovations in woodcarving tools

Woodcarving is a highly creative craft and it is little surprise that the creative people involved find new ways of working, and new tools with which to do it. Many such innovations remain private; others become more widely available. Woodcarving firms are interested in tapping the carving market, and apply their designers to solving problems in new and marketable ways. We carvers benefit from both these sources of new tools but, when it comes to buying any tool, traditional or modern, you need to know what it can do for you – how it can help your carving. Only time will sort out the apparently useful from the really useful (Chapter 6).

The care of woodcarving tools

I have some carving tools which are well over 100 years old; they have the names of several previous owners stamped on the handles. It is sobering to think that you never really own a woodcarving tool – you only have custody and care of it. Eventually it will pass on to someone else who will use it and, hopefully, also take care of it and use it to create many beautiful works.

   If you want a more prosaic reason for looking after your woodcarving tools, they represent quite an investment – of money and time – and are a major contributor to job satisfaction (Chapter 7).

Promoting a degree of confidence in the use of woodcarving tools

When all these points are assimilated, along with those in Part II on sharpening, a feeling and understanding for your woodcarving tools will be established which will underpin both the quality of your work and your enjoyment of carving – and this applies whether you will be carving full time, or just need one tool for a particular purpose.

CHAPTER ONE

TYPES OF WOODCARVING TOOL

AIMS

- To help sort out the wide variety of shapes that are found among woodcarving tools, and describe their purposes

- To explain the numbering systems used by manufacturers to identify the various types

FINDING YOUR WAY AROUND

If you had wanted a tool for carving wood before the Industrial Revolution, you would have needed a willing blacksmith to make you one – and not just any smith, but a metalsmith with the fairly specialized knowledge to make these unusual tools.

In the past, tools were far more precious than they appear to us today, both in terms of what they cost and their comparative scarcity (Figs 1.1–1.3). Having gone to some trouble and expense to have tools made, their owners did not consider them disposable; they would be passed down from master to apprentice, or be kept within a family. They were valued as a key to earning a living in a way that is not easy for us to appreciate. Combining tools with a marketable skill, like carving, ensured a place in what was a harsh world; and proficiency in a craft, even if it would never make you wealthy, was very important when there was little in the way of financial lifelines. It is

Fig 1.1 *This expressive Tudor head in Abbey Dore Church, Herefordshire, shows the simple, decisive tool marks of a skilled worker in oak*

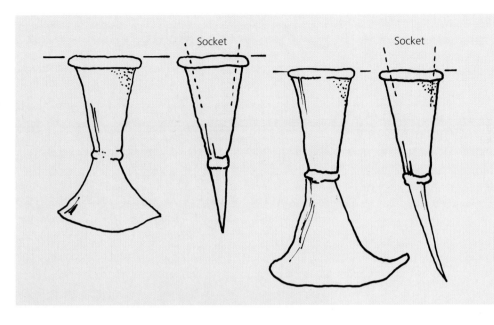

Fig 1.2 *These small socketed chisels were found near Cardiff and are now in the National Museum of Wales. They took a skilled Bronze Age smith time and trouble to make*

Fig 1.3 *Panelwork at Abbey Dore Church which has been vigorously executed with a few simple tools*

interesting to note that the term *craft* has its roots in the Anglo-Saxon word for 'strength in skill'.

Pre-industrial carvers would have particular tools made, some for general work and others for special commissions. In this way an assorted collection of tools would be built up relatively slowly over a life-time. Eventually these tools would be passed on. Such carvers would have thought they were entering a magical cave, full of priceless treasures, if they could see the variety, consistency and ready availability of today's woodcarving tools.

Transported into our replete tool shops, carvers from the pre-industrial past would certainly be able to pick out familiar carving tools, as well as having an

understanding of what the more recently developed ones are for. This would probably be true of any carver from the 4,300 years since the date of one of the earliest surviving woodcarvings – the so-called *Sheikh-el-Beled*, an Egyptian carving in acacia wood dating from the Fifth Dynasty (Fig 1.4). The reason is that the carving and shaping of wood has always involved, and always will involve, overcoming the same fundamental problems inherent in the material. The tools used then would still be appropriate today.

The proliferation of written information about carving is a very recent phenomenon. Carvers of the past would have been taught by true masters of the craft. They in

Fig 1.4 *A dry Egyptian tomb kept this woodcarving of a nobleman from deteriorating, although it has split from shrinkage. Made about 2300 BCE, its great presence and workmanship speak of a well-established craft*

turn would carefully impart trade secrets – closely guarded knowledge – to their apprentices and pupils (Figs 1.5 and 1.6). It is only since World War II that, in Britain at least, the whole tradition of bestowed carving expertise has virtually died out; the last flowering of an innovative 'school' of carving design was that of Art Nouveau, in the years leading up to World War I. This means that those who decide to take up carving today rarely have the chance of intimate access to another carver – someone who will show them the way of the tools, what types there are, how to sharpen and use them to accomplish an intention. The newcomer may be left in the same magical cave of choice, not knowing how to find his or her way around it.

The Industrial Revolution, with its commercial competition, brought the capacity to manufacture a large variety of tools relatively easily. By Victorian times there was the need to satisfy a large and growing

Fig 1.6 *Tilman Riemenschneider's virtuosity placed great demands on the tools available to him. A wide range of sophisticated shapes must have been needed to get into the deep recesses of this angel, part of the limewood* Elevation of the Magdalene *(1490–2), now in the Bayerisches Nationalmuseum, Munich*

number of trade carvers as well as, for the first time, leisured 'gentleman' and 'lady' carvers. The making of woodcarving tools still involved a large degree of hands-on skill, but the numbers and variety of shapes became enormous. By the second half of the nineteenth century a regular catalogue was needed; it was published in the tool-making heart of England and was known as the *Sheffield Illustrated List*.

THE SHEFFIELD LIST

The Sheffield List began as an illustrated price list of the tools and related products being made in Sheffield at the time. Later editions introduced numerical codes to identify particular tools, and, as far as carving tools are concerned, these soon became a recognized, standard system of nomenclature across Britain (Fig 1.7). It is still trade practice to use this numbering system, either as a whole or with some small variations. To some extent a similar system, or a version of it, is followed in other countries.

Fig 1.5 *An outer door in Berkeley Castle, Gloucestershire; the clear, but quite subtle, carving speaks of a long tradition*

This numbering system, which will be described here, will enable you to recognize quite easily 'what's what' within the diverse range of carving tools available – particularly those made in Britain. However, the Sheffield listing is generally only accepted as a guide – individual tools made by different manufacturers may vary, as we shall see. Some firms may add further digits to the number to specify an additional attribute of the tool such as the overall length of blade. For example, a firm may list a longer 'workman's' or 'professional' size of tool next to an 'amateur's' size. This presumably dates from the Victorian expectation that 'ladies' and 'gentlemen' would use more refined and delicate tools for their hobby.

Continental catalogues usually arrange the tool shapes in clusters, one nesting within another, though the range of shapes is essentially the same as in British catalogues where the shapes are spread across the page. Many people find the spread-out chart easier to follow.

An important term to introduce at this stage is the **sweep**, which refers to the curvature of a gouge when this is part of a circle. More will be said on this later (pages 26–31).

NUMERICAL DESCRIPTION

When you pick up a carving tool, look for a number, normally stamped on the shank just beyond the handle (Figs 1.8 and 1.9). Associated with this number will be the manufacturer's name and/or logo, and sometimes the place of manufacture as well. All specialist woodcarving-tool manufacturers in Britain today put such details on, as do those of repute abroad. In fact, generally speaking, this is a good first check on the quality of a tool: if the tool has no stamp on it, then either it is individually hand-made or the maker did not think it worth acknowledging. (Although it should be said that many excellent older makes are not numbered – and it is still not unusual to find good second-hand tools made before the numbering system was introduced.) The number will also appear in the manufacturer's catalogue, and it is

worth having a few of these on file to compare sizes and shapes. Addresses of major manufacturers and suppliers can be found in the advertising pages of magazines such as *Woodcarving*.

This numbering system is essentially a shorthand description of a particular woodcarving tool:

THE BASIC NUMBERING SYSTEM

Number	Shape	
(0)1	Straight flat chisels	
(0)2	Straight skew chisels (corner chisels)	
(0)3–11	Straight gouges	
12–20	Longbent (swan-neck) gouges	
21	Shortbent chisels	
22	Right shortbent corner chisels	
23	Left shortbent corner chisels	
24–32	Shortbent gouges	
33–38	Backbent gouges	
39	Straight	60° (medium) parting tools
40	Longbent	
43	Shortbent	
41	Straight	45° (deep) parting tools
42	Longbent	
44	Shortbent	
45	Straight	90° (shallow) parting tools
46	Longbent	

The appearance of any carving tool is a combination of three factors:

- the *width* of the blade;

- the shape of the blade in *cross section*;

- the shape of the blade along its length (the *longitudinal section*).

NUMBER

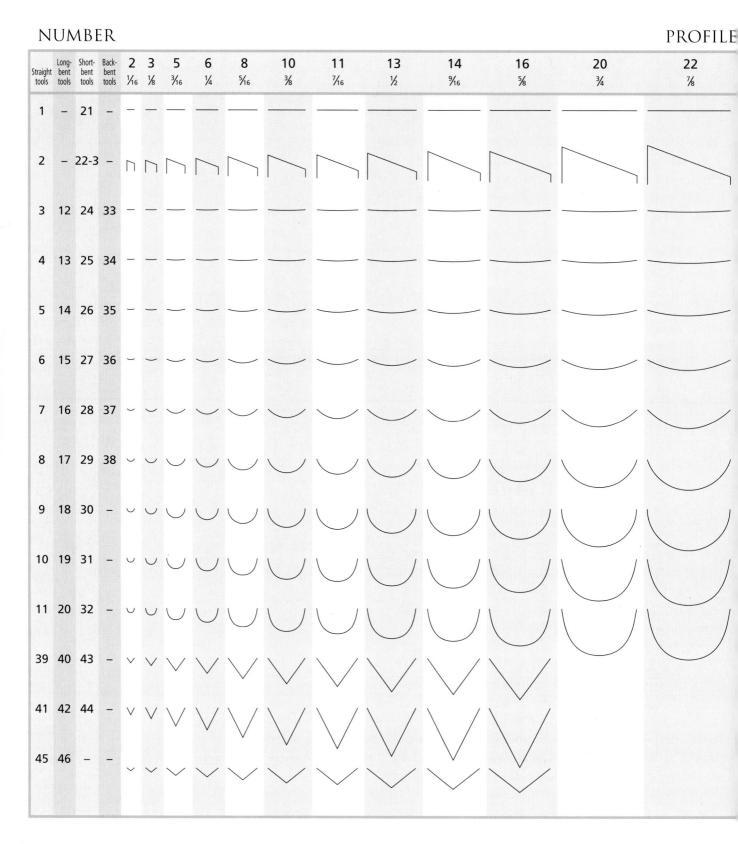

Straight tools	Long-bent tools	Short-bent tools	Back-bent tools	2 1/16	3 1/8	5 3/16	6 1/4	8 5/16	10 3/8	11 7/16	13 1/2	14 9/16	16 5/8	20 3/4	22 7/8
1	–	21	–												
2	–	22-3	–												
3	12	24	33												
4	13	25	34												
5	14	26	35												
6	15	27	36												
7	16	28	37												
8	17	29	38												
9	18	30	–												
10	19	31	–												
11	20	32	–												
39	40	43	–												
41	42	44	–												
45	46	–	–												

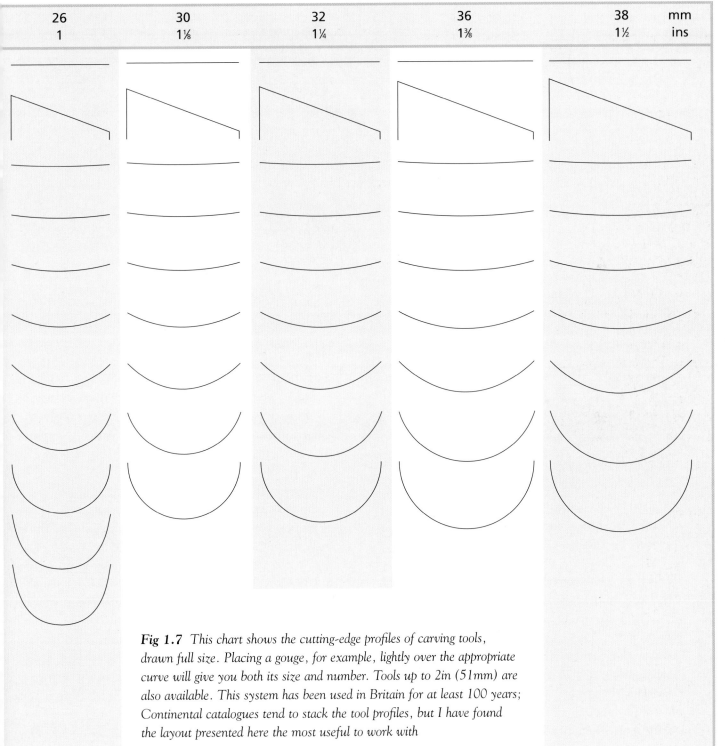

26	30	32	36	38	mm
1	1⅛	1¼	1⅜	1½	ins

Fig 1.7 *This chart shows the cutting-edge profiles of carving tools, drawn full size. Placing a gouge, for example, lightly over the appropriate curve will give you both its size and number. Tools up to 2in (51mm) are also available. This system has been used in Britain for at least 100 years; Continental catalogues tend to stack the tool profiles, but I have found the layout presented here the most useful to work with*

Fig 1.8 *The shanks of a selection of modern tools, stamped with the names and logos of the makers, as well as a tool number*

Fig 1.9 *If important details are marked on the ferrule or handle instead, this information may get lost if the handle ever needs replacing*

It is the variation in these three elements that creates the huge variety of woodcarving tools.

The basic numerical code concerns only two of these factors: the cross section of the blade and the shape along its length. The width is normally given separately in inches (or fractions of an inch) or millimetres (Fig 1.10).

A few manufacturers use higher numbers to designate more specialized tools, such as fishtails (a series from 50 onwards in the original list), but nowadays these are often given a prefix number or letter instead. (The various names and shapes of carving tools will be looked at in greater detail when we come to consider the parts of a woodcarving tool in Chapter 2.)

The range of straight gouges has equivalents in shape and size in the ranges of bent gouges. So, for example, the curvature across the blade of a ½in (13mm) no. 3 straight gouge should be exactly the same as that of a ½in no. 12 longbent gouge, a ½in no. 24 shortbent, and a ½in no. 33 backbent gouge; the same profile will be available in fishtail and other forms as well (Fig 1.11).

Note that where you might – according to the list – expect nos. 39–41 to be backbent gouges, these numbers actually refer to parting tools or V-tools. The reason for this is that the deeper shapes of gouge do not work well as backbent tools, so are not usually made in this form. (These points are explained more fully in Chapter 5.)

Bear in mind that you do not need this list to start carving – so do not worry about memorizing these numbers at the outset. The main use of the listing is for reference: it has a practical application when selecting and buying carving tools.

There is often more than one name for a particular style of carving tool, sometimes several. These names will be noted in the text in the appropriate places.

Fig 1.10 *These tools all specify the same Sheffield List number (01) and differ only in the specification of the width*

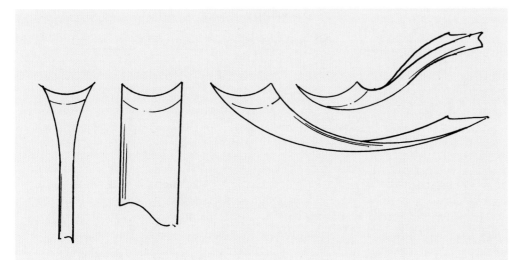

Fig 1.11 *Any curvature across the blade is available in different longitudinal shapes, for different purposes – in this case (left to right), fishtail, straight, longbent, shortbent*

HOW USEFUL IS THE SHEFFIELD LIST?

Well, not as useful as it really could be. Although many firms use it, or something similar, there is a certain amount of inaccuracy in the making of tools: a no. 5 in real life, for example, may correspond to a no. 6 in the catalogue, or even a no. 5½. Then again,

one firm (such as Bristol Design) may use a lettering system instead, as did early editions of the *Sheffield List* itself; another (Pfeil, for example) may miss out some numbers altogether, and use others in non-standard ways.

On the other hand – speaking of well-established firms – the tool for which you are looking will more than likely be available, even if it is not so easy to find. And since most carvers buy tools from a variety of manufacturers – if only for the reason that different makers have different strengths and weaknesses – some cross-maker reference is needed. I suggest you do what I do:

- Choose one, actual-sized, sweep illustration as your standard reference – the one in this book is ideal – and photocopy it.

- Highlight the sweeps of your tools on this reference chart; use one copy for straight gouges, another for bent, and so on.

- Send for catalogues from all the manufacturers.

- Have transparent acetate photocopies made of all the sweep illustrations from these catalogues.

- Using these acetate photocopies as *overlays*, you can compare the sweeps on your standard reference with those of other manufacturers and order accordingly.

- Check the tools when you have received them; don't settle for anything other than what you wanted.

This might seem a lot of work, but it is well worth the trouble to do this, and you only need do it once.

Manufacturers don't change their specifications readily, and you will be in control of what you have, and what you may wish to buy.

When buying tools over the counter, you will find it helpful to take impressions of your existing tools on a piece of wood or card to use as a comparison.

USING THE NUMBERING SYSTEMS

A beginner can start off with any carving tool, making as much use as possible of it and discovering its limitations. What normally happens is that as the carving progresses, you come to a point where it is clear that the tool is no longer suitable – its useful limit has been reached for the work in hand. A change to a different tool is needed to continue. There are usually only three factors which need to be changed (Fig 1.12):

- the width

- the cross section (or sweep)

- the shape along its length (longitudinal section).

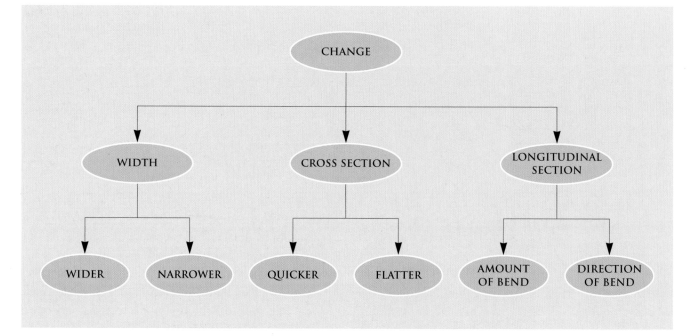

Fig 1.12 *You can work your way quite logically to exactly the tool you need for a particular job*

The following examples show how this might work out in practice, using the Sheffield List numbering system:

The tool is the right width and shape along its length but the sweep (the cross section) is not the curvature you want

Here you can move up or down the numbering system to increase or decrease the amount of curvature.

The tool is the right width and sweep but the shape along its length (the longitudinal section) does not suit the work

In this case the listing enables you to keep the sweep and width you have been using, but switch to a bent or a fishtail form.

The tool is the right sweep and longitudinal shape, but is too narrow or not wide enough

You may have to estimate this by trial and error because, as will be discussed below, it is not just a matter of going to the next width – the curvature actually changes as well. A carver often knows by experience which tool is needed to continue cutting a curve, or may well impel one sweep to do the work of another. If you need to keep the same radius of curvature, you can find the tool you want, but under a different number. Refer to the Sheffield List chart (see Fig 1.7), where the profiles of carving tools are shown full size.

Remember that a degree of hand-forging creates some slight differences between individual tools. A good idea, especially for repetitive work such as mouldings, is to work out which of your own tools have similar sweeps and mark a corresponding numbering system on to the handles. More will be said about this later (see pages 28–9).

THE PARTS OF A WOODCARVING TOOL

Various terms are used to describe the different parts of woodcarving tools. The following describes a 'typical' carving tool (Fig 1.13).

The steel blade is fitted to a wooden handle by its **tang** – it is normally quite straightforward to separate blade and handle. Sometimes the word **blade** refers to

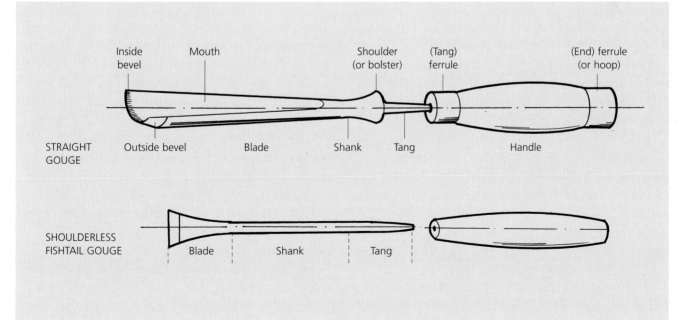

Fig 1.13 *The parts of a typical carving gouge*

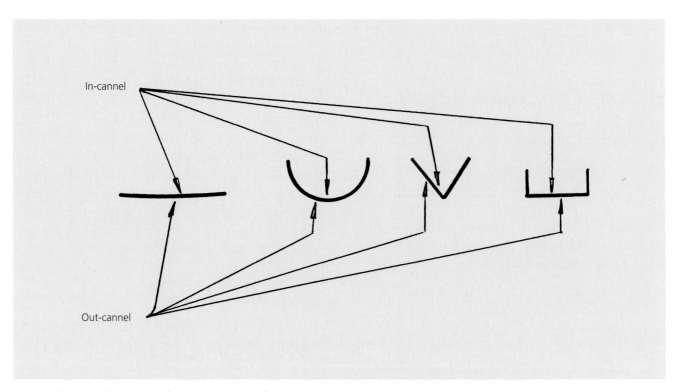

Fig 1.14 *'Cannel' is a useful term referring to the inner and outer faces of any carving tool*

the whole of the tool except the handle, sometimes only to the part below the shoulder, depending on the context.

The handle may have a metal **ferrule** or **hoop** at the tang end to resist splitting. Another, heavier, ferrule is sometimes fitted to the top end, limiting damage to the handle when it is struck with a mallet.

Between the blade proper and the tang may be a shaped lump of metal: the **shoulder** or **bolster**. This prevents the tang from being forced into the wooden handle and splitting it.

Blades are either flat (**chisels**) or curved in cross section (**gouges**) – though carvers often use the term *chisel* loosely to refer to both kinds. A flat chisel has two bevels and each side looks the same, but a gouge will have a **concave** surface and a **convex** one. The concave side is known as the **inside, face, hollow, channel** or **mouth** of the gouge. The other, convex, surface is the **outside, reverse** or **back**.

The terms **in-cannel** and **out-cannel** refer to the inner and outer faces of any carving tool which has them – without specifying an actual tool (Fig 1.14). (When used on its own, **cannel** usually refers to the concave or inside surface of the gouge.) An **in-cannel gouge** (not normally used in carving) has its sharpening bevel on the inside only; an **out-cannel gouge** is bevelled only or mainly on the outside. *Cannel* comes via *cannelure* – the French for 'channel' – and is used in architectural contexts to mean a flute or round-bottomed groove. It is also related to the words *channel* and *canal*, meaning 'a watercourse'. The root of all these words is the Latin *canalis*, 'a pipe or duct'. Although these terms are useful, they are more often used by toolmakers than carvers.

The part of the blade nearest the shoulder is the **shank**; which brings us to the various shapes of blade, as discussed in the next chapter.

At the working end of the tool, a **bevel** diminishes the thickness of the steel into the cutting edge. There may also be a bevel on the inside of the gouge – in other words, there may be an inner and an outer bevel. The corner where the bevel meets the full thickness of the blade is known as the **heel**.

In the next chapter we will look in detail at the various parts of a woodcarving blade – first at the quality of its steel, then how the parts fit together.

CHAPTER TWO

BLADES

AIMS

- To show how to assess the quality of a carving tool in order to know exactly what is being bought

- To show how the shapes of carving tools relate to their function

QUALITY OF STEEL

The five tools shown in Fig 2.1 all look very different, but the differences are largely cosmetic: some manufacturers finish their blades to a high polish and some do not. What makes one blade better than another in practice?

The steel used in woodcarving tools needs to be what is known as **high-carbon**. It is often an alloy with small amounts of other metals, and must be of appropriate quality (purity) to keep its cutting edge. If you put high-carbon steel to a fast grinding wheel, an intense, bright shower of sparks will be produced (Fig 2.2). Anything that produces dull sparks, in small quantities, will be a low-carbon 'mild' steel and useless for carving. Manufacturers keep the make-up and sources of their steels to themselves.

High-speed steel (HSS), which has become almost universal for woodturning tools, has a superior edge-holding ability to high-carbon steel. In turning, the wood is cut at a high speed, concentrating both heat and wear on one small spot – under these conditions carbon steel softens and dulls more quickly. However, HSS is much more difficult to work, and to forge into the various shapes that carvers need.

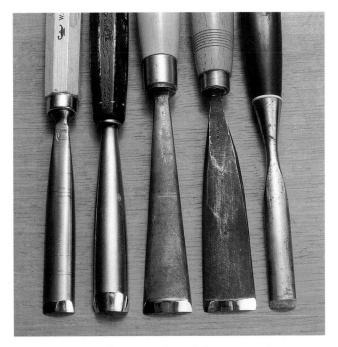

Fig 2.1 *Five similar gouges from different manufacturers, each finishing the tool in a different way – how do you know what the steel is like underneath?*

Turning tools, which are comparatively simple shapes to make, are fashioned by grinding or cutting away excess metal from a round or square blank. For this reason HSS is unlikely to become available in the

Fig 2.2 *The spark test for identifying steel of carving-tool quality*

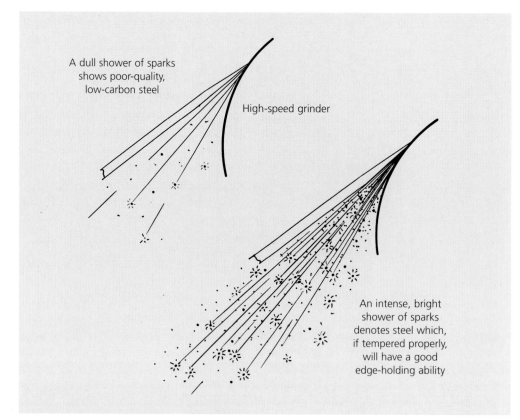

A dull shower of sparks shows poor-quality, low-carbon steel

High-speed grinder

An intense, bright shower of sparks denotes steel which, if tempered properly, will have a good edge-holding ability

same way to carvers, unless some more versatile way of working it is developed. Modern methods of *sintering* – fusing the HSS under pressure into a single shape – may produce tools in the future.

To make a carving tool, a blank of high-carbon steel is heated in a forge and shaped on swage blocks, creating the tang, shoulder, shank and blade. There are different ways of doing this, from crude, mechanical drop forging to the more sensitive, hands-on hammer forging – which is a highly skilled craft like smithing, requiring sensitivity and judgement to shape the blade consistently and correctly (Figs 2.3 and 2.4). Hammer forging creates a finer, stronger grain structure within the metal and is regarded as the superior method, used by the best toolmakers.

After the forging or shaping process, the blade is subjected to heat treatment, achieving the optimum hardness and tensile strength for the job it has to do. Only the cutting blade itself, and not necessarily all of that, is hardened. A greater or lesser part of the metal towards the handle (including the shank, shoulder and tang) is made softer and less brittle; this gives these parts more resilience.

Fig 2.3 *Toolmaking today may still involve a large amount of hand work*

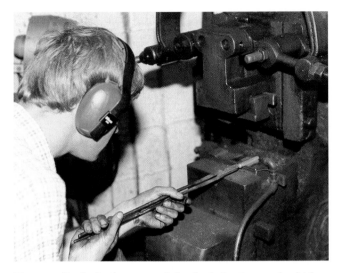

Fig 2.4 Both the forging and the final shaping need a high degree of skill, taking many years to learn

These three factors –

• the steel

• the forging

• the heat treatment

– establish the quality of a carving-tool blade. They determine both its shape and its cutting ability; and variations in any one of these factors can produce a superior or inferior tool.

Woodcarvers love to debate tools: who makes the best; which tools exhibit what qualities; how the steel, forging or tempering in each type of tool compares; the edge-holding properties of the 'old' versus the 'new'; and so on. There is no consensus on these questions. It is worth going a little further into this discussion about what it is in a blade that makes a good tool, so that you can make as good, or at least as reasonable, a choice as possible.

Steel technology and research – and the ability to produce the appropriate quality of steel consistently – have developed a long way since the height of the Industrial Revolution. Modern steel can be considered superior for this reason alone.

Victorian tools are much valued because it is really only from this period onwards that working tools (that is, tools with real working life left in them) have come down to us. As you might expect, these tools are quite often considerably worn by years of good use

(Fig 2.5), which in some cases may have taken the cutting edge back into a softer part of the blade. The steel is the same throughout the tool, but the heat treatment differs: the remaining part of the blade may have less hard, but more resilient, steel. If you have any of these shortened tools, and find that they keep their edges badly, you can resurrect them by re-tempering. The method is explained in Volume 2, Chapter 3.

It is not just for the quality of steel alone that these tools are justifiably prized. The best makers today still shape and forge their tools in very similar ways. But you can often see, when you look at an old carving tool, a considerable difference from some of its modern counterparts (Fig 2.6). It is as if the older tools used thinner metal to get the same strength of structure, and it may be the quality of the steel that allowed this. There is also the matter of individual care: perhaps more time was taken in the shaping. Whatever the reason, old tools are generally regarded as better formed and finished off than many modern ones. But this, again, is arguable, for some modern tools are beautifully made, and some old ones are far from perfect.

The final processes, known as **hardening** and **tempering** – when the steel is rendered into the appropriate hardness for carving – are even more contentious. Suffice to say here that a large tool which

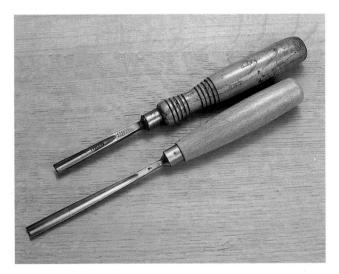

Fig 2.5 The old gouge at the top would originally have been as long as the modern one beneath. The reduction in length represents many years of carving and sharpening

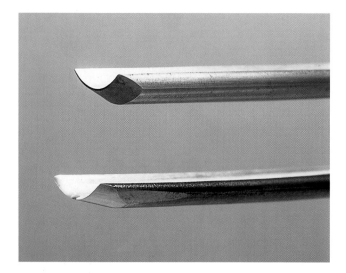

Fig 2.6 Some manufacturers today (top) make their tools of much thicker metal than older ones (bottom)

takes a heavy pounding from a mallet – say a 1in (25mm) gouge – requires a different treatment from one which is used for delicate and precise cutting. It needs to be a little less brittle, and able to absorb the stresses of impact without cracking. The extreme example of this principle is the traditional mortise chisel, made of wrought iron with steel welded on for the cutting edge only.

Different sizes and shapes of tools need to be heat-treated differently; not only because of the use to

Fig 2.7 These two tools are not as different as they look. The maker of the lower gouge chooses to leave the tool black on the outside from the quenching, but polished inside to show the tempering colours; the upper one is uniformly finished all over, with the tempering colours polished out

which they will be put, but also because of the variations which can occur in the quality of steel, despite the intentions of the manufacturers. Producing a large volume of tools economically in a modern factory – compared with comparatively smaller numbers using cheaper labour in the past – means that the tools get an 'average' heat treatment en masse. They are not treated individually, according to how they will be used. On the other hand, there is probably much more precision and consistency today than there has ever been, with heat treatment being computer-aided. The 'average' treatment given to modern tools can be a very good one in terms of quality and consistency. There are also definite differences between the products of different manufacturers, as well as between individual tools within one manufacturer's range.

In the past there were also methods of quenching the hot tools, such as lead dipping, which (for economic and other reasons) are not used today. Such methods may have given an improved crystal grain structure to the blade and allowed for the reduced thickness in the walls that was mentioned above.

Much of this discussion, with its reference to the historical background, may seem academic. The person whose only wish is to get on with carving something might justifiably ask: 'Where does all this lead us, and how am I to decide which are the best-quality carving tools?' Here is my view.

If you compare the tools made by specialist wood-carving toolmakers – those firms which have been working within the tradition of making woodcarving tools for many years (over 100 years in some cases) – the differences between them mostly come down to matters of personal preference. We are talking here of quality tools from reputable manufacturers. There are also carving tools – often imported, but not always – which are much cheaper than the established brands. These look like bargains, but beware: this cheapness has as much to do with poor-quality steel and inadequate manufacturing techniques as with cheap labour and the rate of currency exchange.

It is easy to overlook other factors, in addition to the type of steel and the forging or tempering of the blade, which affect the ability of a tool to hold its sharpness. Three of these factors are:

CUTTING TECHNIQUE

Even top-quality tools may become blunt quickly, whatever the nature of the steel or the tempering, because of poor carving technique. For example, the habit of scraping the edge of the tool across the wood after cutting into it, or prising chips of wood away and not allowing the edge to enter and leave the cut cleanly, is very common (Fig 2.8). As a way of blunting a carving tool on wood, you could hardly do better. Crisp carving of the kind seen in Fig 2.9 can only be achieved by cutting, not by scraping or levering.

Fig 2.9 Tilman Riemenschneider's mastery of cutting technique is quite breathtaking in this detail from the limewood Elevation of the Magdalene *in the Bayerisches Nationalmuseum, Munich*

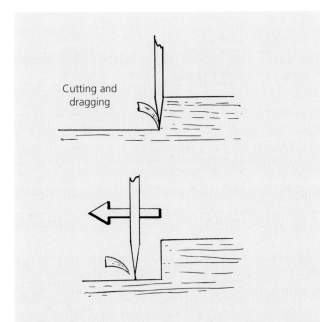

Cutting and dragging

Cutting and prising

Fig 2.8 There are two poor carving techniques which quickly blunt cutting edges – avoid them

LOSS OF TEMPER DURING GRINDING

Heating the blade repeatedly to far more than 'hand-hot' may also lead to loss of edge-holding ability, even if the metal never reaches the well-known 'blue' colour which indicates overheating and loss of hardness. Great care must be taken not to allow the blade to heat up significantly during grinding (Fig 2.10).

Fig 2.10 A 1920s hand-cranked, water-cooled grinding wheel might be slower than a modern grinder, but would never overheat the blade

THE SUBTLE EFFECT OF SOME MODERN GRINDING WHEELS ON THE CRYSTAL STRUCTURE OF THE EDGE

Minute cracks and striations may appear in some sorts of steel from the high-speed impact of the abrasive grit, so making the edge more liable to decay. This is more likely to happen with a coarser stone. Always finish off grinding on the finest wheel, and leave enough metal for hand-working beyond any effect of the grinding. (Grinding is considered in detail in Part II.)

In my experience there is little difference in the steel and edge-keeping qualities of most old and new tools – and I have in use a range of several hundred tools, old and new, but all from the best-quality manufacturers. Individual tools of all ages and makes seem to vary in their edge-holding properties because so much depends on variations in steel, tempering and the treatment of a tool in the processes of carving and grinding. When it comes to the forging or shaping of tools, however, there does seem to be more of a difference between old and new. So, to help you buy the best tools, here is some summary advice:

- Never buy tools just because they are cheap, and definitely not from dubious sources.

- Always buy from firms with a long-standing good reputation to protect, who label their tools, are justifiably proud of what they make, and can supply catalogues and other information.

- When you are beginning, buy your good-quality tools from a few different sources and compare them yourself. Do not commit yourself to buying too many tools of the same make at this stage – you might eventually be unhappy with them.

- If in doubt, ask a few carvers which tools they use frequently and what they think of them. Bear in mind we are all biased to some extent.

- Buy the best tools that you can afford and do not stint on quality. It is better to buy a few good tools than more of lower quality. Tools are meant to last a lifetime, and you do not want to regret what you have bought. Avoid boxed sets (see page 91).

In this way you can be fairly sure of getting tools that are the best currently available – made from the best-quality steel, using the best possible techniques.

THE DIFFERENT SHAPES AND THEIR USES

Now let us look at how the blade can be shaped, in its cross section, longitudinal section and width, for different applications.

CROSS SECTION

Woodcarving blades have only a dozen or so different cross-sectional profiles, although there may appear more to a beginner. Even these dozen or so shapes reduce to three basic varieties:

- straight

- curved

- angled.

It is when these profiles are multiplied by the possible variations along the length and the width that we arrive at the huge numbers of different types that are actually available.

The cross section of the blade is seen by looking end-on at the edge of the tool.

STRAIGHT BLADES

Tools with blades which are straight across the width are called **chisels**.

In normal woodworking, the chisel is a very common tool, having a bevel on one side of the cutting edge and a flat face on the other. Woodcarving chisels differ from those used in carpentry by having a bevel on both sides (Fig 2.11). The reason for this is explained in Chapter 9 (page 137); the carpentry chisel is used mostly for different purposes, although it is usual for carvers to have a few.

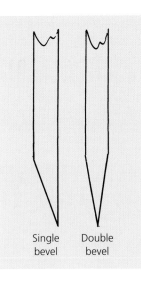

Fig 2.11 *Carpenters' (left) and carvers' chisels require different bevel arrangements*

Single bevel   Double bevel

Another name for the woodcarver's chisel is a **firmer** or **firmer chisel** (Figs 2.12 and 2.13); confusingly, this is also the name of the general-purpose chisel, bevelled on one side only, used by carpenters and others. This term was first recorded a couple of hundred years ago and seems to come from the French *ferme*, meaning 'a roof truss'. It was applied to a chisel with a blade splaying from the handle, and with no distinct bevel, called a *fermoir* –

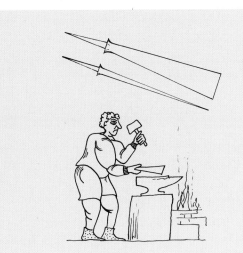

Fig 2.14 *The splayed allongee shape arises naturally as a bar of metal is thinned by hammering to produce a working edge. The earliest chisels may well have kept the original bar, perhaps bound in thong, as the handle, sockets or tangs being later refinements*

presumably connected with the workers of roofs. (According to other sources, *fermoir* is a variant of *formoir*, meaning 'shaper'.) The word *chisel* also comes from the French *ciseau*, which denotes a blade with parallel edges and a definite bevel. Of the two shapes, the long splay – termed **allongee** by carvers – is by far the older (Fig 2.14).

The ordinary straight woodcarver's chisel is designated no. 1 in the Sheffield listing.

When the cutting edge of the chisel is at an angle to the long axis, the tool is called a **skew chisel** (**skewed chisel**), **skew**, or **corner chisel** (Fig 2.15).

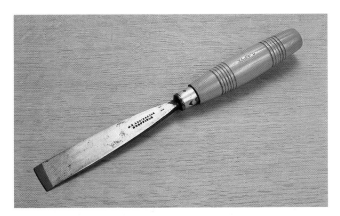

Fig 2.12 *The basic woodcarver's firmer chisel*

Fig 2.13 *An old firmer chisel with a socketed rather than tanged blade, tapering straight to the edge*

Fig 2.15 *The basic skew chisel; the tip of this one has been ground as described on page 148 (see Fig 9.42)*

like depends both on the radius of the circle and on the extent of the sweep – that is, what portion of the circumference of the circle it comprises. Sweeps range from very flat (no. 3 in the Sheffield List), which is almost, but definitely not, a chisel (Figs 2.18 and 2.19), to a true semicircle (usually no. 9); Fig 2.20 shows only a selection from the complete range.

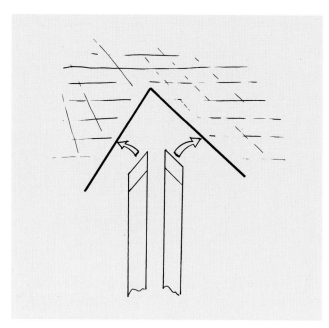

Fig 2.16 *The useful skew can be turned over to get into corners from both directions*

A straight version of this tool, as opposed to the bent varieties, is a no. 2 in the Sheffield List. Like the firmer chisel, it has a bevel on both sides and can be used either side up, with the cutting edge facing left or right (Fig 2.16).

CURVED BLADES

When the cutting edge of the blade is curved in cross section to a greater or lesser degree, the tool is referred to as a **gouge**.

The curvature usually forms an arc of a circle, in which case it is known as the **sweep** of the blade (Fig 2.17). What the curvature of a particular gouge looks

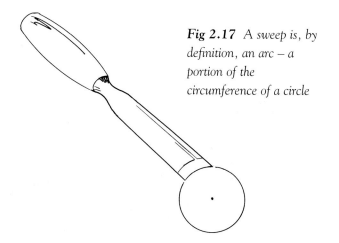

Fig 2.17 *A sweep is, by definition, an arc – a portion of the circumference of a circle*

Fig 2.18 *The flattest gouge (right), seen from above, is almost indistinguishable from the truly flat chisel*

Fig 2.19 *The flattest gouge (right) and a chisel (left), seen end-on. From this angle it is clear that the so-called 'flat gouge' is actually significantly curved*

Fig 2.20 *A selection of sweeps ranging from the flat to the semicircular*

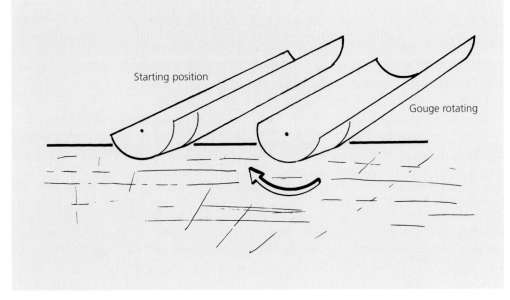

Starting position

Gouge rotating

Fig 2.21 *Only gouges with a sweep which is an arc of a circle can rock or rotate through their cut. This slicing action, in either direction, is a primary carving technique*

The advantage of a circular arc is that the tool can be **rocked** or rotated slightly as it is pushed forward, giving a slicing action which severs the wood much more cleanly than if the tool were merely driven straight ahead (Fig 2.21). The no. 9 is the last sweep in the series that can be rocked through its cut. The smaller representatives – approximately ⅛in (3mm) or less – are sometimes known as **eye tools**; they can be used to form the **eyes** where some types of acanthus leaves meet (Fig 2.22).

Fig 2.22 *A small semicircular gouge is rotated into part of the hollow between acanthus leaves, forming the distinctive 'eye'*

Fig 2.23 *From a semicircle, the walls of the higher-numbered gouges extend to form U-shaped profiles*

The next gouges in the series (nos. 10 and 11) take on more of a U-shape, the side walls elongating and the mouth deepening, with no. 11 having the deepest walls (Figs 2.23 and 2.24).

To go over this numbering system for straight-bladed gouges once more: the flattest gouges are no. 3, the semicircular ones are no. 9, and there is a deepening range of sweeps in between. There are two U-shaped gouges (nos. 10 and 11) with curves based on semicircles and straight, elongated side walls.

This nomenclature is not always as neatly defined as stated here, and some differences occur between makers. For example, a firm may make fewer divisions in the range, or may make no. 10 the true semicircle and only have no. 11 as the U-shape. Remember also, when comparing them with the manufacturers' charts of 'ideal' shapes, that these tools include a degree of hand-making.

It is worth mentioning also that the side walls of U-gouges may be either vertical or splayed outwards slightly – or, for that matter, gently curved rather than straight. This can make quite a difference to their behaviour: a tool with vertical side walls makes consistent, narrow, parallel-sided channels, but is harder to use because the chip is liable to stick in the cannel – and harder to sharpen.

The principle is that the curves progress from flat to strongly curved, and are numbered accordingly. It is a common mistake (and one appearing in many publications) to assume that when each sweep of gouge is given a number, this number applies to gouges that take their curvature from a particular diameter of circle, no matter what the width – in

Fig 2.24 *A selection of deep or 'quick' gouges, from a semicircle on the left to the deeper U-shaped tool on the right*

other words, that smaller or narrower gouges are segments of the larger ones. So no. 6 gouges, whether ¼in (6mm), ½in (13mm), ¾in (19mm) or 1in (25mm) wide, might be assumed to have an increasingly wide segment of the same-radius circle. This is not true.

If you were to join the ends of the cuts made by pushing, say, different-sized no. 6 gouges into a flat wooden surface, the resulting curve would be a spiral, not a circle (Fig 2.25). This shows that the gouges of any designation keep a proportionate depth as they decrease in width. This is true of both Sheffield and Continental systems. How the geometry was first decided appears to be lost, along with the original patterns, in the mists of time. The traditional sweeps are perpetuated because, when the swage blocks that

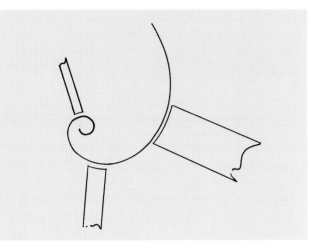

Fig 2.25 *If the sweeps of different-sized tools with the same number are joined side by side, the result is a spiral, not a circle – although the sweep of each individual tool will describe a circle*

are used to form the profiles wear out, a new one can be made using a tool as a pattern; the original information is never needed. Perhaps the curves were based on progressive Archimedian spirals, and not circles at all. However, remember that *every gouge – other than the U-shaped ones – will cut a true circle if*

allowed to follow its own cut (Figs 2.26 and 2.27); this principle is of fundamental importance in certain types of carving.

By stamping the edges of your gouges into a piece of card or tracing paper (or a thin piece of wood), it is possible to find which widths and numbers of gouges *will* join up in the same circle. Do try this yourself; it is quite instructive. A second numbering system of your own, using perhaps Roman numerals or letters, can then be added to the handles. This may be important for repetitive or standardized work such as carved mouldings. For most work, however, carvers come to know which chisel cuts which curve, and will manipulate a gouge to fit a particular cut if exactly the right one is not to hand. (This technique is described in my *Lettercarving in Wood*, page 74.)

A gouge which is so gently curved as to be almost flat is termed exactly that – a **flat gouge**. (If it were truly flat, of course, it would be a chisel.) A gouge with a pronounced sweep is called a **quick gouge**. Carvers talk about 'flatter' or 'quicker' gouges as the curvature varies one way or the other. As the curvature increases, the gouge is said to become quicker. There may an interesting relationship with the phrase

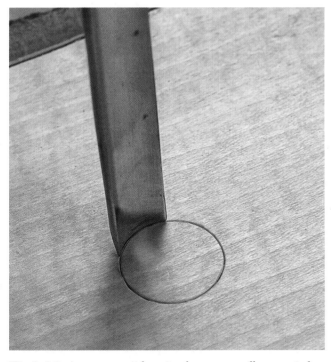

Fig 2.26 *Any gouge with a circular sweep will cut a circle of a size corresponding to its own radius*

Fig 2.27 *U-shaped gouges are obviously not able to do this because of their extended sides*

'the quick and the dead'. A quicker gouge is, in a sense, more 'alive'; in the first rough stages of carving, a quick gouge can remove wood much faster and more vigorously than a flat gouge.

The nos. 9, 10 and 11 gouges, because they are based on semicircles, do not differ from one another in quickness of curvature for any given width: the width of the tool is the diameter of one particular semicircle. These gouges are often, but sometimes arbitrarily, called **veiners** or **veining tools** if they are small (approximately ⅛in (3mm) or less), or **fluters** or **fluting tools** if larger. These terms describe some of the principal uses to which these tools are traditionally put: the no. 9, for example, can be used upside down to shape **reeds** in some decorative work or veins in foliage. A **flute** is a decorative channel cut into a surface, and can be easily formed with these deep or U-shaped gouges (Figs 2.28 and 2.29).

Fig 2.28 *A veining tool (no. 9) can be used upside down to shape the veins in, for example, foliage; fluters, the same shape but somewhat larger, can be used to cut channels, or inverted to make reeds (see next figure). U-shaped gouges (nos. 10 and 11) are not used upside down*

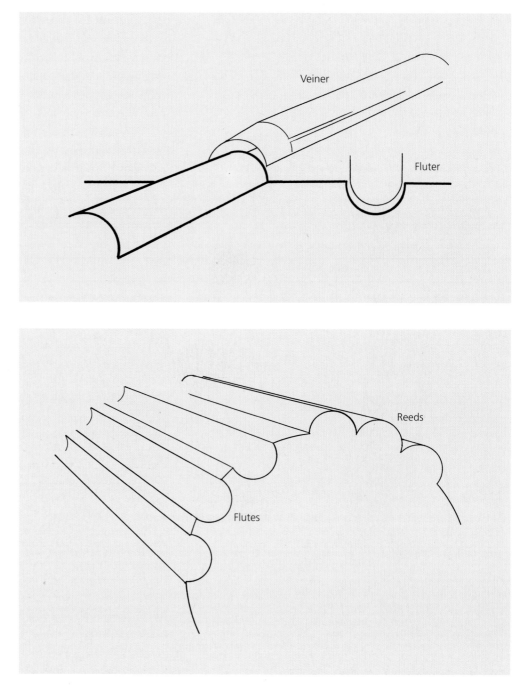

Fig 2.29 *Flutes and reeds*

The gouges which are deeper than a semicircle are often called **U-shaped gouges** or **U-tools** to differentiate them from the regular gouges which can be 'rocked' to give a slicing cut. The extended walls of the U-shaped gouges prevent rocking.

ANGLED BLADES

By far the most common of the angular cross sections is a V-shape. It is helpful to see this tool as two chisels joined together by one edge; for obvious reasons it is called a **V-tool** or **V-chisel** (Fig 2.30).

Another common name for this shape is **parting tool**, because among other things it is used to separate or divide one area of carving from another. This is most easily seen in shallow **relief carving**, where the subject is 'relieved' from its background.

The angle formed between the two sides can be more, or less, acute: the three commonest angles are nominally 45°, 60° and 90° (Figs 2.31 and 2.32), but these may vary considerably in practice – so much so that the narrowest shape is occasionally referred to as 30° rather than 45°. The angle is chosen according to the work for which the parting tool is needed. If you have to choose only one type, the 60° angle is probably the most useful, being the medium shape.

The junction in the bevel between the two faces of the parting tool is called the **keel** and, like the keel of a boat, it has a guiding function (Fig 2.33). In effect the V-tool has *three bevels*: two for the chisels that form the sides, plus the keel where the two side bevels meet. *Grasping this point is vital when it comes to sharpening the V.*

Fig 2.30 *The basic V-tool or parting tool*

Fig 2.32 *The same size of V-tool is available in three different angles: approximately 45°, 60° and 90° (left to right)*

Fig 2.31 *Apart from the standard 60° parting tool, narrower and wider versions are available for different purposes*

Fig 2.33 *The parts of a V-tool or parting tool*

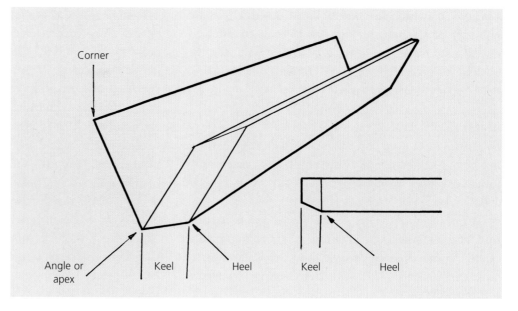

You may come across other, more unusual, tools which have an angled cross section of some sort (Fig 2.34). These were originally developed for particular work in the furniture trade, such as cleaning between the elements of a relief design. They are little used in general carving; most of their work, if not all, can be done with other tools, and they are nearly redundant these days. If you are just starting carving, in particular, these tools should not really be considered. However, they are worth knowing about. Their names are rather fanciful, and it is not hard to imagine some Italian carvers – many of whom found their way to the East End of London in the heyday of furniture carving – having a private joke over their pasta one day which somehow caught on. Some may have been designed by the founder of the tool suppliers Alec Tiranti Ltd.

These angled tools include the following:

The macaroni

This is equivalent to three chisels joined together, with two right angles in between (Fig 2.35). It is sometimes called a **trench** or **trenching tool**, and is a bit like half of a rectangle. It will cut a vertical wall to both the left and the right sides.

The fluteroni

This is a sort of softened-off macaroni with rounded corners. The sides are still straight, but leaning out a little.

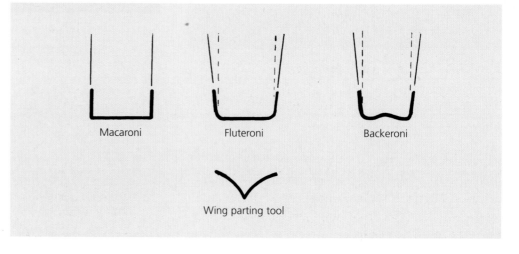

Fig 2.34 *Besides the V-tool, there are other, far less common tools which are angled in cross section*

Fig 2.35 *Shortbent, fishtail and straight macaroni tools*

The backeroni

This is a fluteroni with the central section curving slightly upwards. It is normally made with a bent blade, and could also be described as a backbent gouge with the edges turned up. It is a very specialized tool developed for the furniture trade.

The wing parting tool

This is aptly named, and is the equivalent of two shallow gouges edge to edge, rather than the two chisels that make up the ordinary V-tool. This tool is used to clear wood between two beads, shaping the beads themselves at the same time. (A **bead** or **reed** is a semicircular moulding, the opposite of a flute or channel; the term *bead* is also used for a short segment of such a moulding, carved into a hemisphere.)

Having considered the various shapes of woodcarving tools by looking *across* the blades, let us now turn to the shapes along their length.

LONGITUDINAL SECTION

A blade can be either straight or bent between the handle and the cutting edge, with several variations.

STRAIGHT TOOLS

The sides of these tools may be parallel along their length, or may splay outwards from the handle. Straight woodcarving tools with parallel sides are the ones usually called **straight**.

The splaying or tapering starts either directly from the shoulder of the blade, or begins after some length of narrow shank. The shank can in some cases be quite long, with the blade a mere appendage, fanning out at the end. The tapered tools have their own names, depending on the variable ratio of taper to shank.

Straight, parallel-sided gouges or chisels

These (Fig 2.36) are by far the most common and useful woodcarving tools, although a few specialist carvers may have more of other types. In terms of the

Fig 2.36 *The straight chisel normally has flat faces. The oval shape of the lower tool is an attempted innovation, but I find its smooth corners make it less easy to grip*

Sheffield List, these tools are the ones numbered 1 to 11 as discussed above, and also include the straight parting tools (nos. 39, 41 and 45).

Straight, tapered chisels and gouges

These are lightweight versions of the straight, square-ended tools, while still retaining the same sweeps or curvatures. The consequences of the splaying shape are twofold:

- The corners are made more acute. This is most important for getting into corners, as when lettering.

- They are of lighter weight and give greater visibility. This facilitates more precise cutting and makes them excellent for finishing off.

One obvious disadvantage of splayed blades is that their cutting edge gradually becomes narrower as they are sharpened. This means that they have a shorter effective life than parallel blades.

The names given to these tools vary a bit between manufacturers and some have, predictably, been obscured with time. A fairly uncontroversial classification would be as follows (Fig 2.37):

- The **allongee** tapers, or splays, from the shoulder straight out to the edge (Figs 2.38 and 2.39). As we have seen already, this is probably one of the oldest shapes of chisel, since the act of beating out a lump of metal naturally tends to produce a splayed shape (see Fig 2.15). The name comes from the French *allonger*, 'to elongate'. As straight gouges and chisels get wider, they also become bulkier; for a tool wider than 1½in (38mm) or so it may be worth having the less cumbersome allongee shape, trading the slow loss of width over time for the lighter use.

- The **fishtail**, at the other extreme, has a long, square shank with a suddenly expanding blade at the end, which does indeed look like the tail of a fish (Fig 2.40).

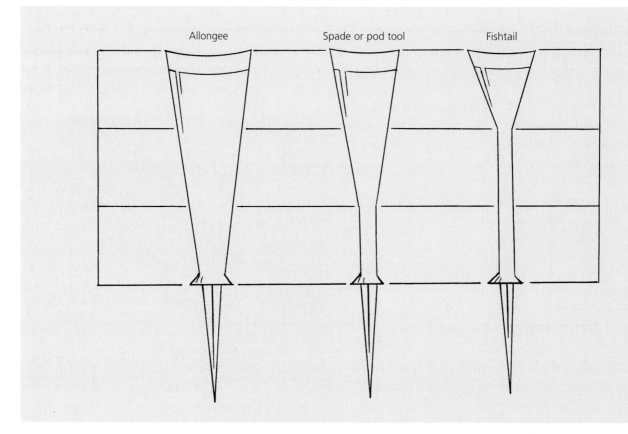

Fig 2.37 *A guide to the nomenclature of tapered carving tools*

- Between the allongee and the fishtail proper can be variable lengths of shank or taper somewhere in the middle (Fig 2.41). Old books often refer to these middle tapers as **long-**, **medium-** or **short-pod tools** or, collectively, as **spade tools** or **spade gouges**. Here the word *pod* may come from *podium*, meaning 'foot' or 'leg', with reference to the prominent shank. Bear in mind that *shank* also means a leg, or at least part of it.

When considering buying any of these splayed tools, it is important to bear in mind that a fishtail to one manufacturer may be a spade tool to another. You

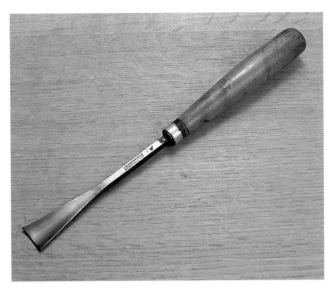

Fig 2.40 *The basic fishtail shape today is more of a 'spade'*

need to check this detail against catalogue illustrations, and not assume that all manufacturers use the same names for the same shapes.

The actual blade sweeps normally correspond to those of the other straight gouges, and the tool numbering reflects this fact. With most manufacturers the last digit (or two digits) of the listing are the same for all straight blades with the same sweep, regardless of the different longitudinal shapes. In this way, if you like the sweep and size of a particular parallel gouge, but would like it as a fishtail, you should be able to get this version of the tool using the numbering system.

Fig 2.38 *The allongee shape*

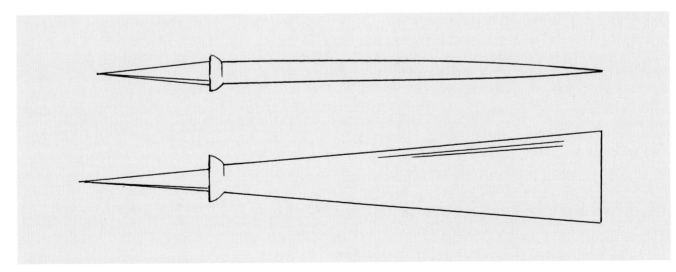

Fig 2.39 *The allongee is a lighter tool for the size of the cutting edge. The side view (above) shows how the taper often merges into the bevel, which may be indistinguishable*

Fig 2.41 A range of tapered gouges, from spade to fishtail; nomenclature varies between manufacturers. You need to decide what you want to achieve, and ask which shape of tool will do it for you

Chisels, as well as gouges, may also be allongee, spade or fishtail with a long shank.

BENT TOOLS

The bend is seen by looking at the side of the blade: it will curve first one way and then the other. The bend itself can start from one of two places (Fig 2.42):

- It can start from the shoulder of the tool, as a long, continuous, snake-like bend: the **longbent** tool.

- It can start much further away, towards the working edge, after a straight shank. This creates a short, crank-like bend: the **shortbent** tool.

The short bend, in turn, can bend in opposite directions as you move from the cutting edge towards the handle (Fig 2.43):

- towards the front first: a **frontbent**

- towards the back first: a **backbent**.

Let us look at these various bent tools in more detail.

Longbent tools

These tools – which are invariably gouges or V-tools, not chisels – have various names: **longbent**, **curved**, **salmon-bend**, **sowback** or **swan-necked** gouges (Figs 2.44 and 2.45). The curvature is long and

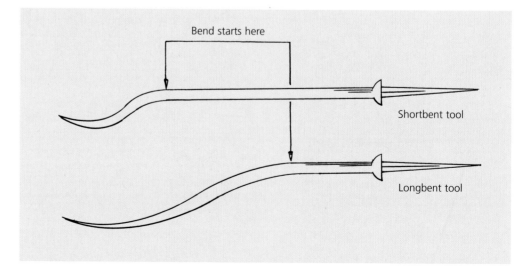

Bend starts here

Shortbent tool

Longbent tool

Fig 2.42 Longbent and shortbent carving tools

elegant, and enables the carver to get into a shallow recess without the handle fouling the wood. Some ranges of 'microtools' (see pages 104–5) include a longbent chisel, but these are not available in the standard ranges.

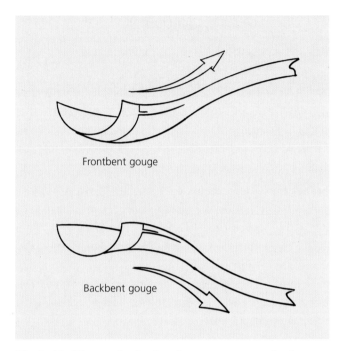

Fig 2.43 *The crank of a frontbent gouge curves in the opposite direction to that of a backbent gouge*

Shortbent tools

Again there are various names: **shortbent, shallowbent, frontbent** and **spoon** or **spoonbit** gouges (Figs 2.46 and 2.47). Sometimes the simple term 'bent gouge' is used; this usually implies the type with the short bend to the front, but this is not necessarily the case. The term is best avoided and replaced with something a little more precise.

Shortbent tools include fishtail chisels or skew chisels with a long shank, as well as gouges.

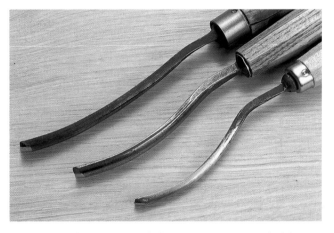

Fig 2.45 *The amount of lengthwise curvature in longbent gouges varies between manufacturers. Some have so little curve as to be little improvement on the straight gouge*

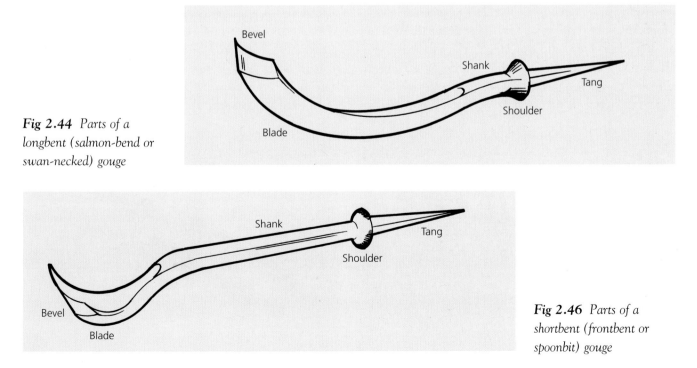

Fig 2.44 *Parts of a longbent (salmon-bend or swan-necked) gouge*

Fig 2.46 *Parts of a shortbent (frontbent or spoonbit) gouge*

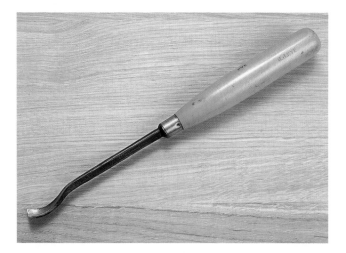

Fig 2.47 *Basic frontbent or shortbent gouge*

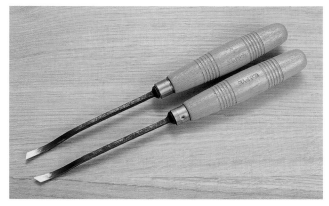

Fig 2.49 *Shortbent skew chisels come in pairs, left- and right-handed, to suit different grain conditions*

The shortbent chisels (Fig 2.48) and flattest gouges are sometimes called **grounding tools** or **grounders**, because they are used to work the backgrounds of relief carving. I have always found the flattest short-bent gouges a better option than the chisels; it is much easier to prevent their corners digging in.

A **shortbent skew chisel** can have the cutting edge skewed to face the left or right; these are usefully bought in pairs (Fig 2.49). V-tools and macaroni tools can also be had in a shortbent form (Fig 2.50; see also Fig 2.35).

The tight bend allows the carver to get into recesses which are deeper than those accessed by the longbent tools – the crank-like shape keeps the handle even further out of the way (Fig 2.51). However, the amount of bend that any manufacturer gives to both shortbent and longbent tools varies considerably – not only between manufacturers, but even between

batches of tools coming from one manufacturer. Sometimes there seems to be so little curve on the tool that it belies the description 'bent', and gives negligible advantage over the straight tools (Fig 2.52). So you need to be a little wary here, especially if you are ordering unseen tools through the post. Try to examine photographs or drawings of what you hope you are getting, and do not accept a tool with a curve that, in effect, does not do the work it is meant for.

Shortbent gouges with the greatest change of cur-vature in the bend are referred to as **knuckle gouges**. These are useful for entering very tight recesses and hollows, such as those found in Gothic carving (Fig 2.53). Unfortunately they are rarely available, either new or second-hand, but they can be made to special order by a firm such as Henry Taylor, or you can make your own using the techniques described in Volume 2, Chapter 3.

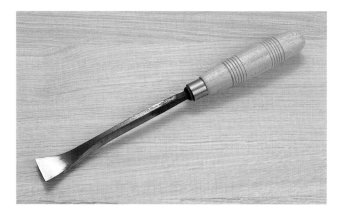

Fig 2.48 *Shortbent chisel*

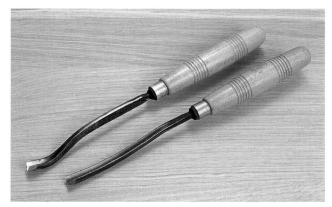

Fig 2.50 *Shortbent and longbent V-tools*

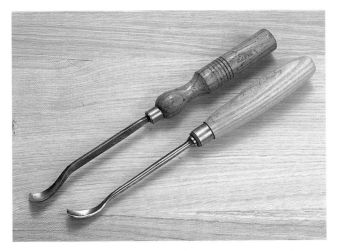

Fig 2.51 *The shank of the frontbent gouge is normally rectangular, facilitating grip. The circular shape looks slicker, but I find that I can grip it less firmly. This sort of personal reason is why it is best to try tools in your own hands first, rather than depend on the catalogue photographs*

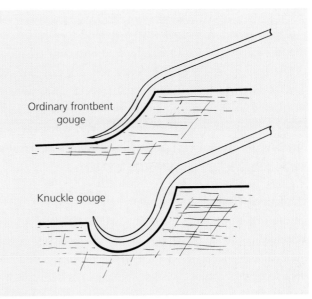

Fig 2.53 *The knuckle gouge is a tightly cranked frontbent gouge which gets into deep recesses more easily*

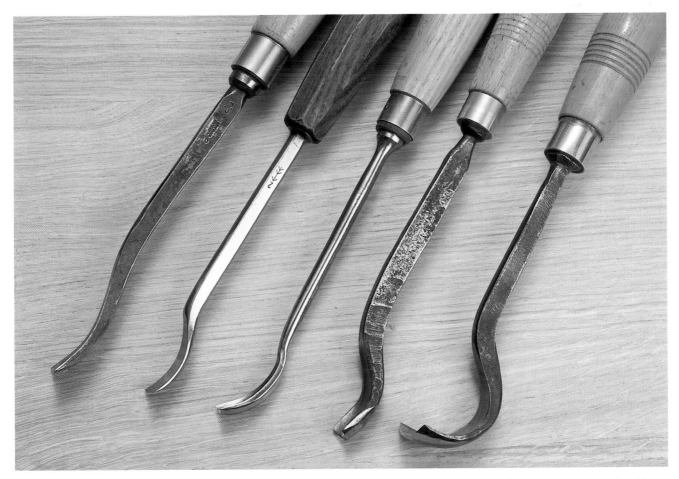

Fig 2.52 *As with longbent tools, the lengthwise curvature of shortbent tools by different manufacturers varies considerably, and some versions are hardly bent at all. The right-hand one was made by the author as described in Volume 2, Chapter 3*

Sometimes, but fortunately not often, a very awkward job requires such a bend that a special tool has to be made – perhaps with so much of a bend that the edge of the tool is actually facing back towards the handle. This is not too difficult a procedure, and Chapter 3 of Volume 2 gives you enough working details to tackle this problem. It is simplest to start with a tool which already has the sweep and width you want, so you need only alter the lengthwise bend.

Backbent tools

These are similar to shortbent gouges, but the curve is made in the opposite way. The odd-looking tool so produced comes into its own when carving a bead or other convex surface which curves concavely along its length – such as when a reed travels into a hollow or recess (Fig 2.54).

To put this another way, a convex surface (such as a reed) can be formed by turning an ordinary straight gouge upside down. Sometimes, though, when working that shape into a hollow, the handle of this straight gouge can get in the way. Cranking the handle back keeps it clear of the wood: this is the backbent gouge (Figs 2.55 and 2.56).

It may sound like a very specialized tool, but I find myself using it quite a lot. It is useful for many surfaces which are concave in one direction and convex in the other; such surfaces constantly occur in natural forms. To anticipate a subject which is covered more

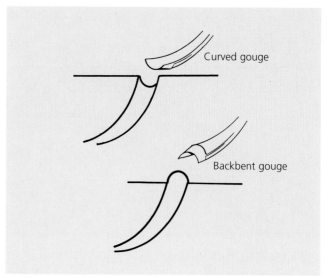

Fig 2.54 *Backbent gouges will deal with convex profiles which in turn curve into recesses*

Fig 2.55 *The basic backbent gouge*

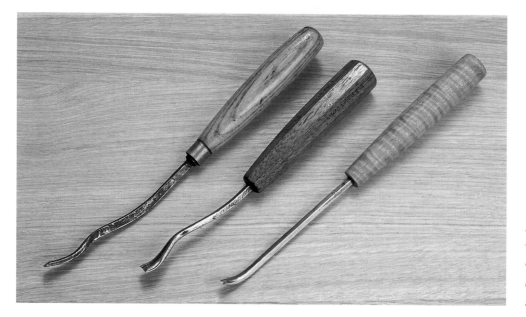

Fig 2.56 *Some home-made backbent gouges, two with the handle cranked back further for a more specialized purpose*

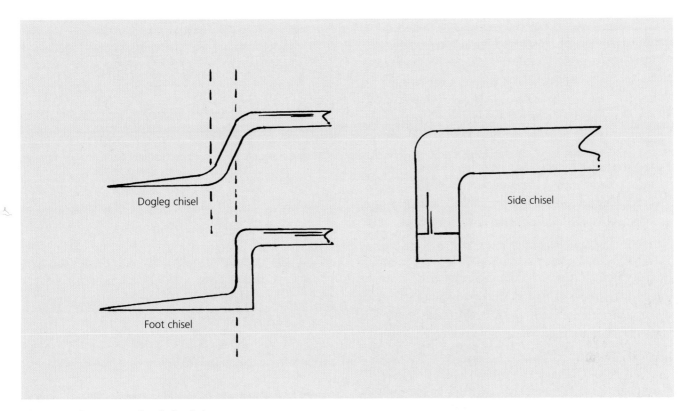

Fig 2.57 *Some specialized chisel shapes*

fully in Part II (pages 136–40), sharpening your straight gouges with an inner bevel reduces the need for backbents.

Generally speaking, all bent gouges can be obtained in the same variety of sweeps as the straight gouges. However, the deepest gouges (no. 11, and also no. 10 if this is a U-shape rather than a semicircle) are not available in the backbent form as they do not really work upside down. For the same reason, the V-tool is also unavailable in a backbent form. As with the tapered tools, some manufacturers may prefix the sweep number with another to specify the type of bend.

Dogleg tools

The **dogleg chisel** has two nearly 90° bends in its shank, towards the working end (Fig 2.57). It is used, like its counterpart the knuckle gouge, to get into very tight recesses, or when undercutting. A **foot chisel** is a more sharply angled version of the dogleg. A **side chisel** has an L-shaped shank; again, it can get into odd corners not reached by other shapes.

WIDTH

All woodcarving tools are available in a large range of widths (Fig 2.58). It is the working edge that is taken into account when measuring the width.

Fig 2.58 *Particular carvers may work with mostly large or mostly small tools, depending on the type of work they prefer, or specialize in*

- Chisels (straight, tapered or bent): the width is measured at right angles across the cutting edge. A skew chisel is measured across the maximum width of the blade, as if it had an edge at right angles – presumably because the length of the cutting edge depends on the angle at which it is ground (Fig 2.59).

- Gouges or parting tools (straight, tapered or bent): the width is measured as a straight line across the widest part of the mouth, at the very edge. This will be from corner to corner, at right angles to the long axis (Fig 2.60).

British manufacturers usually give the width both in imperial measurements (inches) and in approximate metric equivalents (millimetres), but most European tools use only metric. There is a conversion table at the end of this volume.

Widths start from very small, delicate tools of ⅟₁₆in (1.5mm), or occasionally less, and range up to large brutes of 2in (50mm) or more, used for sculpture (Fig 2.61). What widths are actually available varies between manufacturers – no one makes all the tools

Fig 2.60 With the exception of skew chisels, it is the actual cutting edge which is measured, from corner to corner

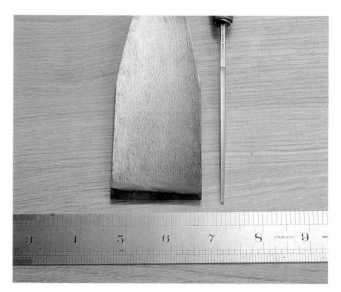

Fig 2.61 Width increments, between the smallest and largest for each type of carving tool, help to account for the enormous numbers that are available

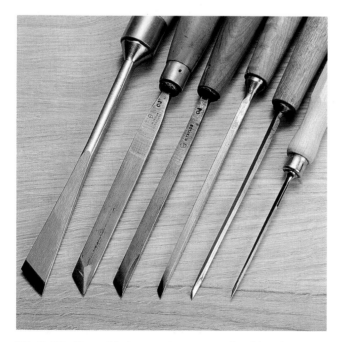

Fig 2.59 Skew chisels come in a range of widths. A newcomer should start with something in the middle (say ⅜in/10mm) and buy different sizes only when they are actually needed – which might be never

that could possibly be made. Most makers stock a wide variety of the most commonly used tools, having made, on economic grounds, some selection of sizes to offer the public. You may have to look around if you need an exact specification for a particular purpose. Some manufacturers will consider producing a tool to your special requirements.

LENGTH

The overall length of a woodcarving tool varies between manufacturers (Fig 2.62); you should also consider the length of the handle. Some make a range of tools in both larger and smaller overall sizes. As a guide, you may expect the blade of a ½in (13mm) gouge to be around 4–5in (100–125mm) from the shoulder to the edge. This is useful when you come across an old tool and are trying to work out how much has been worn away.

The lightweight gouges with mushroom-shaped handles, designed to be held in one hand, are really meant for wood engraving or wood cutting for printing purposes – although they can be used for any small-scale carving (Fig 2.63). The principles of sharpening covered in this book also apply to them. Normal carving tools are always held in both hands. If you are carving, rather than engraving or making

woodcuts, then the larger tools, of sufficient size to allow the free use of both hands, are what you need.

There are cheap sets of 'carving' tools around which are very small and look like the nibs of old dipping pens. They are made of soft metal and are meant for cutting soft linoleum and the like. They are not suitable for carving wood and should be avoided.

Fig 2.62 *Two brand-new tools by different manufacturers; the difference in length is about 1in (25mm)*

Fig 2.63 *Such mushroom handles are for woodblock makers' gouges or wood engravers' burins*

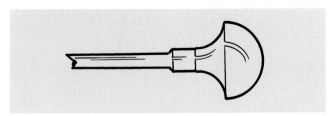

SUMMARY

I have described in this section, in some detail, the sorts of tools that are available, and the various terms you may come across.

- Gouges come in a series of curves or sweeps, ranging from very flat to very 'quick' or deep.

- This range of gouges can either be straight, or bent in various ways along the length of the blade.

- The straight gouges can have parallel sides, or sides which taper out from the shank or handle, splaying to varying degrees.

- The bent gouges can be bent along the whole length of the blade (longbent), or just at the far end away from the handle (shortbent).

- Shortbent gouges can be bent in either of two directions: so that the mouth or hollow of the gouge is at the front (frontbent), or at the back (backbent).

- This array of tools can be generally smaller or larger, and can be obtained in a large variety of widths.

When you buy a tool you will need to know:

- what sort of sweep or curve you want

- whether, and in what way, you want the tool bent or tapered

- how wide you want the tool to be.

Chapter 5, on selecting and buying tools, explains further how the shapes of these tools relate to their function, and includes a discussion of other considerations which need to be taken into account before buying any tools (see pages 80–96).

SHOULDERS

FUNCTION

The **shoulder** of a woodcarving tool, sometimes referred to as the **bolster** or **stop**, is the protuberance in the shank of the blade where the tang penetrates the handle. The word *bolster* seems to be used here in the same way we use the word elsewhere, meaning 'a cushion or pad'.

The flatness of the shoulder, as it meets the wood, prevents the tang being driven further into the handle and splitting it. The shoulder is, in effect, a sort of joint. It is particularly important when a carving tool, such as a large gouge, is struck with a mallet: the impact of a blow on the handle arrives at, and is taken almost entirely by, the shoulder (Fig 2.64). The force pushes on into the blade itself. The tang is not unlike a nail, and mallet blows can be unremittingly

– even unwittingly – heavy, especially on the larger sculpture tools. The shoulder works with the ferrule to stop the sharp tang forcing its way into the wood of the handle. Historically the shoulder predates the ferrule, presumably because making metal tubes was not easy.

Some carvers and manufacturers insert a hard leather or rubber washer between the shoulder and the handle to smooth this transmission of energy (Fig 2.65), but this is not actually necessary with a properly fitting shoulder.

Fig 2.65 *Leather washers like this are more for the sake of appearance than for function*

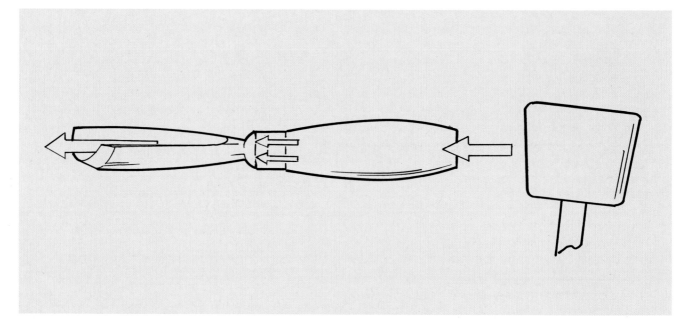

Fig 2.64 *The force of a mallet blow is taken and transmitted by the flat shoulder*

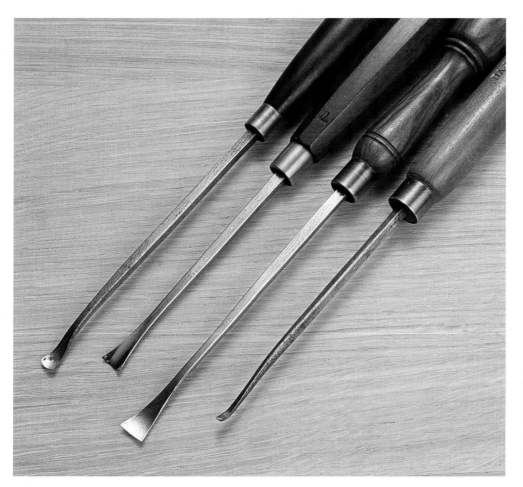

Fig 2.66 *Typically, shoulderless tools are lightweight and are used for finishing and delicate work*

Fig 2.67 *The flat end to the tang of a shoulderless tool (right) acts in a similar way to a shoulder, inhibiting the splitting of the handle*

SHOULDERLESS TOOLS

Not all carving tools have a shoulder. A shoulder is really only necessary, as is the ferrule, when there is a danger of splitting the handle. Light tools, which are only worked fairly delicately by hand, do not need the added protection of the shoulder and ferrule as the pressures on them are small (Fig 2.66). However, one very important feature of these shoulderless tools is that the end of the tang is squared off – this helps resist any further penetration of the tang into the handle (Fig 2.67).

At the most, these tools can be lightly struck with the heel of the hand, as carvers sometimes do. However, avoid the dangers of overusing this technique (see the section on using a mallet in Volume 2, Chapter 1).

A bad practice is to exert sideways leverage on such tools, as this can lead to splitting the handle, if not bending the tool or breaking its edge.

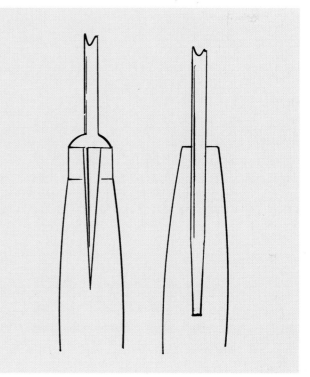

CORRECT SHAPE

The shoulder is formed quite early on when the tool is made, and it seems that the forming is often hurried in the rush to get on with making the blade itself. A look at a broad range of carving tools will verify this – the shoulders come in all shapes and sizes (Fig 2.68). They may be too large and overhang the ferrule; sometimes they are ridiculously small and only the ferrule prevents them pushing, cone-like, into the wood; sometimes they are badly offset to one side. But, to be fair, some manufacturers take a lot more care over the forming of the shoulders, and the tool as a whole, than do others (Figs 2.69 and 2.70).

The main features of a correctly shaped shoulder are as follows:

- The part of the metal in contact with the handle should be flat (Fig 2.71). It is not uncommon to have handles without ferrules, relying entirely on the flatness of the shoulder to prevent the wood splitting.

- The metal of the shoulder should be distributed equally, and evenly, around the shank.

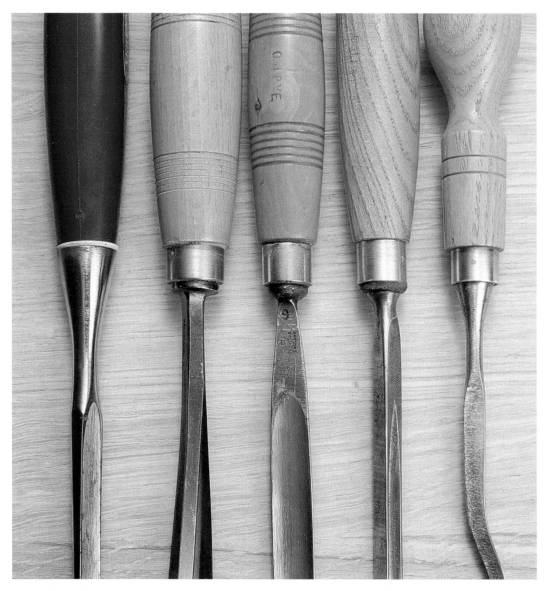

Fig 2.68 *Different manufacturers shape the shoulders of their tools in different ways, some taking more care than others*

• The shoulder size should relate to the size of the tool – larger tools needing appropriately larger shoulders. The shoulder should not overhang the ferrule – although this latter point can have as much to do with the handle being too small as the shoulder being too large.

Fig 2.69 *A beautifully forged shoulder with a good size and shape, seated well on the handle*

Fig 2.70 *The same shoulder from the handle side; it is obvious that trouble has been taken in the shaping*

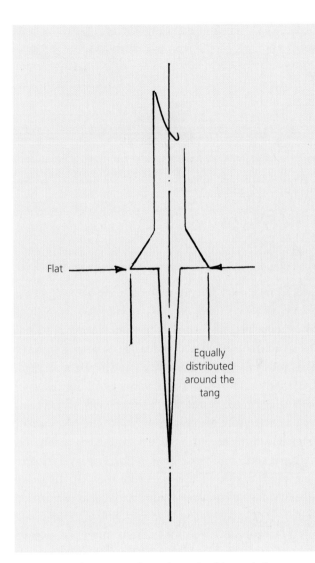

Flat

Equally distributed around the tang

Fig 2.71 *The correct shape for a shoulder or bolster*

TANGS

FUNCTION

The tang is the means whereby the blade itself can be fitted with something more comfortable and amenable to the hand than steel (Fig 2.72). The word *tang* comes, through Danish, from the Old Norse word *tangi*, meaning a point or spike. In dialect, *tang* has also referred to a serpent's tongue and an insect's sting, and, interestingly, connotes a penetrating taste.

The use of a tang is only one option, however. Another method, better in some ways but involving

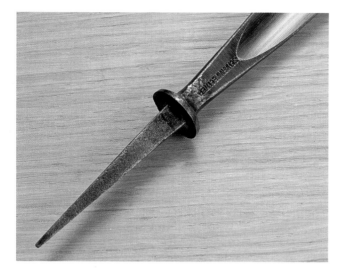

Fig 2.72 *A strong, straight, well-made and purposeful tang*

Fig 2.73 *A socketed shipwright's chisel with an iron end ferrule; such a strong socket will take far more punishment than a tang*

more labour and materials, is to form a conical socket into which the handle is fitted. This seems to have been quite a common method in the Bronze Age, when casting the socket was part of casting the tool itself. You can see examples of these tools, along with tanged chisels and gouges, in the National Museum of Wales, Cardiff. As early as the Iron Age, when the forging of tools had just started, socketed gouges were being made – one of these can be seen at the Lake Village Museum in Glastonbury, with a handle turned in oak. The Egyptians and Romans, whose tools can be seen in many museums, also commonly used sockets as well as tangs on their chisels. Depictions of medieval woodcarvers – including those carved on misericords, which must have been made by people who knew about these things – invariably show socketed gouges. The socket probably fell out of favour eventually because a tang is less labour-intensive to make. However, the socketed blade can still be seen in heavy chisels used to cut mortise-type woodworking joints, and in wheelwrights' and shipwrights' chisels (Fig 2.73), sometimes found in second-hand tool shops; in the USA it is still quite common for general woodwork. Some Chinese and Japanese chisels have both sockets and tangs.

The socket, merging into the blade, gives a much stronger tool that can be repeatedly and forcefully struck – consider that a 1½in (38mm) gouge may only have a ½in (13mm) shoulder and a ¼in (6mm) tang behind it. The strength accorded by the socket was

originally important when the metal of the blade had poor edge-keeping qualities and the woodwork was monumental – heavy work by today's standards.

Before damp-proofing, tools were more prone to rust, especially in the tang, which is hidden away in the handle. If oak was used for the handle, as it frequently seems to have been, the tannin in it would react with the iron of the tang when moisture was around. This corrosion of the tang, even when the handle is not oak, is still seen quite often in old tools that have not been kept in dry conditions. A socket, being a bigger mass of metal, resists this corrosion for much longer.

The socket is, therefore, tougher both mechanically and in its ability to resist the effects of time and damp. Early toolmakers would have appreciated that – bearing in mind the effort involved in making larger, heavier tools – socketed handles were a better investment of effort.

Sockets are still common in many cultures today, but they do make tools heavier. When it comes to smaller sizes, though, the socket tends to merge into the handle and produce an elegant tool. Should you come across any of the old heavy-duty socketed tools, remember that they can be reshaped into large, very tough gouges for sculpture.

Another option, instead of using a tang or a socket, is not to have a wooden handle at all. The whole tool can be made from a bar of steel – like a stonecarving chisel – and is struck with a metal hammer.

The metal part forming the 'handle' can be made more comfortable by binding it with a leather thong or some type of cane. This way of making carving tools is quite useful if you are making your own, as there is significantly less effort involved in working a blade into one end of a simple bar of metal. This can be of particular importance in countries where energy is considered more precious than it is in the industrialized world, and it is in these cultures that this sort of tool is most common.

TYPES

There are two types of tang: tapered and parallel. Both types are most commonly square in section, but the parallel ones are sometimes round (Fig 2.74). These require slightly different approaches when it comes to fitting them into the handle (see pages 69–70). The corners of the normal square-section tang bind into the wood and stop the handle turning on the blade. A round tang cannot bite the wood in the same way, and is therefore not as good (Fig 2.75).

Fig 2.75 *The parallel, round tang is unusual and does not 'bite' the wood like square-sectioned tangs. In this case the tang, and shoulder, are strong and well made, so there should be no problem providing the tang grips the hole in the handle tightly enough*

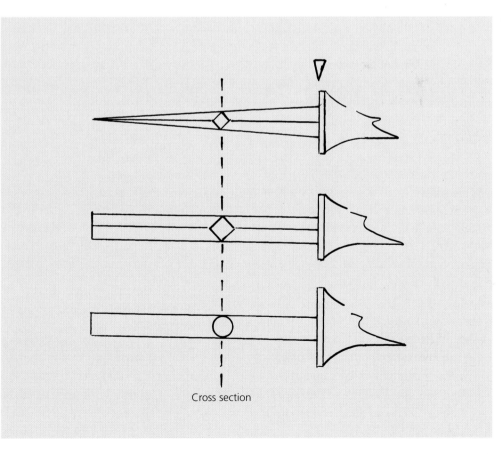

Cross section

Fig 2.74 *In general there are three types of tang, of which the square tapering sort is the most common*

CORRECT SHAPE

A tang can be made well or badly, with some manufacturers performing better than others. The tang has several important functions – often disregarded – and, like the shoulder, the shape of the tang may cause it to function efficiently or inefficiently.

The tang must be made without too many lumps and bumps, and should be straight

The tang must allow the handle to be fitted. Some carvers try to protect the tang from rust by soaking it in oil and pouring a little more into the hole before actually fitting the handle.

The tang must be in a straight line with the rest of the blade

This, if nothing else, is bound to affect the feel of the tool in your hand. From the arm, the hand grips the handle of the gouge in a straight line of intention. This intention wants to be carried straight through to the cutting edge without veering away to one side. Some carvers do put up with tools whose handles are bent at an angle to their blades; only when the handle and blade have been lined up correctly do they realize how much more satisfying the tool feels in this condition.

The tang must not be bent at an angle

I have seen this angle as much as 20° out of true. If such a gouge is struck heavily with a mallet, even with a good shoulder and ferrule, the bend can become gradually worse and the tool may threaten to break (Fig 2.76). The tang, shoulder and shank are made of a softer-tempered, less brittle metal compared with the blade itself. This is quite deliberate, allowing the impact of a blow to be absorbed and transmitted through the metal without its breaking under the stress. Should there be some angling away from the central axis of the tool already, there will be a tendency for the softer metal to bend further. Bending can also happen when the tool is used inappropriately like a small crowbar, to lever pieces of wood away (Fig 2.77).

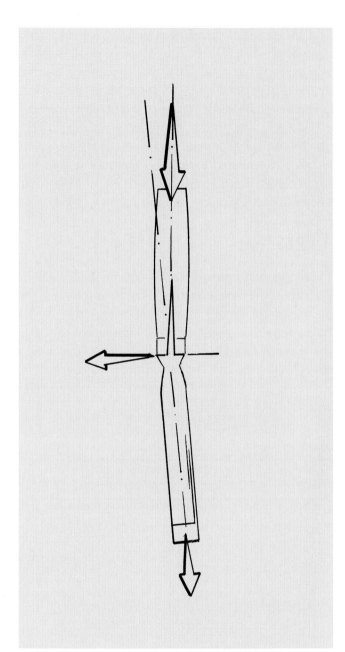

Fig 2.76 *Where the tang is bent at an angle to the axis of the blade, some of the mallet blow or driving force will go into flexing the tool – possibly bending it further*

The tang should not be offset

The tang is correctly aligned when it runs down the central axis of the shank and blade. If it is parallel to this axis but offset to one side (Fig 2.78), fitting a handle without the shoulder overhanging the ferrule becomes more difficult. This fault also affects the feel of the tool, as mentioned above.

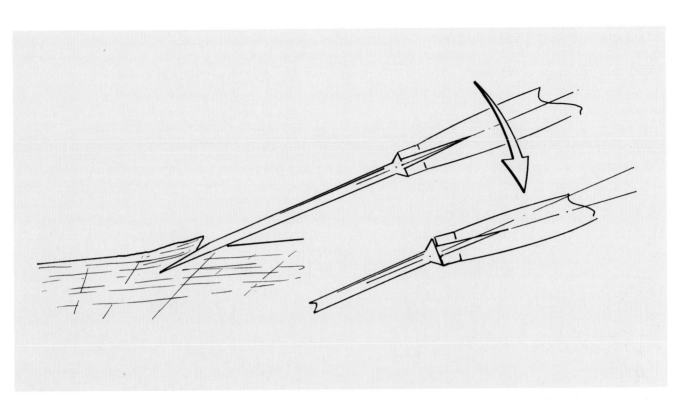

Fig 2.77 *A good way to bend the tang or break the blade is to use the tool to lever away pieces of wood*

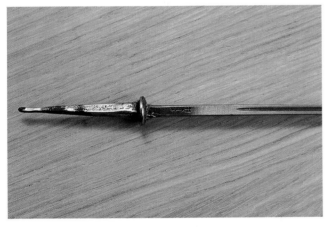

Fig 2.78 *A straightedge applied to the photograph will demonstrate how far the tang is from true*

The tang should be of a size and shape appropriate to the work that the tool can reasonably be expected to do

The tang should not be too short and fat, as this provides little purchase on the handle and interferes with the shoulder; nor should it be too long or thin in a larger tool, as this may be a point of weakness (Fig 2.79).

Fig 2.79 *When we get to carving tools of this size – 2½in (65mm) – a tang only ¼in (6mm) wide is beginning to look a little inadequate, and a socket might be a better option*

51

Fig 2.80 summarizes some of the faults to be avoided. There can also be a problem with tangs in older tools which are partly, or completely, rusted away. All might not be lost: see the section on second-hand tools in Chapter 5 (pages 95–6).

If you ever have occasion to buy tools without handles, carefully inspect the tang along with the rest of the tool, bearing all the above points in mind. Some faults can be corrected, but where they cannot – or perhaps you do not feel you *should* have to correct them – return the tool with the appropriate explanation and politely ask for a better one. Putting up with manufacturing faults does nobody any favours in the long run.

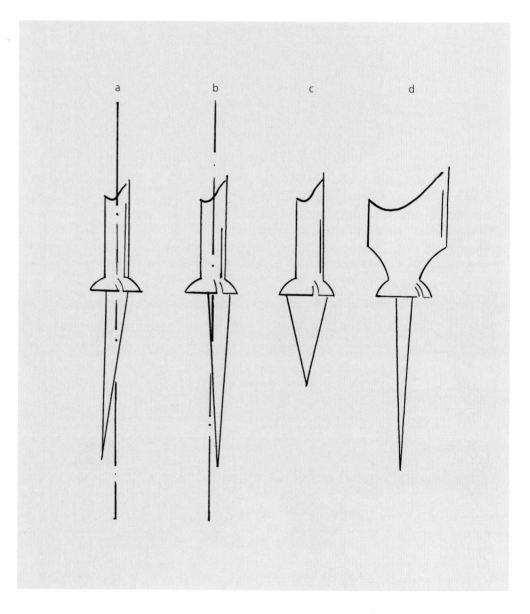

Fig 2.80 *Some faults commonly found in tangs: (a) angled with respect to the axis of the blade; (b) parallel to the axis but offset to one side; (c) too short, with not enough shoulder; (d) too long and thin for the size of the blade*

HANDLES

OVERVIEW

The previous chapter started by looking at carving tools from the end furthest away from us: the blade and shank. Then we turned to the shoulder and tang. Now we come to the nearest part of the whole tool: the handle, which is often undervalued.

Supplying tools with fitted handles is a phenomenon of mass production over the last 100 years or so. There is at least one advantage: if the tool is supplied already 'handled' and – as the tendency is today – already 'sharpened', then, in theory at least, you can consider yourself up and running for the nearest piece of wood.

Carvers used to buy their tools unhandled, with just the steel blade and its naked tang. Unhandled tools can still be bought from some suppliers. The carver would then make and fit a handle personally. This was usually from a square piece of wood, subsequently shaped to an octagonal section and without a ferrule. This meant that – depending on the wood to hand and the mood of the carver – the handles would all be distinct. Without the ferrules the handles may

not have lasted as long, but replacing them would not have been considered a problem. Old handles of a factory-made type often show a variety of marks, glyphs or notches where the carver tried to make some tool handles stand out from others.

Today, manufacturers rarely provide more than three sizes of handle, all exactly the same shape, for the whole range of their carving tools. In fairness, this is probably as much as they may reasonably be expected to provide, as they are primarily makers of carving tools, not handles.

Factory-made handles are therefore convenient, but all the handles are more or less the same; handmade handles involve additional effort, but the result is more individual and personal. This needs to be considered a little further, because there are definite advantages to handmade handles, making the additional effort worthwhile. The handle makes the tool more comfortable in the hand, but there is more to it than that.

The handle lies between the blade, which works the wood, and yourself, who directs the carving. Its very name describes its function: it is the bit you 'handle' and actually hold in your hand (Fig 3.1).

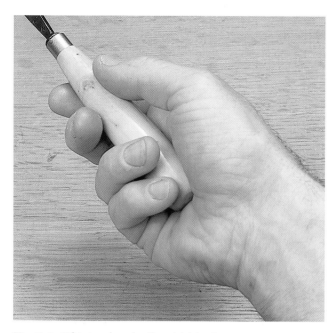

Fig 3.1 This is what the 'hand-le' is about

Lying as it does between the blade and you, it must have a relationship not only to the size and shape of the blade, but also to the hand or hands holding it. The handle plays a vital role in establishing the comfort, strength, efficiency, balance and 'feel' of the whole tool. A tool may be perfectly sharpened but still not 'feel right': it sits awkwardly in the hand; perhaps it is not one to which you feel attracted. This in turn will affect how you carve, in anything from a subtle to a significant way.

It is not the tools themselves which decide whether a carving is successful or not – a whole array of mental factors and attitudes surrounding the act of carving itself come into play as well. A tool appears to respond to the amount of effort, even love, that is put into its care. Such an attitude of care and attention to the tools feeds into the process of carving. It is hard to abuse a beautiful tool, one into which a lot of care and effort has been put. It is as if the tool draws your best effort towards itself. Carving tools are the vehicles through which creativity and pleasure flow. A carver absorbed in carving will forget the tools – at this point you are working directly with the wood, without any tool in the way (Fig 3.2).

This is the first reason for making your own tool handles, or at least some of them: you are making the tool personal in a way which is not possible with the

Fig 3.2 Effortless carving by the great master Riemenschneider: St Barbara (Bayerisches Nationalmuseum, Munich) carved about 1515 in limewood

blade itself. After all, it is your hand on the handle, not a mass-produced, average hand. Besides this, there are several other reasons for not buying factory-made handles:

A mass-produced handle looks like every other mass-produced handle

It is quite possible to have 40, 50 or more carving tools arrayed on the bench and at work. Every carving tool that you possess may be on the bench among wood chips, sawdust, pencils and other tools. In such cases similarity between gouges and chisels can cause confusion and irritation (Fig 3.3). It is important for efficiency and continuity of purpose that individual tools are readily recognized and picked up. This is accomplished far more easily if the shape, size, type of wood or colour of the handles is varied (Fig 3.4). It helps to distinguish at least some of the handles on your carving tools, even if you do not do it for all of them.

54

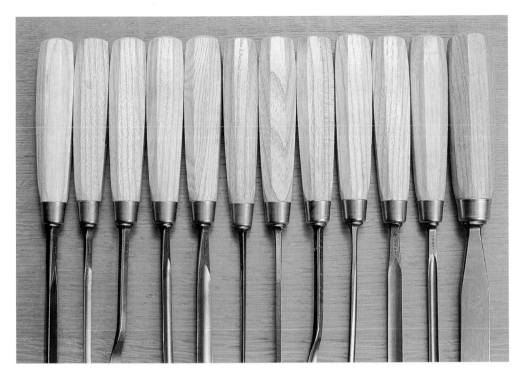

Fig 3.3 *Although there is nothing 'wrong' with the handles in themselves, when such mass-produced handles are aligned on the bench, their similar appearance can be confusing*

Fig 3.4 *Differently shaped handles, also in different types and colours of wood, make tools more immediately recognizable on the bench*

The overall length of the tool can be controlled by varying the length of the handle

For example, a particularly short tool can be given a better overall working length – and a longer useful life – by increasing the length of the handle (Fig 3.5). Another example would be fitting an extra-long handle to a large flat gouge; this gives the tool greater slicing leverage and speed for cleaning and finishing backgrounds (Fig 3.6).

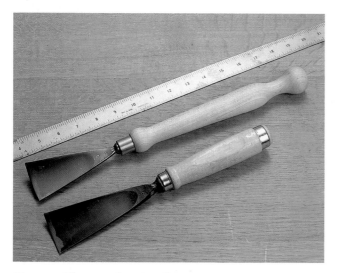

Fig 3.5 *It is possible to lengthen a short tool to the normal overall length by means of a custom-made handle*

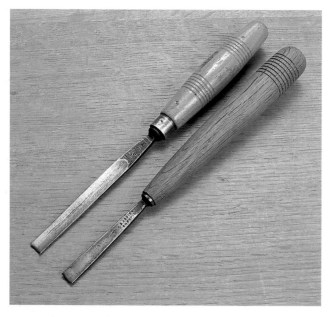

Fig 3.6 *The extra-long handle on one of these shallow gouges facilitates the flattening of backgrounds*

The handle can be suited to both the hand and the blade

Because of the limited range of mass-produced handles compared with the large variety of carving-tool shapes and sizes, such handles can often be entirely the wrong size or shape for the tool. Since hands vary as well, the handle may also be uncomfortable.

The handle of a sculpture gouge needs to be gripped comfortably and held easily for long periods. There are shapes which are more suited to mallet work, tending to bind into the hand better and not sliding through (Figs 3.7 and 3.8).

Fig 3.7 *This design of handle which I have developed for sculpture gouges . . .*

Fig 3.8 *. . . fits into the hand well. In use it tends to grip more firmly than other types*

By flattening one side of the handle of a straight gouge, the handle can be lowered that little bit extra, which gains vital access for the cutting edge in a hollow when a bent tool of the same shape is not available.

IMPROVING BOUGHT HANDLES

Bought handles very often have a thick layer of varnish which can cause your hand to become unpleasantly warm and sweaty, even slippery (Fig 3.9). There may also be ridges and sharp corners to make the hands sore – these are often found at the very end of an octagonal handle (Fig 3.10). Octagonal handles are good shapes for setting down on an inclined plane – for instance, when lettering a panel – as they do not roll so easily; but end corners, if they are not softened, can work into the palm of the pushing hand.

Varnish can be removed with sandpaper, followed by oiling the wood; sharp edges and corners can be filed or sanded away. This allows you to take some control over some of the qualities of your carving-tool handles – the next step would be to make your own handle from the beginning.

If you have quite a lot of tools with mass-produced handles, consider remaking the handles a few at a time, starting with favourite tools. You may be able to see some ways of reshaping or altering the existing handles to make them more personal, distinctive or better-functioning.

It is not difficult to make your own handles for woodcarving tools, and the time invested is not much compared to the years over which you may be using them. Once the importance of handle quality is realized, no further encouragement will be necessary.

Of course, there is nothing to stop you going straight ahead with mass-produced handles and producing wonderful carvings. At the end of the day handles are not carvings, only part of the means towards that end. What I am trying to promote here is an attitude of positive regard for carving tools, in the hope that this attitude will make the carving itself more satisfying and successful. This attitude or approach works *with* creative potential, rather than against it.

Fig 3.9 *A thick layer of varnish over the whole handle has congealed into a glob on the ferrule. Removing it may make the handle much more comfortable*

Fig 3.10 *Octagonal handles can have quite sharp corners (top); round them over to make them more comfortable*

SHAPES AND IDENTIFICATION

From the illustrations in this chapter it can be seen that handles can have many possible shapes – some very traditional, some a little more unusual. When you come to choose the shape and size of handle, you will need to bear in mind the shape and size of the blade to which the handle will fit, the 'roughness' of use to which the tool will be put, the size of your hands, and so on. There is a large degree of free choice, with no hard-and-fast rules, but here are some useful guidelines:

SIZE

• A good overall length for a woodcarving tool is somewhere between 9 and 10in (225–250mm), so you need to adjust the length of handle to suit. Around 4–5in (100–125mm) for the handle is common (Figs 3.11 and 3.12).

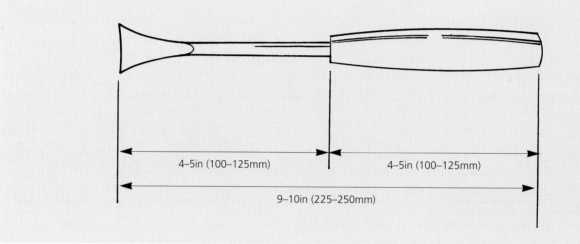

Fig 3.11 *The overall length of a carving tool will involve a balance between the length of the blade and that of the handle*

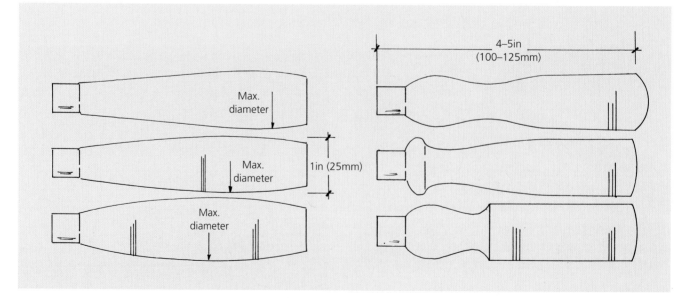

Fig 3.12 *Some possible handle shapes and approximate sizes. The maximum thickness of the row on the left can, of course, be varied to suit the tool or the user*

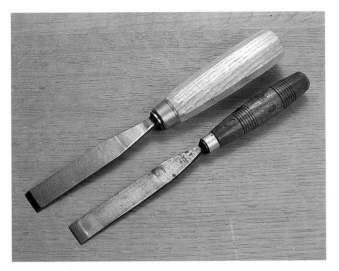

Fig 3.13 Roughly the same size of tool, fitted with different sizes and shapes of handle by different manufacturers. The choice comes down to individual preference

- The width of the handle is usually ⅞–1in (22–25mm) at its maximum point, but should be larger for bigger hands (Fig 3.13).

SHAPE (Figs 3.14 and 3.15)

- Large gouges need larger, heavier handles.

- Thin, delicate gouges suit longer, thinner handles.

- Short, small gouges can have the length of the blade made up in the length of the handle.

- A carving tool that is struck a lot with a mallet might be held better with a more wedge-shaped handle – a shape which grips into the hand. The wedge does not want to be too conical; this in itself can feel uncomfortable. Fatter, barrel-like shapes tend to pop out of the hand. The concavity of a wedge-and-ball, **London pattern** or pattern-maker's handle (bottom right in Fig 3.12) gains a good purchase for the first finger and thumb.

- Make sure there are no hard corners to dig into the palm of the hand that is pushing the handle.

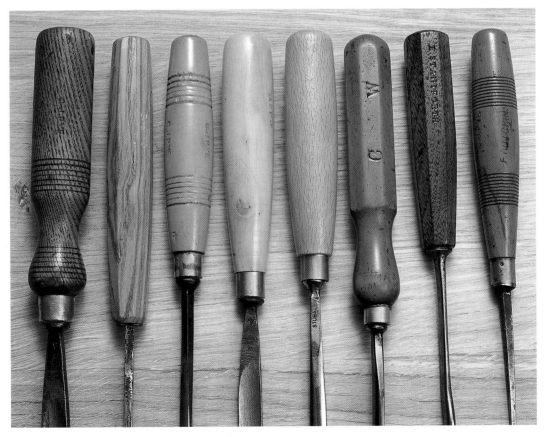

Fig 3.14 Some classic handle shapes

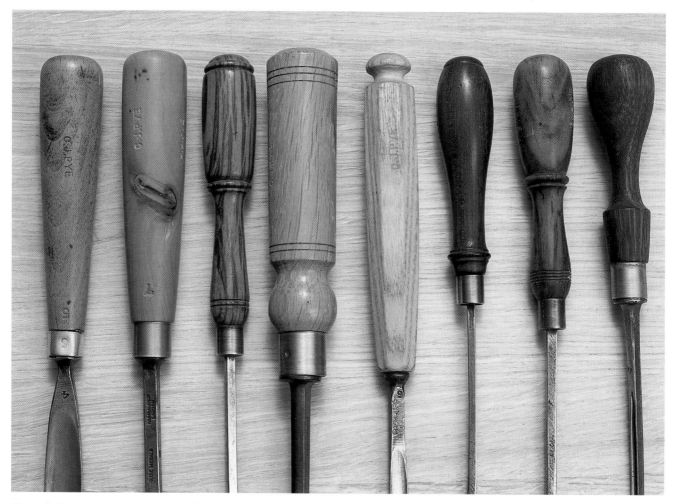

Fig 3.15 *Some more unusual handle shapes*

- With barrel-shaped (**carver pattern**) handles, the point of maximum bulge can be varied in its position along the length. So can the amount of this bulge in relation to the length. This will be a matter of what feels right. A wide end is more easily struck with the mallet (Fig 3.16).

- Octagonal handles are gripped much more securely than round ones, and do not roll on the bench. They can be made by shaping a square-sectioned piece of wood, rather than by using a lathe. Turned handles go back to Roman times, and no doubt the octagonal ones are equally old. To put a ferrule on an octagonal handle shaped by hand involves some accurate whittling, so invariably these handles did not (and still do not) have ferrules. If they split, then it is not too much effort to make another.

Fig 3.16 *The wider end of the upper handle is a better target for the mallet than the other, which reduces towards a point*

REINFORCEMENT

- A tool used for light work will probably not need a ferrule, or even a shoulder. However, make sure the handle is made from tight, straight-grained wood.

- A larger tool, doing more work, will benefit from a ferrule at the tang end to make sure the wood does not split here.

- If the tool is expected to take a great deal of pounding from the mallet, an additional ferrule on the top end of the handle will cause it to last longer, preventing the wood splitting and mushrooming out.

WOODS

Handles need a resilient hardwood with close, straight grain, that has been properly seasoned (definitely not green). Certain factors are important in determining the suitability of a piece of wood to be used for making handles.

RESILIENCE

Wood can either be taken from near the centre of the tree (**heartwood**), or towards the outside (**sapwood**). The wood taken from towards the outside, even though the tree is still called a **hardwood**, can be soft and open-grained. Wood for handles should be taken from the tougher heartwood, although not from the actual centre of the tree. This would be the toughest, hardest option. Some woods, like ash or hickory, have a natural resilience or springiness.

STRAIGHT GRAIN

The grain of the handle should run along its axis, not diagonally across it, even in part. This is especially important if a mallet is to be used: cross grain in the handle can split from a blow on the end (Fig 3.17). Uneven, difficult grain can also create problems when fitting the tang into the handle. Knots may be a problem, depending on where they are, their size, and whether they are 'live' or 'dead'. They can be an attractive feature, as can **burled (burred)** wood, but you need to be careful when using the mallet.

CLOSE GRAIN

Trees which have grown very quickly produce broad **annual rings** and relatively light, soft wood – the heartwood can be as soft as the sapwood. Use a tight, close grain, where the tree has grown slowly. Usually it is just a matter of selecting and putting aside odd bits of wood for use as handles when you need them.

SPECIES

The following list, which is by no means complete, may be useful in selecting wood for a handle:

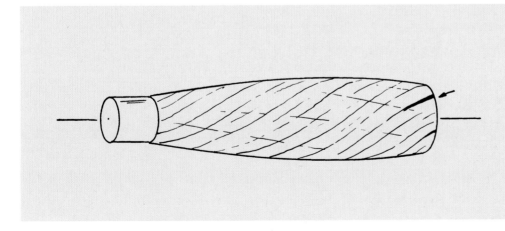

Fig 3.17 *Short or cross grain in a handle is susceptible to splitting, especially when a mallet is used*

- For tools struck heavily with a mallet: box, ash, hickory, pau marfim.

- For tools occasionally struck with a mallet: any of the above, plus beech, well-seasoned oak, fruitwood (such as cherry, apple or plum), maple, sycamore, hornbeam.

- For tools rarely or never struck with a mallet: any of the above, plus rosewood, teak, mahogany.

FERRULES

A ferrule is a metal collar binding the end of a handle to strengthen the wood against splitting. The word itself relates both to the Latin *ferrum*, meaning 'iron', and to the Old French *virelle*, meaning 'a bracelet'. Many terms show the great importance of the Norman and French influence both on stonecarving and woodcarving in Britain.

The ferrule can be fitted at either the tang end (a **tang ferrule**), or the free end of the handle (an **end ferrule**).

TANG FERRULES

Such ferrules reinforce the wood against the tang being driven, spike-like, into the end grain. When force is exerted sideways on the blade, the ferrule prevents the handle splitting. More delicate carving tools, and those with good, flat shoulders, do not actually need a ferrule – although one is often fitted to the handle as a matter of course.

Manufactured ferrules are normally made of brass, which resists stretching and does not corrode. If you cannot buy purpose-made, loose ferrules, then a strong piping or tube with walls about $\frac{1}{16}$–$\frac{1}{8}$in (1.5–3mm) thick will substitute. A short trip to a scrap yard or metal supplier's will produce enough ferrule metal to last a lifetime.

The size of the tang ferrule should relate to the size of the blade, particularly its shoulder and tang (Fig 3.18). The shoulder can rest on the edge of the ferrule, but an overhanging shoulder is uncomfortable. The amount of wood between tang and ferrule should be neither too great, in which case the wood gives, nor too little (for instance, if the ferrule is very thick), in which case this part of the handle is weakened.

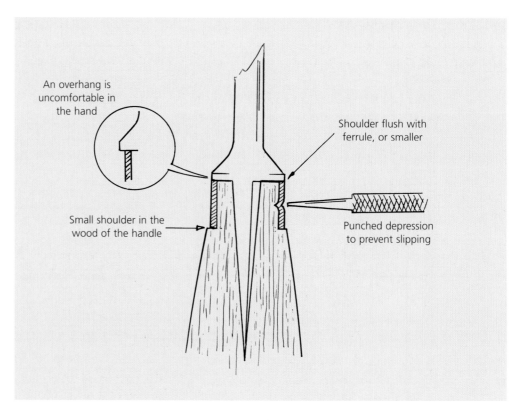

An overhang is uncomfortable in the hand

Small shoulder in the wood of the handle

Shoulder flush with ferrule, or smaller

Punched depression to prevent slipping

Fig 3.18 *The relation of the shoulder or bolster to the ferrule*

One important feature of a ferrule is that it has a bevel on the inside of one end. This end is offered to the wood of the handle, which is made a touch over-size. When it is tapped home, the inside bevel pinches the wood tightly and the ferrule compresses the wood, so it will not work loose if the handle eventually shrinks a little (Fig 3.19).

Fig 3.19 *Close-up of a brass tang ferrule, showing the inside bevel. The bevel is offered to the handle first, and jams the ferrule in place by compressing the wood*

Fig 3.21 *A favourite shoulderless tool benefits from a lovely bit of ferrule improvisation*

Manufactured handles today sometimes have an internal ferrule, which may be visible only when the blade is removed (Fig 3.20). Home-made handles may be protected against splitting in a variety of ways (Fig 3.21).

END FERRULES

When a mallet is used, the top of the handle takes a great deal of punishment and is easily damaged (Fig 3.22). It is sometimes possible to salvage a damaged handle by paring away the broken part, or by gluing splits before they develop too far (Fig 3.23).

Fig 3.20 *Internal ferrules like this are mostly found on the mass-produced handles of continental Europe. The offset hole in this example is not intentional*

Fig 3.22 *Repeated mallet blows may eventually split pieces off the end of the handle*

Fig 3.23 *Damage to the end of the handle may be trimmed off (top) or glued. The circlip on the lower handle was an emergency repair to allow the doomed handle to be used a while longer*

Fig 3.24 *Two sculpture gouges fitted with end ferrules*

Fig 3.25 *Even an iron ferrule can itself burr over after weeks of hard mallet work*

If a tool is going to be struck heavily with a mallet, the life of the handle will be considerably extended by banding the free end with a thick ferrule (Figs 3.24 and 3.25). This needs to be thicker-walled than a tang ferrule, and preferably made of iron. Many types of piping will be suitable.

With a steel or iron ferrule on the end of a large sculpture gouge, a soft-metal **dummy mallet**, such as is used by stonecarvers, can be used instead of the normal wooden mallet. This sort of mallet is made of soft, annealed iron and has the advantage that a good weight is possible without bulking up the size.

MAKING AND FITTING FERRULES

Mark the selected tube and cut it squarely with a hacksaw or a pipe cutter. Clean up and remove any burrs on a benchstone or grinding wheel. (Be careful here: grip the tube in self-locking Mole grips, and apply it *lightly* to the side of the wheel.) An inside bevel can be formed with a round file or a small, conical grinding wheel, such as those designed to fit into an electric drill.

For a tang ferrule, the end wood of the handle, onto which the shoulder of the blade sits, should finish flush and square with the free edge of the ferrule. Flatten the end wood with a sanding block after the ferrule is fitted.

For an end ferrule, allow the wood to extend a little way out of the metal tube. With use the wood will eventually mushroom over, taking the metal of the ferrule with it, giving rise to less wear and tear on the mallet. You may like to start this process by planishing over the corners with a hammer first.

When any type of ferrule is fitted, it should butt onto a little shoulder formed in the wood (which must be made at the same time as the handle), just wide enough to merge the wood comfortably with the metal.

Sometimes, as an added precaution, a centre punch is used to make one or two depressions in the side of the ferrule – this locks it on in case the wood shrinks or the ferrule works loose.

MAKING HANDLES

The hole into which the tang will fit must be aligned along the central axis of the handle (Fig 3.26). To achieve this, bore the hole first, whatever shape of handle you are making. If the hole is first made true, and the shape then worked around the hole, the tang – and the blade – will align correctly along the handle (provided the tang is true to the blade).

It is also helpful, but not necessary, to start with a square-sectioned piece of wood which is a little oversize and overlength. The wood does not need to be

Fig 3.26 *Accurate boring is needed if the blade is to be concentric with the handle*

planed, but can be accurately bandsawn; a little care taken over the initial accuracy of the blank makes the following stages easier. Mark the centres at each end of the wood by drawing diagonally across the corners, and use a point to punch a small starting depression at the point of intersection; this will prevent the drill bit wandering as it starts to bite. Once you have a squared-up, centred block, you can bore the hole.

BORING THE HOLE

Whether the tang is tapering or parallel in section, it helps to drill an accurate pilot hole first, no more than ⅛in (3mm) in diameter. It can then be enlarged with a drill of the appropriate diameter to fit the tang.

- If you have a parallel round tang, make the final hole an exact tight fit along its whole length.

- For a parallel square tang, bore the hole to a size which is halfway between the diagonal of the square and one of its sides (Fig 3.27). Test the fit of the hole first on a piece of scrap wood. The corners of the tang bite and lock into the wood of the hole.

- For a tapered tang, bore a guiding pilot hole about ⅛in (3mm) in diameter and use the 'twist' method of fitting the handle which is described later (page 70). This method also works for parallel square tangs, though it is not possible to adjust the angle of the handle in the process, as you can with a tapered tang. If the wood is something like box, with a propensity for

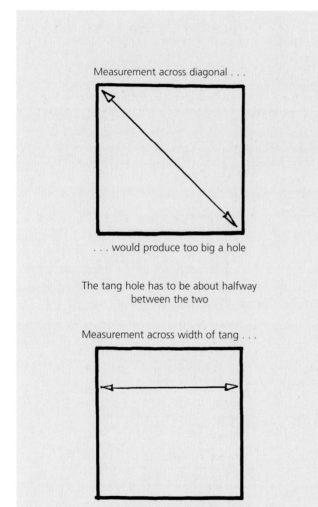

Measurement across diagonal . . .

. . . would produce too big a hole

The tang hole has to be about halfway between the two

Measurement across width of tang . . .

. . . would produce too small a hole

Fig 3.27 *Estimating the correct size of hole for a parallel square tang*

splitting, then enlarge the hole to about a third of its depth by boring with a larger drill. Take a measurement of the diagonal of the tapering tang a third of the way down from the shoulder, and make this the diameter of the second drill.

There are various ways to bore the hole accurately. The easiest method (whether you are intending to turn the handle or not) is to bore the hole on a lathe; the wood automatically lines up axially between the centres (see opposite).

The next-best method is to use a pillar drill, which is, in effect, a lathe turned vertically. The handle needs to be aligned correctly using a simple jig. Pass a screw perpendicularly through a plate of plywood, MDF (medium-density fibreboard), etc. Clamp the plate to the pillar-drill table so that the drill bit descends dead on the point of the screw.

To use the jig, place the centre of one end of the wooden blank onto the screw point and lock the pillar drill to start a little above the other end. For the pilot hole of ⅛in (3mm), you can hold the wood in position with one hand and lower the drill with the other. Clear the hole of sawdust regularly and there will be little problem with the wood twisting in your grip. If some clamping method is available with the drill, then do use it.

If you have neither lathe nor pillar drill, bore the hole using an ordinary wheel brace (hand drill) or a hand-held electric drill. The problem still remains of how to bore the hole true; the tried methods of a helper's eye, or a set-square placed as a guide on the bench next to the drilling, can work well here. In any case, it is best to bore the hole while the wood is over-size; it can then be fitted partway on to the tang and the axis of blade marked on it before shaping.

Once the pilot hole has been drilled, the size of the hole can be incrementally enlarged as necessary. Hold the wood in a vice and allow each bit to follow the hole made by the preceding one.

SHAPING THE HANDLE

OCTAGONAL HANDLES

Try and get these as accurate as possible, although what really matters is the feel of the handle – test this often. There should be enough width of wood remaining at the tang end for any shoulder to seat correctly. Bore the hole first, bearing in mind my earlier comments on the shape of the tang (pages 49–52).

1 Start with a square piece of wood, accurately sawn (and planed if possible), with the centres marked at each end.

2 Draw the profile of the handle on one face of the wood and cut the waste off cleanly using a bandsaw or coping saw.

3 Use adhesive tape or masking tape to reattach the bits sawn off and, turning the wood over 90°, draw the profile again.

4 Saw off the waste a second time and you should end up with a four-sided profile of the final handle.

5 Smooth the faces squarely with a spokeshave, rasp, file, etc.

6 Chamfer the corners by eye in the same way to give the eight sides. It may be helpful to make a V-shaped cradle to hold the handle securely, as shown in Fig 3.36 (page 72).

7 Octagonal handles, as mentioned before, normally do not have ferrules. If you do want to

fit one, it is either a job for the lathe, or a matter of paring or rasping the wood into shape.

8 Sand the handle smooth; round over the end that will push into the palm of your hand, and seal the wood as for the turned handle described below.

TURNED HANDLES

1 Bore the hole first, with the drill bit held in a Jacobs chuck at the drive end of the lathe. Use a slow speed, and feed the wood from the tailstock to the necessary depth (Fig 3.28). Mark the depth of the various drill bits with masking tape. If several handles are being made, bore them all as one procedure.

2 Remove the wood and the Jacobs chuck from the lathe, and fit the normal drive centre. Reverse the wood on to the lathe so the point of the revolving centre is in the hole, and tighten up.

3 Rough the handle to a cylinder, then move in the toolrest as close as possible.

4 Fit the ferrule next; mark its length and a little extra on the end of the wood. Using a square chisel and callipers, carefully reduce the wood

Fig 3.28 On the lathe, a hole can be drilled easily and accurately between centres

Fig 3.29 *Sizing down to a close fit for the ferrule*

to the *outside* diameter of the ferrule, keeping the shoulder square (Fig 3.29). Stop the lathe and try pushing on the ferrule; remember to offer the end of the ferrule with the inside bevel to the wood.

5 By trial and error, creep up on a final diameter where the ferrule pushes on tightly. You may need to take the handle off the lathe and, with the ferrule on the edges of a vice or piece of tube, tap the ferrule home.

6 An end ferrule, if required, is fitted in a similar manner.

7 Now, with the ferrule in place, shape the handle. Round the end to fit comfortably in your hand. Do not run the wood completely down to the ferrule, but leave it a shade proud where they meet – a definite, but *small*, shoulder should remain.

8 Sand the handle and then burnish with shavings. The wood can be left like this, acquiring the natural patina of use, or sealed with a coat of cellulose lacquer, varnish or shellac. Cut the sealer back finely. Do not give the surface a shiny or glossy finish: this makes the grip uncomfortable, slippery and possibly dangerous.

9 Use the point of a turner's skew chisel to trim back the excess wood at the ferrule end, but take care not to cut into the revolving centre (Fig 3.30).

Fig 3.30 *Cleaning the end of the fully shaped handle with the skew*

⑩ Part off the handle and remove it from the lathe. Hold it in a vice and finish off both ends with a chisel and sandpaper. Flatten the hole end so that the blade shoulder fits flush to the wood. Seal the ends in the same way as the rest of the handle.

⑪ Finally, punch a locking depression in each side of the ferrule – a nail will do for this. A thick end ferrule may need a small hole with a nail tapped in.

FITTING HANDLES

Faults with the blades, and especially the shoulders and tangs, need to be corrected as far as possible to give the best chance of fitting a handle well. These are dealt with in Chapter 4.

Old carving tools can be found with quite large and not particularly accurate holes for the tangs, filled with gutta-percha (a resinous gum from a Malayan tree). The tang has been pushed accurately into the gum which has then set like hard, black horn, fixing the blade neatly and securely in position (Fig 3.31). This is a trick worth remembering. Modern equivalents (such as the two-part plastic fillers intended for car bodies or wood) will repair a handle, perhaps correcting too large a hole, or one that is offset. The only snag is that if the tool is struck with a mallet, the tang will work loose; but for lighter tools this method is quite adequate.

To knock on a handle, the blade must be held properly. If you were to set the blade upright so its cutting edge was against a resistant surface and then thump on the handle, there would be a problem: the tool would have nowhere to travel and, as the energy from the mallet blow could not be released, the blade might crack. This is particularly true of U-shaped blades, where the bevels on either side act as wedges, squeezing the sides together.

Instead, grip the chisel in a vice by the shank of the blade, so that *the shoulder is supported on the jaws of the vice* and the tang points straight up in the air (Fig 3.32). A metalworking vice with soft metal linings is the best sort to use; but a woodworking vice is an alternative, if you first pack out and protect any wooden linings with scrap hardwood.

Fig 3.32 *To fit a handle, hold the tool so that the shoulder rests on, and is gripped by, the jaws of a vice, with the tang vertical*

Fig 3.31 *An old carving tool in which the blade has been fitted to the handle with gutta-percha*

The other point to mention is not to thump too freely, but take the fitting of the handle in a relaxed and easy way.

The method varies for parallel and tapered tangs:

PARALLEL TANGS

If the holes are the right size, the parallel tangs, both round and square, should knock straight on with a mallet.

TAPERED TANGS

❶ Tap the handle, with its pilot hole, on to the tang a little way then twist it around both ways – the tang is being used to ream out the hole (Fig 3.33).

Fig 3.33 *The 'tap and twist' method of fitting a handle*

❷ Tap the handle a little more and twist again. Remove the handle and tap out the dust.

❸ Keep repeating this process with the handle in one hand and the mallet in the other, taking the handle off now and then and tapping out the dust. You will fairly quickly get a rhythm, and before long will have set the handle down on the tang to within ⅛in (3mm) of the shoulder.

❹ At this point clear the dust out one last time and select which part of the handle – perhaps a pleasing bit of grain – you want to appear where. More importantly, if the tang and hole are at all offset, now is the time to look for 'compensating errors' – the handle may well fit straighter one way than another.

❺ Now tap the handle home, and there should be no problem of splitting. If your tang and holes are true, the blade will be aligned along the axis of the handle.

One final point: the method by which the tang is heated and burnt into the handle is only appropriate if a hole cannot be bored and you are really desperate. While no doubt it is fun, it also chars the wood inside, allowing the handle to work loose; it can be messy and not without its dangers – both to the lungs and to a wood-filled workshop; and it can, if care is not taken, damage the tempering of the tool. It is also much slower than any method described here – all in all it is not a technique to be recommended.

REMOVING HANDLES

Although problems of sticking do arise with old tools and rusty tangs, the handle of a woodcarving gouge or chisel normally comes off without much difficulty. This is especially true of tools that have tapered, square tangs – these lock securely in place during use, but release from the wood fairly easily when required.

For the following methods of removing handles, grip the tool in a vice by a substantially strong part such as the shank, just beyond the shoulder. If an engineer's vice with metal jaws is being used, pack the jaws with hardwood pieces to protect the blade from being marked.

Never grip quick gouges – and especially U-shaped ones – across the blade. The pressure of the vice can crack the metal which, having been hardened and tempered, is more brittle than flexible.

METHOD 1

With the blade held firmly in the vice, try the handle a little while gently twisting it. Sometimes this is all that is necessary. Be careful, as the handle can come off very suddenly; so make sure that nothing is in the way of your elbow as it travels backwards.

METHOD 2

A wedge of hardwood, shaped like a large screwdriver head and long enough to grip, is applied to the ferrule if it is visible around the shoulder (Fig 3.34). Strike the wedge firmly with a mallet. If nothing happens, apply the wedge to the other side of the ferrule and repeat. The handle should knock off fairly easily. Beware, again, that if you are too enthusiastic the handle can disengage from the tang suddenly and take flight across the workshop. Using an actual screwdriver for this purpose can damage the ferrule, which is normally only made of soft brass.

Fig 3.34 *Using a wedge of hardwood to knock off the handle. Keep your hand clear of the cutting edge!*

METHOD 3

When the shoulder sits tight up to the edge of the ferrule, the wooden wedge cannot get a purchase on the handle to knock it off (Fig 3.35). You need to approach the joint between the shoulder and the wood from the side with a screwdriver or one of your less valued chisels, trying to loosen the handle and gain enough space to apply the wooden wedge. Be careful not to damage the ferrule with the chisel or screwdriver. If you do, the ferrule may need filing or touching up on a grinding wheel.

Fig 3.35 *Problems in removing the handle may arise when the shoulder is very tight to the ferrule*

METHOD 4

Sometimes warming and drying the handle a little with a hair dryer causes it to expand sufficiently to release the tang.

METHOD 5

If all else fails – say with an old tool where it is certain the tang has corroded and practically bonded with the wood – the handle has to be sacrificed. First use a hacksaw and pliers to remove the ferrule, sawing diagonally along its length. Grip the blade in the vice by the shank, with the shoulders resting on the jaws and the handle straight up. Split the handle from the top end using one of your second-best chisels. The wood can then be pared away to reveal the tang.

FINISH

Smooth the handle with fine sandpaper so it feels well in the hand. Sandpapering and burnishing with another piece of the same wood, or wood shavings, is an adequate finish in itself.

A coat of varnish, cellulose lacquer, sanding sealer or shellac – rubbed back with fine wire wool – can be used to seal the wood; this can be done on the lathe. Thick, heavy varnish should be avoided, as it becomes uncomfortable and slippery when the hands are warm. It is not necessary to wax the handles as, if frequently used, the wood naturally becomes burnished and acquires its own patina. Bought handles which are already glossily varnished can be rubbed back to the wood with sandpaper and refinished.

If woodcarving tools are unused for some time, a light wipe with linseed oil (raw) on the handles will take care of the wood; but be aware that this may encourage mould growth if the tools are stored in damp conditions.

Soaking the end of the handle overnight in varnish or thinned PVA (polyvinyl acetate) glue – which penetrates the end fibres – helps to increase the resistance of the wood to damage and splitting when it is hit with a mallet. On the other hand, there may be a danger of skin sensitivity with handling.

NAME PUNCHES

It is not a bad idea to stamp your name on your tool handles, or in some way mark them personally. If you have acquired old gouges and chisels and intend to continue using the handles, then you can add your name to any already stamped on. There is a great sense of continuity, seeing tools passed through several hands and being aware of contact with a carver who may be long dead.

Support the handle in a V-shaped trough of wood to stop it rolling (Fig 3.36). Line up the punch and try

to mark both sides of the handle with a single sharp strike using a hammer.

Name stamps (Fig 3.37) are available by mail order from a number of suppliers; look for their advertisements in the woodworking magazines.

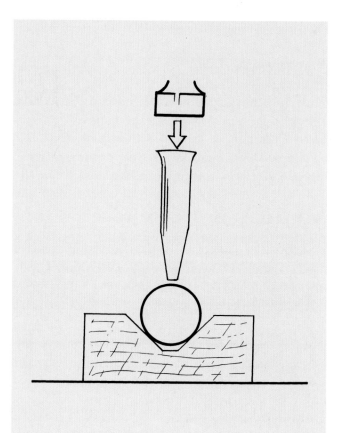

Fig 3.36 *A former of wood is used to hold a round handle safely while it is name-stamped*

Fig 3.37 *Name punches*

72

CHAPTER FOUR

CARVING-TOOL FAULTS AND THEIR CORRECTION

AIMS

- To identify the kinds of faults which are most commonly found in carving tools

- To suggest ways of correcting those faults which can be corrected

A 'fault' in a carving tool may be defined as anything that interferes with its working efficiency. This might include, among other things, the carbon steel being of inferior quality – perhaps with unsatisfactory edge-keeping ability from the original tempering; incorrect forging of the shape; or a poorly fitting handle. Faults may also include poor sharpening – but more of that in Part II.

Some variation in quality may not be seen as a fault. And faults may, or may not, be something you wish to correct – some matter more than others. I am suggesting here that a critical look should be taken at your carving tools to see if there is any way of improving their performance or feel; or even how they may be made more attractive to use.

Most often the fault lies in the actual shaping of the tool when it was forged: in the blade, shank, shoulder and tang. Some manufacturers consistently produce superbly shaped carving tools; others, sadly, do not.

At the risk of producing anecdotal evidence, I started carving with a dozen tools, but in a few months I had built up a list of tools that I could usefully carve with. I duly sent off an order for about 40 tools to a reputable firm (but one which can remain anonymous). When I examined the tools, I found that I needed to send back nearly half of them; distributed among these tools were all the faults which will be dealt with below. The steel and edge-holding properties themselves were excellent, but the shaping of the blades was unacceptable. The tools had been carelessly made and should not have passed the factory inspection. Out of the tools I was sent as replacements, I had to return another six…

The faults which follow have occurred both in my own tools and those of other carvers, and the reasons they may be considered faults – the effect of the fault – will be given. The question is whether the 'fault' or condition makes a difference to you as the user. Some carvers do very good work with tools I would have considered faulted to a degree that would make me want to do something about them.

So, to some extent, it is a question of attitude. The approach I would like to promote in this book is one where manufacturers make tools to the best of their ability and carvers love the tools with which they work, their quality and efficiency.

So, check over your tools, both old and new, as they are acquired. Work through those that you have, and gradually bring all your carving tools up to a level where you can justifiably be proud of them. But do not be obsessional about them – they are a means to an end only.

If you do need to return a carving tool to the retailer or manufacturer, point out the reason quietly but assertively and there should be no problem with getting a replacement; it is to be hoped that your comments are also helping the manufacturers improve their products.

Starting with the blade, working through to the tang and then to the handle, here is a check list of some common faults, together with some notes on what might be done about them. Old and second-hand tools have their own problems, and these will be dealt with in Chapter 5 (pages 93–6).

BLADES

STEEL QUALITY

One of the advantages of not buying too many tools of the same make at the beginning is that a comparison of steels, through direct experience, is possible. There is not much you can do yourself if the blade is discovered to have poor edge-holding qualities, other than attempt to reharden and temper it. This process is explained in Volume 2, Chapter 3, and can often be quite successful.

It is also possible for a tool to have a 'soft spot' where it seems to lose its edge very quickly. **Blueing** of the metal by over-aggressive grinding will produce the same result; refer to the section on bench grinders in Chapter 10 (pages 156–8) for advice on how to avoid this.

A WINDING BLADE

A winding or twisted blade is a problem mainly found in tapered chisels and gouges – such as fishtails – and shortbent tools. The blade has been forged so that, if the edge is looked at directly end-on, there is a degree of rotation or winding around the true axis (Fig 4.1).

The resulting tool feels less certain, more 'self-conscious' in the hands than when the blade and edge are aligned properly to the square shank. The winding must always be kept in mind and compensated for, and the tool will line up inappropriately for **setting-in** and finishing cuts.

There is not much to be done without reheating and shaping, although a bold approach would be to attempt a cold reshaping, using a vice and heavy grips. This may be possible, provided the bending is to be done in a soft, annealed part of the blade, such as the shank. Otherwise, if the shape is not acceptable, the tool will have to be returned.

ASYMMETRY OF THE BLADE

Here the blade, with or without winding, bends away to one side (Fig 4.2). Again, this is more often, but by no means always, to be found in tapered tools. If it is a small problem, a tapered gouge or chisel

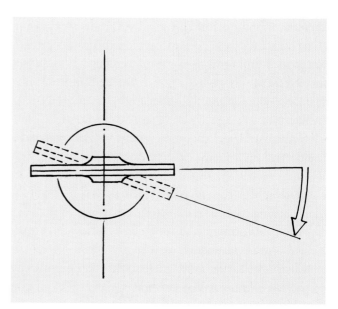

Fig 4.1 *A winding fishtail blade. The same rotation fault can be seen in poorly forged shortbent tools*

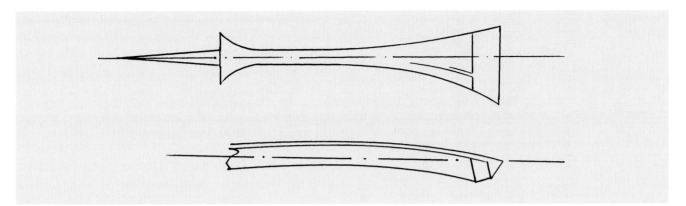

Fig 4.2 *Asymmetry in a fishtail chisel (above) and a parting tool (below)*

may be ground back to symmetry – with some loss of useful life – or a cold bend attempted. But, for the most part, any significantly asymmetrical tool should be returned.

UNEVENNESS OF METAL THICKNESS

When the blade is forged by hand or machine from the hot metal blank, the red-hot metal is placed in one (concave) half of a former and hammered with a matching (convex) shape – the result is a particular shape and sweep of blade.

If the two parts of the former have been accurately lined up, the sweep will have an even wall thickness across the width. The cannel (the inside curve or V-groove) will also line up symmetrically along the axis and not wander, or be offset, to one side. Sometimes, however, less than the desired accuracy of matching is achieved at this stage, and the tool may pass from the factory to the point of sale without being removed by quality controls (Figs 4.3 and 4.4).

If the metal of the wall is of uneven thickness, it becomes very difficult to set the bevel correctly or sharpen the edge evenly. The edge towards one side, being thicker than the other, will need a longer bevel to get the same cutting angle (Fig 4.5).

This problem is especially frustrating with the V-tool – difficult enough to sharpen evenly at the best of times – where walls of different thicknesses can make the tool impossible to sharpen correctly. Another problem with the V-tool is when particularly thick metal is left by the maker along the junction of

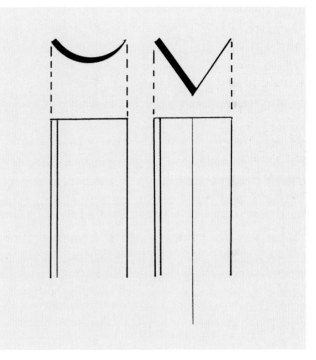

Fig 4.3 *Uneven wall thickness occurs in the forging process when the in-cannel forming block is misaligned*

Fig 4.4 *Differences in thickness between the walls of a V-tool make their equal sharpening difficult*

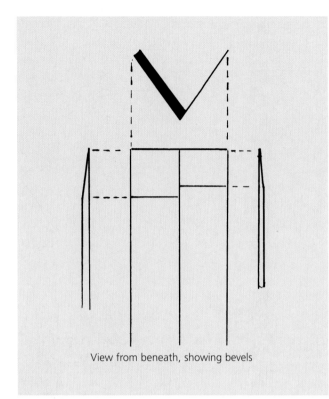

View from beneath, showing bevels

Fig 4.5 *To achieve the same angle on each side of a parting tool with uneven wall thicknesses, the bevels always end up different lengths*

the two sides, as a precaution against the tool cracking at this point when it is bent in the forging. It may be possible to reduce the wall thickness to an acceptable level of evenness by grinding; otherwise, replacement is the only option.

Bad alignment of the cannel, so that it is not parallel to the axis of the blade, can have the same effect on a V-tool (Fig 4.6) This makes the sharpening an unhappy experience, but is less of a problem than uneven wall thickness.

BENT TOOLS

Bent tools are bent for one purpose only: to enable the carver to get into recesses where the straight tools have difficulties. The principle is: bend the blade further and get in deeper. You will find a range of bends being offered by manufacturers, and a range of definitions of what a 'bend' is.

With so many tools ordered by post today, tools are often only seen as drawings or photographs in catalogues and are not actually handled before purchase. They can arrive looking quite different from what was expected. Two tools of the same width and sweep, from the same manufacturer, may have dissimilar bends. Some manufacturers make spoonbit gouges with such a shallow bend that the tools offer little advantage over the straight versions.

What matters is how useful the shape of a carving tool is to you – as the carver actually using it. Shallow bends have their place, as in working shallow backgrounds (**grounding**), but deeper bends are also needed – and when you order one, a deep bend is what you should get. If what you have received is unacceptable, return the tool with a note of the problem; if there is

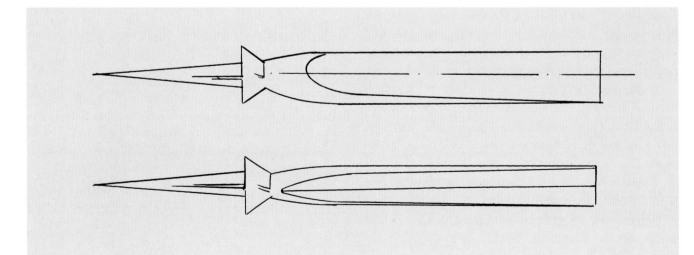

Fig 4.6 *Poor alignment of the in-cannel with the axis of the blade again produces uneven wall thickness*

76

Fig 4.7 You cannot cold-bend the hardened part of a blade, however misaligned, without this happening

no improvement, try another maker. Do not attempt to change the shape by cold bending, as the relevant part of the blade is too near the area of tempered metal and is liable to fracture (Fig 4.7).

BLADE SURFACE

Some makers take a lot of trouble to polish up the surfaces of their tools to make them attractive. Others leave the outer faces with the rough, black, oily surface resulting from quenching the hot metal, and only polish the inside to show the straw colour caused by the tempering. New, polished tools are often protected from damp by being given an oily, or greasy, coating.

Oily surfaces on carving tools are more of an irritation than a problem, as there is a tendency for the grease or black oil to get on to the work via the hands. Rub the blade with a degreaser like paraffin (kerosene) until no more oil comes off. Fine emery paper can be used on the more dense black finishes, as well as to smooth off sharp corners and edges along the length of the blade.

For pitting and roughness of the surface, see the section on second-hand tools in Chapter 5 (page 95).

SHOULDERS

INAPPROPRIATE SIZE OF SHOULDER

Shoulders, or bolsters, can be filed or ground down if they are too large. Too small a shoulder – more of a protuberance than a shoulder – may be forced into the wood by mallet blows. If the tool is for light work only, for all practical purposes this will probably not be a problem. For heavier work, this state of the shoulder is unacceptable and the tool should be replaced.

ROUNDED FACE

The **face** is the surface of the shoulder in contact with the handle. It should be flat and sit tight against the end of the wooden handle (Fig 4.8). If the face is badly rounded, not only will there be a gap between the shoulder and the wood – which is uncomfortable to hold – but there is a danger of the metal being forced further into the wood and splitting it, especially if there is no ferrule on the handle. If the face of the shoulder is not truly flat, it is easier to make the handle *look* as if it is fitting properly.

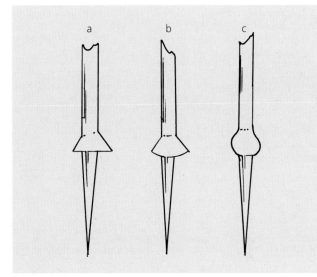

Fig 4.8 Some faults with shoulders: (a) unevenly distributed around the blade; (b) rounded face; (c) misshapen altogether

To create a flat face on the underside of the shoulder, grip the blade in a vice (preferably a metalworking vice) with the tang pointing upwards and the shoulder resting on the jaws. Take a washer which has a hole slightly larger than the diameter of the shoulder, and drop it over the tang so that it rests on the vice. More than one washer may be needed. Adjust the shoulder of the tool so that its face stands out a little proud of the hole, with the tang perpendicular to the washer. With the washer acting as a jig, a file can now be used to flatten the face of the shoulder (Fig 4.9), creating a true face to sit on the wood of the handle. Take care when filing not to bite into the tang.

TANGS

TANG NOT IN LINE WITH THE BLADE

To get a blade dead in line with the handle, the tang must be on the central axis of the blade. The consequences of a bent tang have been discussed in Chapter 2 (page 50).

The tang may have been bent in the original making, or afterwards by rough use. It is still possible to align the handle by boring the hole at a compensating angle (Fig 4.10) – in effect, compensating errors – but this is not easy to get right. It is far better for the tang to be straight in the first place.

An angled tang can often be straightened by cold bending. The blade should be gripped in the vice as described for flattening the bottom of the shoulder, and tapped gently with a hammer, working from the shoulder end. Remember that a tang – or any metal – will not take much bending backwards and forwards before it weakens.

If cold bending feels risky, use a gas torch to heat the tang up to dull red and then bend it. While you are doing this, protect the blade itself from the effects of the heat by wrapping it in a wet rag.

If the tang is of adequate bulk and length, grinding and filing is also an option.

TANG PARALLEL TO CENTRE LINE BUT OFFSET

This is a problem created in the initial forging, and is at its worst when the shoulder overhangs the ferrule.

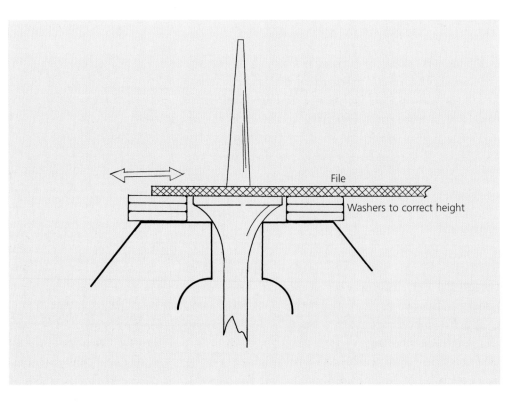

Fig 4.9 A file and washers can be used to flatten the face of the shoulder so that it seats well on the handle

Proper fitting of the blade along the true axis becomes impossible.

Options for dealing with this problem lie in grinding and filing the tang into the central axis – if there is enough metal in it. If not, consider offsetting or packing the hole in the handle. Otherwise, if you do not want to live with it, send the tool back.

INAPPROPRIATE SIZE OF TANG

It may seem obvious that a large gouge needs a large tang to fit strongly into the handle, and that other sizes of blade need an appropriate amount of tang. But the first you may know about a tang being too small is the handle bending about the shoulder. It is more often a problem with larger tools.

If you are making your own handles, you will buy the tool unhandled and can immediately inspect the

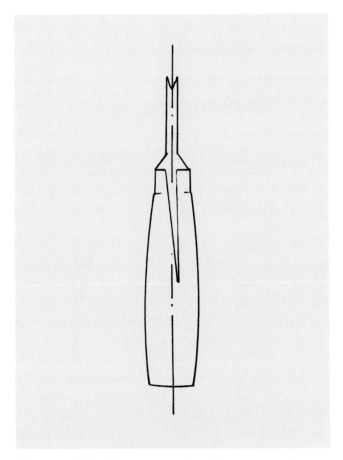

Fig 4.10 *When the tang is misaligned, a compensating direction of hole in the handle enables the blade to be lined up correctly along the axis of the tool*

tang; otherwise you will have to knock off the handle to have a look. Send the tool back if it is a new one.

If the tang is corroded – as it may be in an old tool – a few more options are described in the next chapter (pages 95–6).

HANDLES

HOLE OFFSET OR TOO LARGE

For either of these conditions it is best to make a new hole. Plug the old one with a dowel of the same size – and the same wood if possible – gluing and tapping it in. Find the position for the new hole by lining up both ends of the handle between centre points, and rotating it. An oversize or offset hole can also be packed to the side with slivers of wood.

INAPPROPRIATE SIZE OR SHAPE

Look at whether the size of the handle is too small or too large; whether the shape is what you want; whether the wood is appropriate for the use of the tool; and whether a ferrule is needed at the tang end, or another to protect the handle end against the mallet.

To some extent, if there is wood to spare, handles can be remade. If not, it may be a case of making an entirely new handle, keeping the old one for a different tool.

VARNISH

As mentioned previously, some manufacturers cover their handles with thick varnish. This is not a pleasant surface compared with thinner, less glossy finishes. Varnish like this can be removed with fine sandpaper or paint stripper (followed by washing), after which the handle can be burnished with another piece of wood. Wipe over the surface occasionally with a little linseed oil, or seal it with a thin coat of shellac or varnish, rubbed back with fine wire wool. The best finish and patina comes from the effect of being regularly used in the hand.

CHAPTER FIVE

SELECTING AND BUYING WOODCARVING TOOLS

AIMS

- To explore the functions of the various traditional tool shapes

- To advise on choosing your first set of carving tools

- To consider the special problems involved in buying second-hand tools

SHAPE AND FUNCTION

The subject of woodcarving itself (that is, how to carve) is not the principal theme of this book – although information about carving will inevitably suffuse it. Carving as such is covered in more detail in my other books.

For the newcomer to woodcarving, it is not just the choice of carving tools that is bewildering, but the fact that being able to choose the right tools means knowing, at least to some extent, what to do with them. What carving chisels and gouges are in an academic sense is fairly straightforward, but how does one actually *use* them? The following information is included as a brief guide to newcomers to the craft. In this section are some pointers to the functions of the various carving tool 'families' and what they can be expected to do. This is by no means an exhaustive guide, but should help you decide what tools you need for the work you have in mind. In the following section is an approach to buying the tools you need to start carving.

One point to remember is that when a carver is working, carving as such is only taking place when the tool is actually cutting the wood. So the more 'down time' (that is, time sorting out another tool to use), the slower and more irregular the pace of working. In trade carving on a number of repeat items, or in lettering, a rhythm is built up after a while; the order in which each tool is used is established and refined so that maximum efficiency is achieved. The cuts proceed in a set order and the down time is reduced to a minimum – and the resulting work appears as swiftly as possible, with a uniform appearance.

When a one-off piece is being carved, the down time is kept as low as possible in a different way.

The carver uses the tool in his or her hand for as long as possible and makes the one tool do the work of several others – not putting the tool down until another is really necessary. Against this, though, it should be said that there is a danger of making the work look uninteresting by using the same cut too often; the more variety in the tool cuts themselves, the more lively the resulting surface may be (Fig 5.1). There is a creative balance to be struck.

So the functions of individual tools are not completely fixed and static. One gouge can be made to perform functions more naturally ascribed to another, and the normal 'brief' of each tool is to some extent flexible. But there are also times when you must have one particular tool for the work at hand, and no other will substitute.

Some guidelines for newcomers follow, describing what you may expect each particular family of woodcarving tools to do.

STRAIGHT CHISELS (FIRMERS)

To begin with the obvious: firmer chisels are used when straight lines are needed – as in cutting letters or setting in straight edges. Lettering may need a wide range of chisel sizes to cut the varying lengths of uprights, diagonals and horizontals. (Figs 5.2 and 5.3) Use chisels for working over lightly convex areas to produce a finished surface; if they are presented in a slicing or skewed fashion, they will also trim the outside edges of curves. The chisel is *not* normally used to form wide, flat surfaces, such as the background of a relief carving, because the corners of the chisel would tend to dig in and leave unsightly 'tramlines' on the surface. For this reason the flat gouge is preferred, even though the surface it produces is slightly undulating and only approximately flat.

Fig 5.1 *A variety of tool cuts, depths, open and filled spaces and rhythms are used in this detail from Riemenschneider's* Crucifixion *altar in Detwang, outside Rothenburg on the Tauber, Germany. Many of the tools that were used are clearly apparent*

Fig 5.2 *Straight chisels play a very important part in most lettering; they are central to a formal, roman style like this*

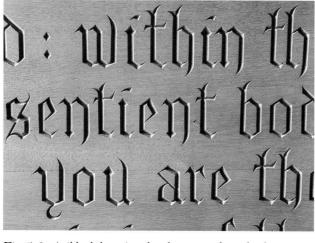

Fig 5.3 *A 'black letter' style of script such as this has minimal curved elements, so chisels are bound to be used more than gouges*

STRAIGHT SKEW CHISELS (CORNER CHISELS)

The essential working part of this tool is its long, pointed corner, enabling it to enter and clean corners and angles where normal square-ended tools – chisel or gouge – cannot reach (Fig 5.4). Different angles of skew will give the skew chisel a longer or shorter corner, for dealing with different recesses; the skew angle can be adjusted in the sharpening process.

The skew chisel, held something like a pencil, can be used in a knife-like way for running and shaping

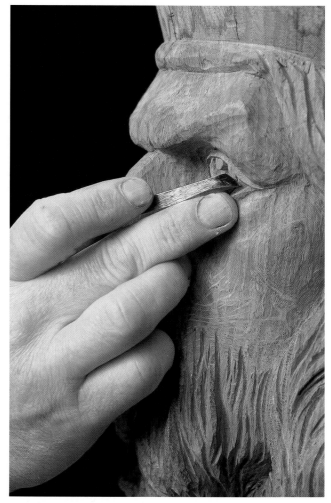

Fig 5.4 *The skew chisel is ideal for cleaning up an otherwise inaccessible corner*

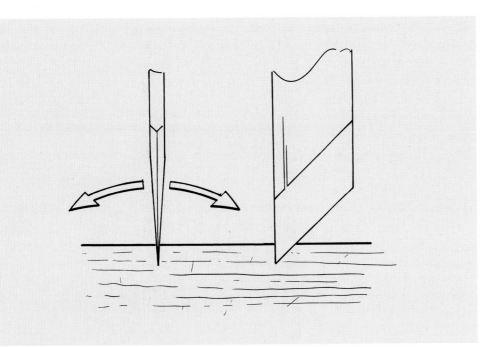

Fig 5.5 *A good way to snap the point off a skew chisel is to rock it from side to side while it is embedded in the wood*

curved edges. It will shape the corners and edges of grooves left by a V-tool. This produces a very flat relief; used in this way, the skew is quite a delicate tool. It can also smooth lightly convex surfaces, giving more of a slicing cut than the square firmer.

Remember that the longer the point of the skew chisel, the more fragile it is. If the point is rocked from side to side when it is sunk in the wood, it is very liable to snap off and remain embedded (Fig 5.5).

SHORTBENT CHISELS (GROUNDERS)

A grounding tool or grounder is primarily concerned with finishing the backgrounds in relief carving (Fig 5.6). **Grounding** describes the deeper, flat-bottomed cutting that is needed to sink a background.

A grounder may be a shortbent chisel, or a shortbent gouge of the flattest sweep. The flat gouge profile

is the preferable cutting edge – the corners are free of the wood throughout the cut, and there is less tendency for them to tear the fibres compared with a flat chisel. The amount of bend in the grounding tool (or any bent tool) dictates how much it can be used, in what circumstances, and how well the cutting edge can get into an appropriate position to cut.

Shortbent chisels can also **undercut** in other contexts, and can clean grain where straight tools cannot reach. Use them to chamfer or clean the insides of curves, as, for example, in Gothic tracery.

SHORTBENT CORNER CHISELS

These tools, sometimes called **corner grounders**, can get into recesses and corners where square-ended tools cannot reach. They come into their own where undercutting has been created and deep corners need to be got at.

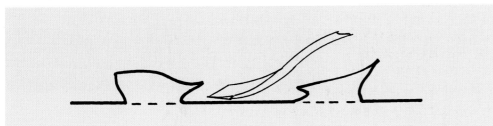

Fig 5.6 *A small grounder works the background flat in a relief carving*

The skewing of the edge in relation to the rest of the tool can be to the right or the left – one reaching where the other cannot, or where the grain needs a particular direction of cut. As both directions inevitably need to be cut at some time or another, buy them as a matching pair. Shortbent corner chisels are the sort of tool that may not be used very often, but when they are needed it is because nothing else will do.

SPLAYED CHISELS (FISHTAIL OR SPADE TOOLS)

The spade or fishtail version of any tool gives two extra benefits over the parallel-sided form:

- The corners become more prominent, allowing cuts to continue into angles normally inaccessible to the parallel tool. For example, use fishtail chisels to cut the flat ends of serifs in lettering.

- These splayed tools are much lighter than the straight tools – they feel more 'dextrous' and so are used mainly for finishing work: for example, in smoothing rounded surfaces.

There is a cost to these benefits, however: the cutting edge loses its width with sharpening and these blades have a shorter working life than parallel-sided ones. For this reason, and because of their lightness, they are unsuitable for rough work. Keep these splayed tools for the lighter, final stages of carving, allowing other tools to take the brunt of the preliminary work.

V-TOOLS (PARTING TOOLS)

These very useful tools are made with different angles, producing grooves or straight-sided channels with different degrees of openness (Figs 5.7 and 5.8). Use the V-tool on its own to run a shallow, decorative and finished groove in the surface of a carving, either to incise a design in a flat surface such as a bread board, or to delineate hair, feathers or leaves.

Chamfering the edges of V-grooves creates a type of **low-relief** carving. The tool can also be used together with special knives to produce **chip carving**, a form of geometrical surface decoration.

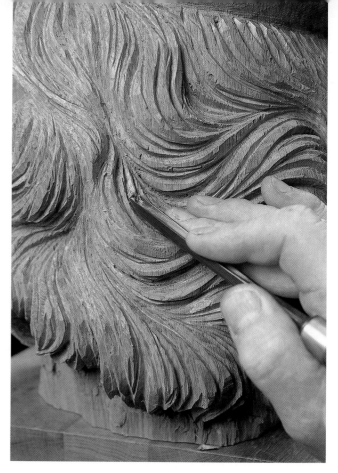

Fig 5.7 *Simple grooves with the V-tool will add a lot of flair to subjects such as hair or foliage*

In relief carving, much preliminary work involves outlining and defining an area to be blocked out (Fig 5.9). The V-tool is indispensable here, and its alternative name of 'parting tool' suggests this use. If the tool is tilted to one side, a degree of simple undercutting is possible, for example under carved leaves.

Fig 5.8 *A frontbent V-tool cleaning the deeply hollowed grooves between locks of hair*

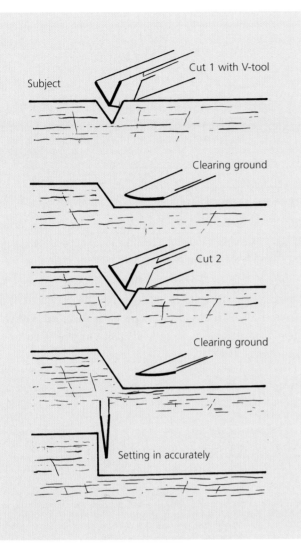

Fig 5.9 A V-tool can be used to outline a relief carving in successive levels to the required depth. A gouge is used to remove the waste, and other gouges or chisels to set in to a predetermined line

STRAIGHT GOUGES

The parallel-sided gouges, of all sweeps and sizes, are the general carver's most called-upon tools. They are at work right from the start of a carving, with the preliminary roughing out, through to establishing the main forms and masses (bosting in) and on to the final surface finishing. It may be helpful to elaborate a little on how gouges are used.

The 'quicker' carving tools do indeed remove wood in more bulk – and therefore more quickly – than the flatter gouges. Flat gouges in turn produce

shallow, polished facets which can be worked over the surface of the wood – **modelling**, smoothing and completing it (Figs 5.10 and 5.11).

In making a gouge cut, one principle is not to let the corners dig in; this is why, as mentioned earlier, the flat gouge is preferred to the chisel for finishing flat surfaces. The middle part of the sweep cuts, but the corners remain in the fresh air, slightly above the surface (Fig 5.12). (This is a different technique from deliberately using one of the corners to make a slicing cut in the manner of the skew chisel.) If the corners of a gouge are buried in the wood during its cut, then not only is some control lost, but the wood fibres are torn, which produces a ragged surface. There is also

Fig 5.10 Quicker gouges will leave a pattern of deep cuts on a surface

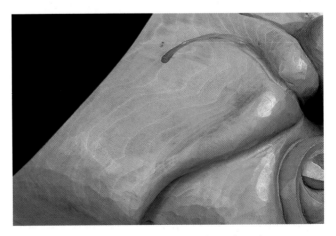

Fig 5.11 Flatter gouges will reduce these deep facets to a smoother finish

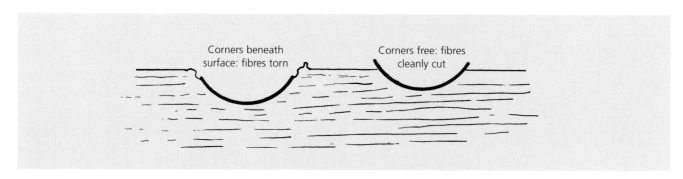

Fig 5.12 *Allowing the corners of the gouge to dig in will tear the wood fibres instead of cutting them*

the danger of breaking an embedded tool. If deeper cuts are needed, select a deeper gouge.

Another important use of the gouge involves matching the particular sweep, or curve, of the cutting edge precisely to a matching curve to be cut in the wood (Fig 5.13). Clean, precise shapes can be outlined in this way and accurately repeated; one important application of this technique is in carving mouldings.

Setting in involves outlining a main subject from its surroundings, as when cutting away the background. Setting in uses the sweeps of carving tools in a similar way to that mentioned above, and this is one of the reasons why carvers build up large numbers of carving tools in different sweeps and sizes. The principle of tool profiles matching the curves of the edges being cut also brings clarity and a precise beauty to the carving of letters in wood.

The term **bosting in** comes from the French *ébaucher*, meaning 'to sketch'. It describes that stage in the carving process which is a little further into the work than the preliminary roughing out. It is used when the main forms and masses are being defined or 'sketched in'. What is being sought are the primary planes, forms and movement of the work – the masses and forms that underlie and support the final details. A variety of straight gouges, often fairly flat, or even chisels, are used extensively in this vigorous stage. Getting these early masses and moving forms correctly established is an extremely important – if not the *most* important – stage in a carving. There is a tendency for beginners to start working the final details before the main body of form has been expressed. Not only will those details which have been carved too early be cut away as the work progresses, but these

details may well be in the wrong place altogether. When the underlying form is established first, the details fall naturally into place.

With the exception of the very deep gouges, all gouges give *two* cuts in addition to the vertical stabbing cut already described: one with the tool entering the wood in the 'normal' fashion to give a concave

Fig 5.13 *Matching the curve of the gouge to an exact requirement to set in a clean, sweeping edge; curved elements in a carving can easily be matched by using the same tool for each*

Fig 5.14 *Gouges can be used in either a 'normal' (left) or an 'upside-down' position*

cut, the other with the tool reversed ('upside down'), which produces a convex cut (Figs 5.14 and 5.15). So, in buying one of these tools, you are getting more value than you thought for your money.

Fluters and veiners, making deep cuts, grooves or channels, can be used to produce decorative work in their own right (Fig 5.16). They will also create a softer outline to a relief form than the V-tool can (Fig 5.17). An object, or area, can be faded or blended more readily into the background if it does not have a hard junction where the two planes meet.

As a final note, there is a distinct risk of U-shaped gouges cracking if they are powerfully embedded in

Fig 5.15 *The beads in this old carved moulding were cut with a gouge in the reversed position*

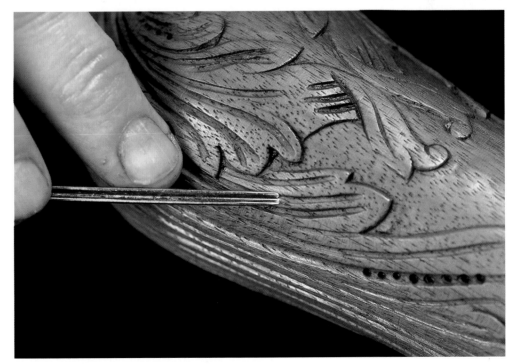

Fig 5.16 *Veiners will produce a 'softer' cut than the V-tool*

Fig 5.17 *A softer edge to a relieved plane is achieved with a deep gouge (veiner or fluter)*

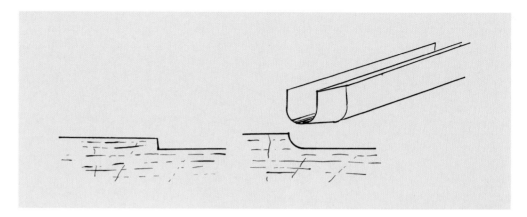

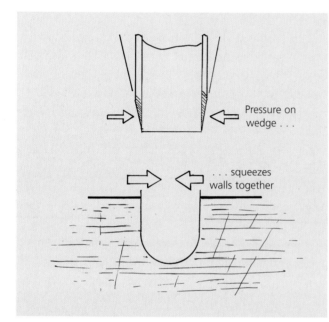

Pressure on wedge . . .

. . . squeezes walls together

Fig 5.18 *Sideways pressure is exerted on the wedge-like bevels of a U-shaped gouge, and if the tool is buried deeply in the wood the walls may be squeezed together sufficiently to crack the metal*

the wood; the outer bevels act as wedges to squeeze the walls of the gouge together (Fig 5.18).

SPLAYED GOUGES (FISHTAIL, SPADE OR POD TOOLS)

What was said about spade and fishtail chisels applies to these tools as well. Being thinner, the splayed gouges are quicker and easier to sharpen than parallel-sided gouges, and hold a finer edge. But for the same reasons they are less economic, becoming slightly narrower with each sharpening.

Fig 5.19 *A flat fishtail gouge must have helped clean the central leaf into the corner in this old oak moulding*

Splayed gouges are not suitable for heavy work, but are excellent tools for finishing. Their lightness and shape makes them easier to manipulate, as they obscure less wood; and their prominent corners will run surfaces into sharper angles and recesses (Fig 5.19). Fishtail fluters negotiate curves more easily than the straight, parallel fluters; the blade following through after the cutting edge has less tendency to jam in the wood. Fishtail gouges have great value in lettering, for example curving end serifs.

LONGBENT GOUGES

The bend in these tools enables the gouge to enter deeper recesses and hollows than a straight tool can (Fig 5.20). Because the sweeps match, when the blade or handle of a straight gouge fouls the wood around a recess a simple change can be made to a similar

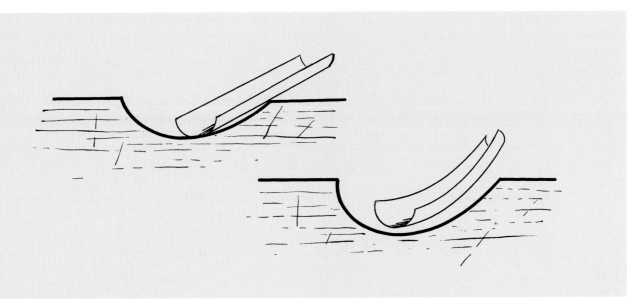

Fig 5.20 *As the recess is deepened, the straight tool will start to foul the edge. The same sweep and size of tool in a curved form will make the cut without fouling*

curved gouge. Bent tools can only rarely be used upside down.

SHORTBENT GOUGES

These will enter yet deeper hollows than the long-bent gouges (Fig 5.21). The deepest hollows are entered by the most sharply cranked tools, whose name – knuckle gouges – expresses their shape.

In practice, the handle of a shortbent gouge often swings through a large arc to produce what is quite a small cut. Make sure the cutting edge is travelling through the wood, and not just being levered at the bend.

Shortbent gouges are used in high-relief carving where the ground is sunk well back; in undercutting; in pierced work, such as Gothic tracery, working the inner curves especially; and in modelling internal curves at any stage in a carving where the hollow is more than a straight tool can cope with.

BACKBENT GOUGES

Earlier, in reference to straight gouges, it was mentioned that two types of cut can be made by presenting the blade in different ways to the wood. A concave groove or facet can be cut with the inside of the gouge

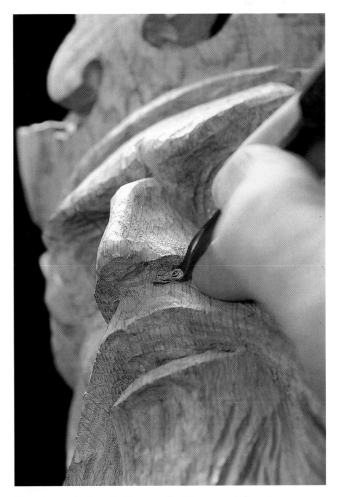

Fig 5.21 *A deep hollow worked by a small frontbent gouge*

Fig 5.22 *A straight gouge used 'upside down' shapes a convex surface (top). A backbent gouge (bottom) will negotiate a convex profile where a straight gouge cannot reach*

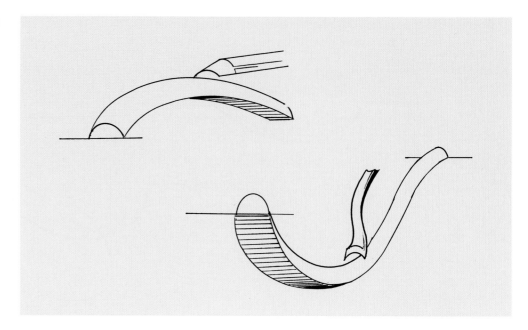

facing upwards (the 'right way up'). This type of cut is the one normally associated with gouges; and long-bent or shortbent gouges, as needed, will take the carving into deeper and deeper hollows.

The second way of cutting involves reversing the tool so that the inside of the gouge points downwards ('upside down'), against the wood. This presentation produces a rounded or convex cut (Fig 5.22). Now, just as the longbent and shortbent configurations enable a gouge in the first position to enter hollows, so the backbent shape allows a similar access for a gouge in the second, more difficult, reversed position (Fig 5.23).

Fig 5.23 *The backbent tool enters hollows in the upside-down position, shaping a surface which is concave along its length but convex from side to side*

SELECTING AND ORDERING

MAKING THE CHOICE

The contents of Part I so far will have helped you gain an understanding of the 'anatomy' of woodcarving tools, how they work and what might be done with them. But if you are starting off without any carving tools at all, there comes a point when you need to take the plunge and buy some. Which ones, and how many? Or what if you want to expand your range? Here are some notes that might help you in making your choice.

Buy only a few carving tools to start with

Time is needed to understand each tool as you carve, so that you become familiar with it and discover what it can do for you. Time will also be needed to sharpen the tools, which can be slow and at times frustrating to begin with. On the other hand, too few tools can be frustrating as well, and your work may be limited by not having the right tools.

As a guideline, around a dozen or so carefully selected tools is a good starting number. A suggested list, with the reasoning behind it, is given in the table on page 92.

Base your choice on need

At the start you may have no idea of what it is you want to carve – how big it will be, or how complex. You will almost certainly need more tools than you initially buy. The best approach – whether you have no carving tools or many – is to increase their number as and when the need arises.

Make the most use of what tools you have available, and make a few notes as you go along. If you feel that a particular gouge would be right for the job, if only it were wider, narrower, bent or shaped in some way, you can use what has been said earlier in this chapter to define the difference you need accurately.

Use your gut feeling

Having said that the choice of carving tools is best decided rationally – basing your need on previous experience – there is also a place for a more intuitive approach, especially if you do not know what you actually want to carve. So if you see a carving tool that 'grabs you', or fills your head with ideas of what might be done, or that you can feel and see yourself using, then the chances are that your heart is speaking to you, and you should listen.

SELECTING THE TOOLS

At the start, you need to make some decision as to what tools to buy. At the risk of duplicating what has been said earlier, here are some guidelines:

Avoid cheap tools

Cheap tools are almost always made of poor steel, badly tempered and incapable of holding an edge for long – even if they have been polished up to look smart. They are often shorter than usual, with cheap-looking ferrules.

Expense is relative. Top-quality carving tools may *appear* expensive, but they are meant for a lifetime's use. Through them you may have years of pleasure and creativity, and perhaps even earn your living. If there is still any doubt as to the value of carving tools, consider the relative cost of a few hours at the cinema, eating out, or setting up in other crafts.

Buy from reputable manufacturers

Buy from well-established firms with a reputation to protect in the marketplace. They will have useful lists of their tools and additional information available.

It is particularly useful if they are using a standard numbering system such as the Sheffield List, so that you can refer between makes. Better still, if you are able to inspect the tools personally, take along an impression of the cuts of your present carving tools, made by stabbing their edges into a flat piece of wood or cardboard. With this in hand, you can make a comparison between the sweeps you have at home, the variation of sweep or shape you want, and what is on offer.

Try various makes to start with

Different makers seem to have different strengths, for example in the bends of their tools, the thickness of metal or the finish. Some makes of tool are more attractive to some individuals. But before settling into the well-known rut of 'brand loyalty', do try out different makes. It is worth experimenting this way even if you have quite a few tools already.

Avoid boxed sets

This is the way many people start: a boxed set of woodcarving tools given as a Christmas or birthday present. This can work out well, but equally often, does not. The giver will usually be unaware of the quality of the tools, and may have bought some of the cheaper tools to be found on market stalls. Even when the quality is excellent, the choice of tools has been made by other people: firstly by the manufacturer and secondly by the giver of the set. Poor quality, or poor selection, can cause a lot of frustration and, sadly, has been known to put people off carving right from the start.

The choice of tools is a very personal issue, as has been stressed before. In effect, the tool kit grows with the carver. However, if you already have a boxed set, do not despair: they may be exactly what you need. If they are not what you need at the moment, but they are good-quality tools, sooner or later you will use them.

Inspect the tools

Use the information given in Part I – and summarized in the next section on second-hand tools (pages 93–6) – to check over your tools for faults when you buy them. There is no reason to accept substandard tools when by returning them you should get the quality you are paying for. On the contrary, by keeping manufacturers on their toes with your discrimination, carving as a whole is being done a long-term service.

A SUGGESTED STARTING KIT

Having just spent the last few paragraphs suggesting that other people should not be allowed to make decisions about the carving tools you need, this section may seem a little out of place. However, my experience has shown me that although a beginner may understand all that has been said so far about woodcarving tools – about quality, the different shapes, what they do, and so on – there can still be an initial lack of confidence when it comes to buying some to start with. This is not such a surprise, as confidence will only really begin when you actually lay your hands on the tools and start using them.

The following tool selection is based on several things: my teaching experience, both private and in adult education; discussions with other carvers; what *I* started with; and what tools are on my bench more often than any others. My initial selection of carving tools should be sufficient to perform basic, useful functions. From here onwards, acquire tools by working out your own needs.

Bear in mind that any book on woodcarving will give you a different set of tools with which to begin. There are at least three reasons for this:

- the apparent vastness of choice among carving tools and makes

- the wide-open field that is carving design, with different projects requiring different tools or approaches

- the unique preferences, not to say prejudices, that individuals (including myself) have about what we like and what we think is right – about anything, never mind carving tools!

Eventually, you will know yourself the work to which you are inclined – the scale, size and degree of detail. Perhaps it will be lettering or wildlife, huge bowls or duck decoys, abstract sculpture or netsuke.

What you must do is *start* – with something, anything – but start. Problems then become something to get your teeth into. And this is also a good way to see your first carving as well. It is easy to worry about different aspects of what you want to do before you have started carving. Once you get going, you have experience to learn from, and what previously seemed difficult becomes tangible and approachable.

The tools I suggest you buy are listed in the table below, where the numbers refer to the Sheffield List.

AN INITIAL SELECTION OF WOODCARVING TOOLS

No.	Width (in)	(mm)	Description
02	⅜	10	Skew (corner) chisel
03	¼	6	Flat gouge (straight)
03	½	13	Flat gouge (straight)
03	¾	19	Flat gouge (straight)
06	¼	6	Medium gouge (straight)
06	½	13	Medium gouge (straight)
06	¾	19	Medium gouge (straight)
09	¼	6	Quick gouge (straight)
09	½	13	Quick gouge (straight)
09	¾	19	Quick gouge (straight)
39	⅜	10	V-tool (parting tool)

Consider also buying the following tools:

- right and left shortbent skew chisels, ⅛in (3mm)

- large fluter and small veiner

- bent and fishtail tools in any of these sweeps and sizes.

You may also wish to make some variations, according to your particular interests as a woodcarver:

LARGE-SCALE SCULPTURE

You may find that the smallest tool you need is 1in (25mm), going up to approximately 1½in (38mm). It is possible to buy 2in (50mm) tools, but in practice they require a lot of effort with the mallet. In the long term the smaller tools, while apparently slower, are less tiring to use, and eventually more work is achieved with the same effort.

MINIATURE CARVING

The shapes above are still more than likely to be needed, but in this case the range is reduced in size. Most of the tools might be around ¼in (6mm) and below, though a few larger ones will still be needed.

LETTERING

Lettering requires more straight chisels – if not a full range in small increments – as straight lines are a prominent feature in many styles of lettering. The curves of the letters will need to be matched to some extent, and fishtail gouges and chisels will be used for the serifs. For detailed information, see my *Lettercarving in Wood: A Practical Course* (GMC Publications, 1997) .

MISCELLANEOUS

Other interests such as violin-making or carving duck decoys suggest their own requirements: curves to match the scroll of the violin, or fine veiners and V-tools for featherwork.

BUYING BY MAIL ORDER

Today, ever larger numbers of carving tools are bought through the post; often it is not possible to see and handle woodcarving tools locally. You will, therefore, need a good idea of what tools you want.

Get hold of catalogue information

Good manufacturers and suppliers readily distribute their catalogues. Study them and check that their particular numbering system coincides with what you want and what you expect to receive.

Keep an accurate record of your order

Mark the sweeps of the tools you have sent for, and the date you sent the order. You can record the exact shapes of your existing blades by pressing them into a board of thin wood; it is then easy to compare these impressions with what the manufacturers are offering.

Check over the carving tools when they arrive

First, see that the sizes and shapes are exactly what you expected. Secondly, inspect for faults and problems using the information in Chapter 4. Decide whether any fault is something you can deal with simply or not; return any unacceptable tools, with a polite explanation, asking for a replacement.

Perhaps I am giving the impression that faults in woodcarving tools are common; they are more common than might be expected. Fortunately, toolmakers have been improving their quality as the market grows and the competition increases. My main reason for giving information on faults or problems is to save you being at a loss when they occur, by informing you of what sorts of remedies are possible.

SECOND-HAND TOOLS

Because of the increasing interest both in carving itself and old tools in general, second-hand carving tools are not as common as they used to be – nor are they necessarily cheaper than their new equivalents. However, they still crop up in markets, second-hand tool shops, car-boot sales and so on, and are worth looking out for. Once people know of your interest in carving, you may well find that you are given tools and wood. There is a welcome feeling today that it is reprehensible to waste such assets. So you may well acquire some old tools, and with luck they will bear such illustrious names as Addis & Sons, Herring Bros. or Ward & Payne.

With a new tool you can be reasonably sure of its shape, size, quality and so on, but these old tools can have certain problems that actually make them less than attractive propositions. It is these problems that will be dealt with in this section, thus helping you to make an informed decision as to their worth to you as a carver. Unless you like collecting these old tools, do not buy a tool merely because it is old. Reviving older woodcarving tools and putting them back into successful service, however, can be a very satisfying undertaking.

Bear in mind all that has been said previously about assessing new carving tools – these observations can be applied to old tools as well. In addition, the following points should be looked at:

LENGTH OF BLADE

It is a fact that the most useful tools are those that wear down quickest because of continual sharpening. Therefore, it is often the case that the blades of the most useful-looking old woodcarving tools are considerably reduced in length. Not all of a blade is tempered for cutting wood – a section towards the handle is left softer and more resilient. Whether a carving gouge has worn beyond the tempered steel, or not, can only really be assessed by using it. (Soft metal *can* be retempered: see Volume 2, Chapter 3.)

Some tools, such as parallel-sided gouges, can take a lot of sharpening, and thus shortening, in their stride. If they become inconveniently short, a longer handle will solve the problem (Fig 5.24). With other tools – fishtail and shortbent carving tools, for example – the effect of sharpening can be seen more quickly (Figs 5.25 and 5.26). The effective life of such tools is shorter, as it takes far less time to reduce the blade beyond its useful shape or workable hardness. When a carving tool is no longer useful for carving,

Fig 5.25 *The older fishtail tool at the top started life about the size of the lower one*

it will be reborn as something for opening paint tins or making holes.

Heavily used tools can therefore present two serious problems:

- They may no longer have any useful temper or hardness, making it impossible for them to hold an edge.

- The shape may be so shortened that it is no longer of any use.

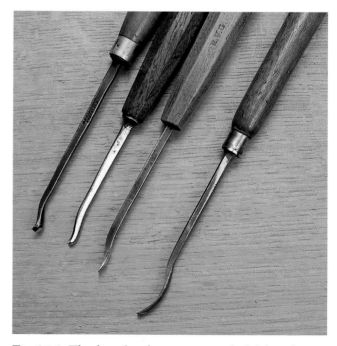

Fig 5.26 *The three frontbent gouges on the left have been worn back considerably compared with the somewhat newer tool on the right*

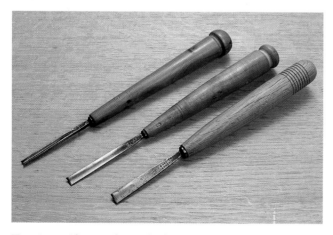

Fig 5.24 *Short tools can be brought back into circulation with handles of extra length*

The cure for both these problems is heat treatment: either retempering or reshaping, as described in Volume 2, Chapter 3. Assuming the steel is good quality, and you are willing to take the time and trouble, there is no reason why such tools cannot be usefully reborn within the realms of carving.

RUST

The effect of storage in a damp place – unfortunately the lot of many old tools – is corrosion of the metal parts. The iron, taken originally out of the earth as iron ore, is naturally returning to its stable compound, ferrous oxide. Corrosion appears as smaller or larger areas of pitting or flaking in the surface. In second-hand shops, tools are often given a wipe of oil to inhibit the corrosion, so the rust will not necessarily look reddish-brown; it may appear dirty black instead.

The extent and, more importantly, the *depth* of pitting has to be assessed. Because carving tools have bevels – usually both on the inside and the outside – the actual cutting part of the steel is *within* the blade. Take, for example, a carver's firmer chisel with equal bevels on both sides, where the cutting edge is formed in the very middle of the blade; only very severe corrosion would reach this far in (Fig 5.27). Although a blade may look corroded, the point is that if, after sharpening, the actual cutting edge is free from pits, there will be no marks or scratches in the wood following its cut. Effectively the tool is as good as new (Fig 5.28).

With gouges, the amount of bevel set on the inner surface varies depending on the tool and how it is used. It does no harm to go beyond any pitting on the inside by forming a longer than normal inner

Fig 5.28 *A badly rusted surface on a gouge blade, but not pitted enough to affect the cutting edge, which lies more towards the centre of the steel*

bevel – so, again, pitting of a gouge blade may easily be overcome (see Chapter 9, pages 136–40).

If the pitting is so deep that it appears in the cutting edge when the blade is sharpened, the effect is to leave a scratch in the wood. This is not acceptable for work which is to be left straight from the tool and not sanded. A tool may be worth grinding back, beyond particularly bad pitting. The metal can be cleaned up with small grinding wheels (such as those fitted to power drills), slip and bench stones, and grades of emery paper. Certainly the tool can be soaked in oil or an anti-rusting agent to prevent further damage.

RUSTED TANGS

Corrosion affects the tangs of old tools as well as the blades. If the blade of a carving tool with a handle is affected by damp in this way, assume at least a similar effect on the tang. The handle may protect the tang

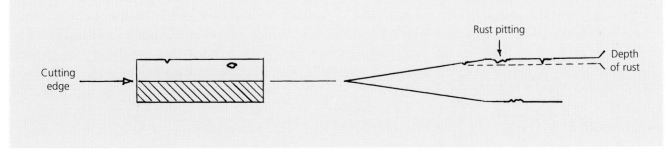

Fig 5.27 *With a double or inside bevel, rust pitting may not be deep enough to affect the actual cutting edge*

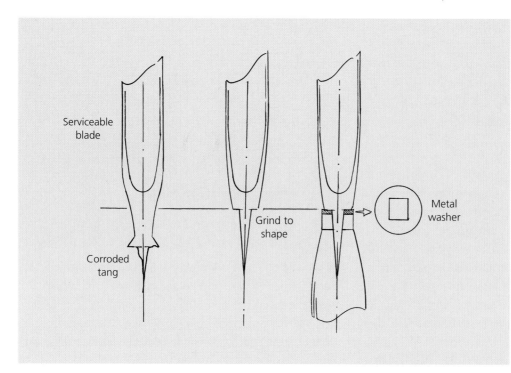

Fig 5.30 *A gouge which had lost its tang through rust, now back in use*

from moisture, but equally the wood can hold moisture in, and against the metal. Badly rusted tangs may appear as looseness of the handle – which may give a surreptitious opportunity to inspect the tang. The tang can be so badly corroded as to be thinned almost to nothing – stopping short at the shoulder and making the tool weak and liable to bend or break.

What is most important is the blade, as this is what does the cutting and finishes the surface. The tang is only a means of holding the blade, with the help of the handle.

If the blade is usable, form a new tang by grinding one into the metal in its normal position, but of necessity closer to the cutting edge (Fig 5.29). Substitute for the shoulder (bolster) proper by grinding two shoulders into the metal, and seating these on to a washer. Make the diameter of the washer that of the ferrule, and file its hole square to take the new tang. Take care to grind the new tang in line with the axis of the tool and to make it big enough; at the same time make the new shoulders square and in line. While grinding, dip the blade in water or wrap it in a wet rag to keep it cool. It does not matter if the tang itself heats up, as this needs to be softer anyway.

This way of reinstating the tang works well (Fig 5.30). Because the blade is effectively shortened, the loss of overall tool length can be made up by fitting a longer handle.

BROKEN BLADES

This is usually to be seen where some sad old carving tool has already been used to open paint tins or as a screwdriver. Judicious grinding can sometimes salvage these blades, but be careful not to overheat the steel and draw the temper. Remember that the steel is thicker towards the shank of the tool, so a longer bevel is needed to get the cutting angle that is wanted. Retempering the blade may also be necessary (see Volume 2, Chapter 3).

Broken tangs may be approached in the same way as badly rusted ones.

CHAPTER SIX

INNOVATIONS IN CARVING TOOLS

AIMS

- To assess some recent additions to the range of woodcarving hand tools

Human beings are highly creative; they can never leave the status quo alone for long. Thus in the carving world today it is exciting to see many new ideas being tried: new methods and ways of doing things; new effects and the pushing of boundaries in design; and new technologies and metals meeting restless minds.

Some ideas seem to be just 'the tyranny of the new' and marketing-led. Some are personal to a carver and will never see the light of day in the marketplace, but may be shared between carvers. Others seem to be standing the test of time and are gaining popularity – carvers are actually using them, and this must be the proving: if a new tool is used for a short while then left to moulder in a drawer for evermore, it cannot be counted a success.

Additionally, carving tools are now beginning to appear in the West from other, previously disregarded, carving traditions, particularly that of China. I have included them here because they are unfamiliar in the West – though they can certainly not be described as 'innovations', since China has a rich and distinguished history of woodcarving. These tools have been regarded with a little suspicion at first, but perhaps demand will grow as their value to Western woodcarvers comes to be recognized.

This chapter describes a few innovative and imported woodcarving tools that are in the process of becoming established. Interesting though they are, I would encourage you to become thoroughly familiar with conventional tools before experimenting with these less familiar ones.

FLEXCUT CARVING TOOLS

Flexcut tools are the brainchild of carving instructor Rich Rymer and carver David Bennett, of Falls Run Woodcarving Inc., Philadelphia, USA. These tools certainly *are* an innovation – a thorough overhaul of conventional carving tools – and a comparison with traditional types is in some ways not so easy as might seem at first sight. They look quite different from conventional carving tools, to begin with: thin blades with unusually flat, flexible shanks and unique, 'ergonomic' handles.

Flexcut carving tools are currently available in three forms (Fig 6.1):

- *Palm tools*: smaller than conventional tools, and with a handle fitting very comfortably into the

Fig 6.1 *The three varieties of Flexcut tools (from left): mallet gouge; standard gouge; palm gouge*

hand; for use in a one-handed whittling fashion (with the other hand supporting the workpiece), or for close work in general.

- *Standard tools*: more regular-length blades with proportionally larger handles; used in both hands with the workpiece clamped in a vice, say. This is the tool with the most flexible blade.

- *Mallet tools*: the least flexible and most like a regular carving tool, with an octagonal (but still distinctively shaped) handle and large ferrule; for use with a mallet in larger projects or in harder woods.

As these tools become more popular, so the range of widths and sweeps increases. The tools are high quality and come well sharpened with a flat bevel, good cutting angle and straight cutting edge, but no internal bevel.

These tools have gained great popularity in the USA, particularly with carvers who favour a somewhat caricatured 'folk' style influenced by Scandinavian traditions. Perhaps American carvers are more open-minded than Europeans; this is not a value judgement, but a possible reason why traditional carvers in the UK seem less enthusiastic about

these novel tools. As with all tools, there are pros and cons, some of which have as much to do with the background and attitude of the carver as the tools themselves.

When Flexcut tools were first introduced, the flexing of the blade was a strong marketing point: the idea was that the user could convert a straight gouge to a bent one by pressing down on the handle (Fig 6.2). However, since the blade itself is stiff and only the rear shank part can flex, the advantage over a correctly used straight gouge is very small when it

Fig 6.2 *Exerting downward pressure flexes the blade and gives a scooping action to the cut*

comes to creating a hollow. In fact, I don't think this is the strong point of these tools at all.

The metal of the blades is thin – among the thinnest around – and well tempered. This gives a sense of delicacy of touch, and the cutting edge passes through the wood easily. The handles are most comfortable in a low-level, two-handed grip, and those of the palm tools – which I have found useful for undercutting – work extremely well.

The flexible blades feel very different from conventional tools, and some may find that pressing down to make the flex feels unnatural. The flat metal blade and oval-section handle may tend to dictate how you manipulate the tool, compared with the uniform shank and handle of a conventional tool; and the shaped handle may feel less comfortable when the blade is offered 'upside down'. The mallet tools, not having the flex, are much more like conventional tools, and come in sizes large enough to be used in a normal fashion, two-handed or with a mallet.

My feeling is that Flexcut tools suit certain approaches to carving better than others. A newcomer with a desire for traditional ornamental carving would find the range and style of conventional carving tools far more suitable; but for those with a less traditional approach, or a style that emphasizes cuts and facets, Flexcut tools would certainly be worth exploring.

THE RAY GONZALEZ HOOKED SKEW CHISEL

This tool, designed by the well-known British carver Ray Gonzalez, is made by Ashley Iles. It comes in two forms (Fig 6.3):

- *Short shaft*: with a mushroom-shaped handle for holding in the palm, and principally for use with one hand in whittling fashion.

- *Long shaft*: with an octagonal handle, making a normal-length carving tool intended for use with both hands.

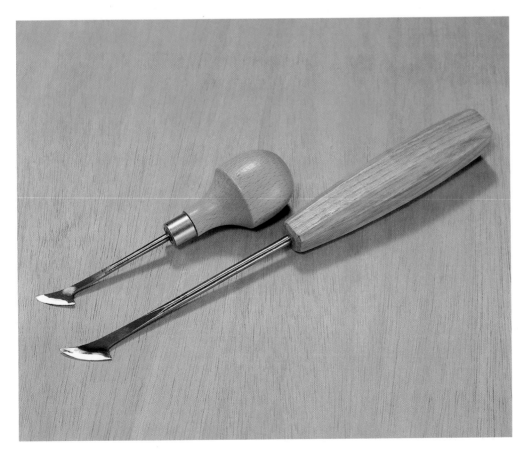

Fig 6.3 *Gonzalez hooked skew chisels: palm type with mushroom handle, and regular-size tool*

99

The narrow shaft is ⁵⁄₃₂in (4mm) wide and expands into a crescent-like blade, available in widths of ⅝in (16mm) and ¾in (19mm). The cutting edge is curved, forming a crescent from corner to corner, and both corners are hooked and available for use, unlike a normal skew chisel (Fig 6.4).

This tool can be used to slice, groove or scribe by pushing or pulling, just like a knife or a skew chisel. The rounding and skewing of the cutting edge allows it to carve a surface by paring while it slices, giving a very clean result. The hooks themselves get into corners that are normally inaccessible, making it capable of small, intricate cuts in confined spaces.

Make sure the mushroom (palm) handle is fitted with the flat on the *underside*, at right angles to the blade, so you can use it equally in both hands. If the flat were facing left, say, you would find the tool comfortable only in your right hand. My own preference is for the long-shafted version, fitted with a lighter, narrower handle than the manufacturer's own; I find this more in keeping with the light, delicate nature of the tool.

The very low cutting angle of 5° gives a delicate blade, capable of shaving off wood very finely. How-ever, this very thinness and delicacy means you must *never rock or wobble* an embedded corner or edge from side to side: it will easily snap.

SHARPENING

Felt and cloth wheels will snag the hook, so powered means such as this cannot be used. In addition, the blade is very fine and of a sensitive shape, so benchstone sharpening is by far the best.

The 5° angle at which the tool is offered to the stone is very low. Otherwise, sharpen like a normal skew, with the cutting edge (or rather, the imaginary line from corner to corner of the cutting edge) at right angles to the length of the stone, first one side, and then the other (see pages 193–4). Because of the curve, you will have to tilt the cutting edge first towards the point and then towards the heel, so as to ensure that the whole of the edge and bevel is covered.

After checking the cut in a piece of carving wood, strop well in the normal way. Again, maintain this very low angle and keep the cutting edge square on, as you did with the benchstone.

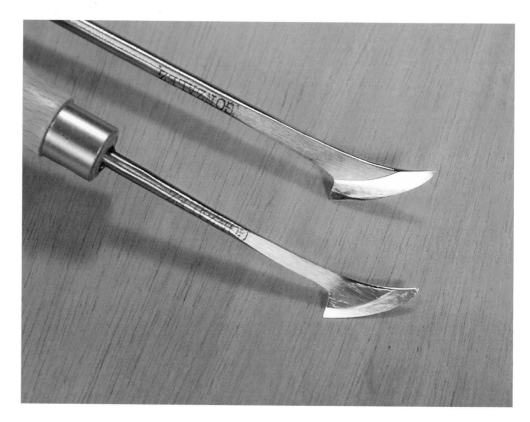

Fig 6.4 *The delicate working ends of the Gonzalez hooks*

COGELOW TOOLS

These are made by Henry Taylor to the specifications of the American carver Fred Cogelow. When a skilled carver, with an international reputation, more or less goes back to the drawing board and redesigns wood-carving tools, the results should be looked at carefully. As with Flexcut tools, I find that I can achieve the same results with more traditional carving tools; however, many carvers whose background and approach are different from mine have found Cogelow tools very useful.

Cogelow gouges are made to quite exacting specifications. They come in a limited range (Fig 6.5), and their features include:

- extra-long blades to increase leverage

- edges skewed to left or right to give an automatic slicing action to the cut, which is helpful for working against the grain

- a small forward or backward bend in the shank behind the bevel to aid the 'scooping' action of the gouge as the blade leaves its cut

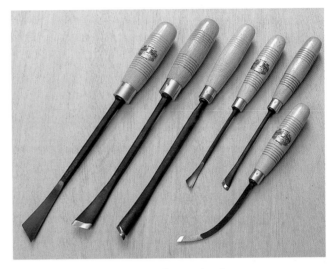

Fig 6.5 *A selection of Cogelow tools; these come in a variety of lengths, shapes and bends, including the bent skew chisel shown on the right*

- slightly thicker metal on the point side of the skew to aid the passage of the blade through the wood.

The 'bent skew', which somewhat resembles the side chisel, is a useful tool for cleaning up the root of deep grooves or hollows.

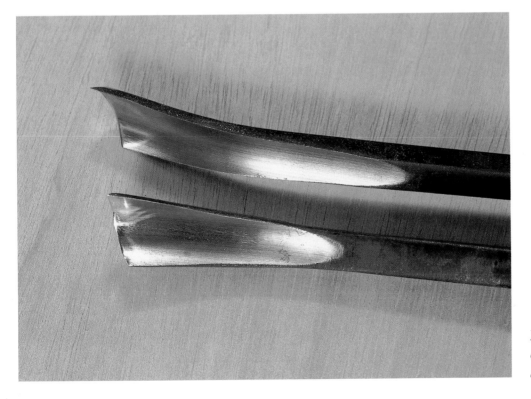

Fig 6.6 *The working ends of these Cogelow gouges are skewed and slightly bent*

The result is a range of unusual-looking tools designed to solve many of the problems that new-comers to carving may come across. In the main, it seems that most carvers who have worked a long while with traditional tools find these unnecessary, whereas newcomers take to them more readily. Nevertheless, since carving is such a personal occupation it really is a case of trying what tools are available and seeing what they can do for you.

CHINESE CARVING TOOLS

In Volume 2, Chapter 3 is a drawing of a Chinese woodcarving tool, some 150 years old, in the Science Museum in London. This skew chisel has a socket made from folding excess metal around a spike, instead of the tang and shoulder of the tools with

which most of us are familiar. Surprisingly enough, a small range of rather similar tools is still available today (Fig 6.7).

The tang by which most of our Western carving tools are fixed to their handles is simply a spike. It is often quite small, even when the blade itself is large, and I have seen large sculpture gouges bent at the shoulder, either through incorrect alignment of the tang or through using the blade as a lever. I have often thought that a socket would be a much better option for big gouges. The reason sockets are not used is that they are laborious to make and use considerably more metal; also, fitting the handle is less straightforward.

The Chinese tools shown here have been hand-made by the Jang family for four generations; there are some 20 stages in the making of each tool, which may be beaten up to 2,000 times; and the three tool-makers in the family make only 30 carving tools in a nine-hour day. The resulting tools may look a little

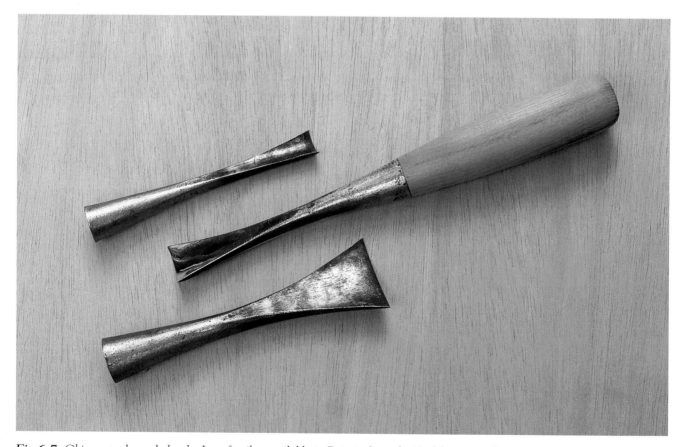

Fig 6.7 *Chinese tools made by the Jang family, available in Britain from the Toolshop, Needham Market, Suffolk. They are supplied unhandled, and the unsophisticated finish hides many excellent attributes*

unsophisticated with their rough-ground finish, and the uneven ends of the conical sockets need refining somewhat before use. The sweeps and widths also vary to some extent from what is listed in the catalogue. There are also some surprisingly sophisticated features, however, and if you are prepared to invest more than the normal amount of time in putting them into commission, the results are excellent and quite handsome-looking tools.

The fishtail blades are truly symmetrical and, uniquely in my experience, the blades have been given a gentle inside bevel in the factory. Their edge-holding properties stand comparison with other carving tools. Given the labour involved in making these tools, they are relatively inexpensive. This compensates for the amount of work needed to clean up the blade and fit a handle, which is not supplied with the blade.

No flat gouge or skew chisel is available, but these can be ground from the flat chisel if necessary. To make a flat gouge, form the inside bevel first.

MAKING A HANDLE FOR A SOCKET CHISEL

These directions will apply to any socketed tool. Since you must go to the trouble of making your own handle, pick a good-looking wood. The easiest way to make the handle (and the method of choice) is by turning it on the lathe. Grip the wood for the handle in a chuck at one end, leaving the other end free to form the taper.

❶ Make sure the very end of the socket is flat and true; use a file to dress it if necessary.

❷ Take accurate measurements of the internal length and diameter of the socket; assume for the moment that the taper is straight.

It is best to form the taper to fit the socket first. Note that there is a shoulder or lip to support the socket end and add stability. (An alternative method which is sometimes recommended is to leave a gap between socket and shoulder to allow for the handle being driven further in by shrinkage or mallet pressure, but I have not found this necessary.)

❸ Smooth and flatten the end of the wood that will reach furthest into the socket.

❹ Create the lip or shoulder, shaping the taper a little larger than your measurements.

❺ Carefully and lightly push the socket onto the rotating, tapered wood; this will mark the high spots where irregularities in the metal prevent the wood seating properly.

❻ Clean these marks away and, with a little trial and error, you should arrive at a snug fit.

❼ The chances are, though, that there will be a slight wobble when you stop the lathe to check; the internal metal will have a slight belly. This can be fixed later.

❽ Shape the handle proper, running the line to merge with that of the metal socket. Make it a fraction oversize at the wood–metal junction; again, the roundness of the metal is bound to be less regular than that of the turned handle.

❾ The handle should be a jam fit; the likelihood is, however, that the internal metal of the socket is not flat (having a belly in the middle), and the metal wobbles on the wood slightly. Smear the taper with a fine sawdust and wood glue mix, push firmly on and align the seating. Leave to set.

❿ As you left the handle slightly oversize to begin with, shave and smooth it down until you can no longer feel the end of the wood and the beginning of the metal socket.

If you don't have a lathe, you can get a fairly accurate cast of the hole by pushing warmed clay or a modelling material such as Plasticine into the socket. Use this as a pattern to whittle the shoulder; bring it close to the finished taper before resorting to metal marking as in step 5 above. Once the socket is dealt with, carve and rasp the main part to shape. The result should be a snug fit with no movement. If there is any wobble, then correct the loose fit as in step 9 above.

The results are beautiful and unusual tools to use, relatively heavy – particularly the smaller ones – until you get used to them.

MICROTOOLS

This is a term in circulation (but not quite established) for very narrow carving tools and, in particular, tools which are *much shorter overall than the regular gouges*. Being short, microtools are mostly used with one hand, or gripped somewhat like a pencil.

For delicate work the length and handle weight of the regular gouges can be an encumbrance. Microtools are welcome and useful tools for the carver of intricate detail – although there is nothing to stop you adapting a narrow gouge of the ordinary, readily available type.

Several different makes are available, with each manufacturer providing only a limited range of what they believe to be the most useful and popular tools. As far as I know, there are no proper shortbent tools to be had, or gouges in the flatter range – though, to be fair, it is difficult to differentiate sweeps at this size. You can make a flat gouge easily enough, though, by taking a micro chisel and carefully reshaping with bench- and slipstones. Three types which I have found useful are:

DOCKYARD TOOLS

Made in Colorado by the Dockyard Model Company, these are available in several sets (for example gouges only, or mixed and graded by size). Wire-like shanks emerge from a simple unferruled handle (Fig 6.8). These inexpensive tools are light and delicate, well shaped and easily manipulated. The smallest tool is $\frac{1}{16}$in (1.5mm) wide. They take a little getting used to, as the shank, at around $\frac{1}{32}$in (1mm) thick, flexes a little disconcertingly – it can even kink or bend at the handle if you do not use a light, straight touch.

KIRSCHEN

In contrast to the simple Dockyard tools, the Kirschen Zier-Schnitzeisen ('fine' or 'dainty' carving tools) are more like standard woodcarving tools

Fig 6.9 *Kirschen microtools: small versions of their full-sized tools*

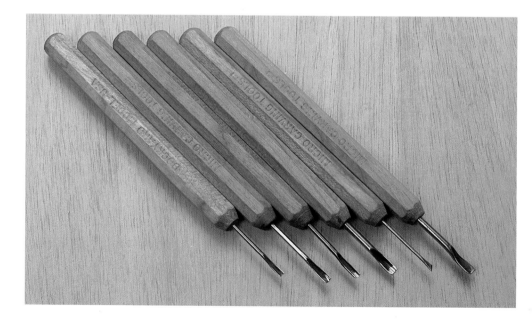

Fig 6.8 *Dockyard microtools: simple, light and slender*

Fig 6.10 *Close-up of the working ends of Kirschen (left) and Dockyard tools*

with octagonal handles, ferrules and shoulders (Figs 6.9 and 6.10). These features make them a little more expensive. The smallest tool is ⅟₅₀in (0.5mm), although most are in the order of ⅟₃₂–⅟₁₆in (1–1.5mm).

ASHLEY ILES PALM TOOLS AND BACKBENT V

The manufacturers term these 'American Palm Cutting Tools', reflecting a style of carving common in the USA, stemming from a whittling style. The handles are mushroom-shaped for use in one hand. (But do remember that you can always change the handle of any carving tool to suit, if you don't like the one with which it was issued.)

Although a small gouge is included in this range, the most unusual feature is the range of V-tools, which includes small (⅟₁₆in/1.5mm) 45° and 60° *backbent* V-tools. The blade shape is the reverse of a longbent (salmon-bend) tool, rather than the reverse of the shortbent as I have been using the term in this book (Fig 6.11). Nevertheless, Iles are the only firm that I know of making any backward-curving V-tool. In the past I've had to make my own for a particular purpose, when nothing else would gain the access

I needed. These small tools are excellent for fur, hair, feathers, etc., where the shape of the animal or bird makes some areas awkward to get at.

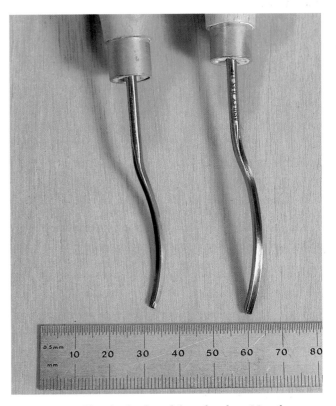

Fig 6.11 *Ashley Iles back and front longbent V-tools*

CHAPTER SEVEN

CARE OF WOODCARVING TOOLS

AIMS

- To consider how best to preserve carving tools from damage and deterioration

- To describe appropriate and convenient ways of storing carving tools

Carving tools need looking after:

- when you get them

- as they are being used

- during the times they are idle.

This is most simply achieved by cultivating good habits. Before dealing with specific ways of storing and looking after carving tools, a few more general thoughts might be useful.

Deal with mechanical faults and problems with your carving tools straight away

Rather than let a lot of small concerns build up, deal with each problem as and when it is noticed if at all possible. The object is to get your tools feeling so comfortable and working so well that you need hardly give them a thought. This includes making a habit of sharpening your carving tools as you buy them, so that they are ready for use whenever the need arises.

Maintain a good level of sharpness

The emphasis here is on *maintenance*. Aim for the best level of sharpness you can achieve, then maintain or improve this level, rather than oscillating between good and bad conditions.

Put the tools away in the state in which you would like to get them out

It is frustrating to get out a carving tool only to find that it needs sharpening – or dealing with in some way – before it can be used. Far better to have tools sharp, working well and ready for immediate use. So have a rule: tools are not to be put away unless they are as sharp as you would like them to be when you next pick them up – this will save more effort than it creates.

Protect the carving tools properly at all times

Essentially this means respect: respect for the carving tools and what they can do. Protection applies to mechanical damage, especially to the cutting edges, and to the effects of damp. Carving tools which are used continuously do not rust, so the longer the tools are left unused, the more protection they need from damp. This matters most to carvers working in garages and sheds at the bottom of the garden. If at all possible, bring the tools into the house between carving sessions.

Never lend out tools

Make this a rule – even to friends. Woodcarvers have a degree of specialized knowledge and personal concern for their tools that is rarely shared sympathetically by others. It is not unknown for the 'friend' to be looking for a screwdriver while ostensibly asking for a chisel. The exception may be another carver whom you can trust to return the tools in the condition in which you lent them.

STORAGE POSSIBILITIES

GENERAL POINTS

Put carving tools away, and out of the way

Large numbers of tools on the bench at any one time are in danger of being damaged if their edges knock against one another as you are working. By all means leave out the tools you are immediately using, but make a habit of clearing away redundant tools – and make sure they are put away sharpened.

Periodically wipe the tools with an oily rag

If tools are not being used for some time – or perhaps towards winter if the workshop is not heated, or is a little damp – this will keep them 'sweet'. Wipe the blades clean with a fresh cotton rag before handling them again.

Store them safely when not in use

There are several methods of storing woodcarving tools – all attempt to store them out of harm's way, but ready when they are needed. The methods described below all have advantages and disadvantages. You may find a mixture of these the best way of storing your particular range of carving tools.

TOOL ROLLS

This is an old and well-tried method of storing and transporting carving tools. The handles of the tools are held in opposite rows of pockets, which are staggered so that the blades of one side lie between the handles of the tools on the opposite side (Fig 7.1).

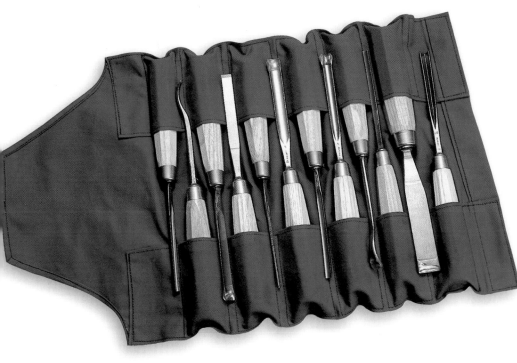

Fig 7.1 *In a tool roll, the handles in one set of pockets support and protect the blades of the tools on the opposite side*

The handles support the blades and edges and, when rolled up, the tools nestle together and are prevented from knocking against each other. The material itself can help protect the tools from damp; good choices include felt, or canvas or linen which have been washed to remove any dressing.

Some measurements for an average roll are given in Fig 7.2, but consideration could be given to having larger or smaller rolls with dimensions appropriate to your own tool sizes. You might try lining up a few sample tools and gauging the pocket sizes with a flexible tape measure.

Tool rolls are easily made with a sewing machine (Fig 7.3). Use baize for the inner pockets, with an outer piece of tough material such as canvas. This should fold over the ends of the blades for additional protection, as well as strengthening the outside of the tool roll. Sewn-on tapes are used to tie the rolls up when not in use.

A good, manageable size might take between 24 and 30 tools. With larger numbers, the rolls start becoming a bit cumbersome; several smaller rolls are a better option. These tool rolls need replacing every so often, as, with the best will in the world, the sharp tools will cut them.

Without good organization, you will be continually opening and closing your tool rolls to put tools away or get them out. One idea is to fill the rolls according to the frequency with which the tools are used. A roll can be left open on the bench, but then a lot of bench space is being taken up by tools that are not in use. It is better to leave the tool roll open somewhere away from the bench, but close by.

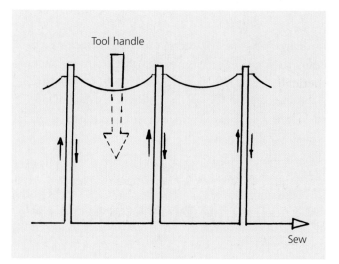

Fig 7.3 *Making a tool roll: for more strength, sew a double line that crosses the edge of the pockets*

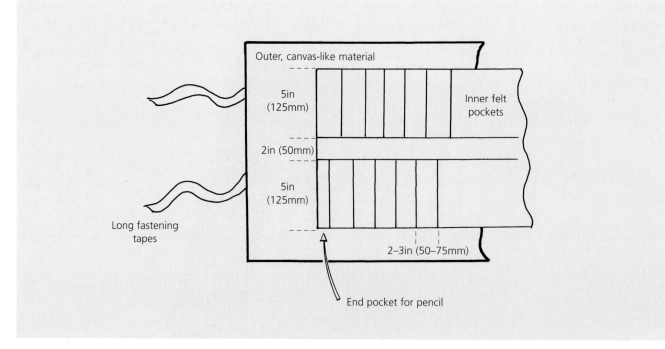

Fig 7.2 *Basic plan of a tool roll*

The greatest advantage in storing woodcarving tools inside fabric rolls is enjoyed by those who do not have a permanent workplace. The tool roll can then be stored wherever convenient – perhaps in a wooden box such as a carpenter's toolbox, with other equipment.

A type of tool roll which contains a row of elastic loops along the centre can be bought commercially, but is not recommended. Passing the sharp edges through the loops without cutting them – or your fingers – can be quite a palaver. Also, the blades themselves are looser than in the pocketed tool roll, which increases the risk of the delicate edges being damaged. This sort of roll may have its place for other bits and pieces, however.

RACKS

This method of holding carving tools can be very convenient. The tools are within easy reach, and can be easily returned after use. The bench can be kept less cluttered and the tools at your disposal can be easily seen.

Two types of rack are frequently used:

LOOPS OF MATERIAL

Leather strips or old car seat belts are tacked at intervals along a board at the back of the bench. Blades are inserted edge down, and the tool is supported by its handle (Fig 7.4).

There are some problems. For this type of rack to work, the tool handle must be wider than the blade, or the tool will fall through the loop. This limits the size of tools to about 1in (25mm) or narrower, depending on the size of the handles.

The blades also need to be heavier than the handles in order for the tools to hang upright. As some blades are quite small and light, their handles tend to fall over and across others. The edges beneath can then touch or knock against one another, with possible damage. You should consider protecting the edges of some tools with vulnerable corners – such as fishtail and skew chisels – by means of a cork pushed on to the end (Fig 7.5). I prefer plastic corks over the natural ones as they don't absorb wine, the acid of which I have found to corrode the embedded edge.

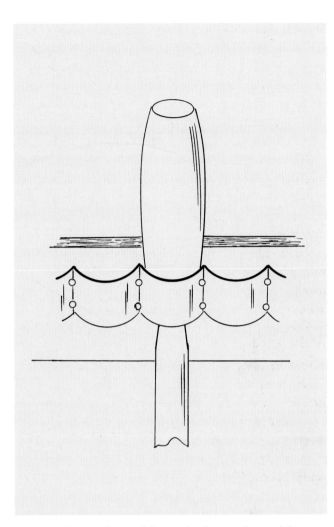

Fig 7.4 *Loops of stout fabric or leather can be used for storing tools*

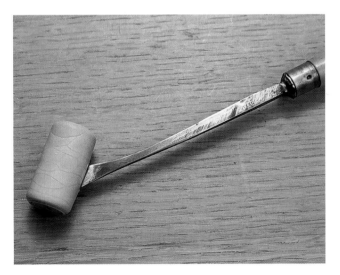

Fig 7.5 *A cork, preferably plastic, will protect delicate corners, either on the bench or when the tool is stored*

WOODEN SHELF

An alternative to loops is a rack made by boring and cutting various-sized holes and notches into a shelf of wood (Fig 7.6). The holes take tools where the blade is smaller than the handle, the notches where the opposite is the case, normally gripping the blade by the shank.

This is a firmer, safer arrangement than the loop method of holding tools, but not so easy to adjust. To begin with, guesses have to be made as to what tools you may eventually have, and the holes, notches and necessary clearance between blades need to be estimated. A more elaborate solution would be a shallow wall-mounted cupboard with racks inside and on the insides of the doors.

DRAWERS

This works very well as a storage method, especially if the drawers are part of the carving bench or close at hand. Use different drawers, or parts of drawers, for particular sweeps or shapes of tools. Home-made drawers can be shallow boxes made with simple butt joints and plywood bases; they do not need to be elaborate. Making the bases wider than the boxes, so they can run in grooves in the sides of the carcass, is easier than making conventional drawer runners.

Metal multi-drawer cabinets which are sold for office filing are exactly the right size for storing woodcarving tools. These units are available with 5, 6, 9, 10 or 15 drawers and can be bought second-hand. The drawers can be easily labelled and, being metal,

they will last indefinitely. Such drawers will need lining to protect the edges of the tools. Self-adhesive cork floor tiles are useful for this; the unvarnished ones are better for protecting the contents of the drawer from damp.

If all the tools are laid out neatly pointing in one direction, there is little danger of the blades clashing against each other when the drawer is slid open or closed. Alternatively, you can fit more tools in by laying them in opposite directions (Fig 7.7), though in this case you may have to take a little more care to avoid cutting yourself as you take them out. The smallest tools, especially those with round handles, may roll a little, but a few wooden dividing strips, acting as racks, will prevent this.

A traditional alternative to drawers is a lockable wooden box, with trays fitted in one above the other in the manner of a needlework box. This would be easier to make than a set of drawers, though perhaps less convenient to use. You would need to keep your favourite tools in the top layer.

LONG-TERM STORAGE

There may be an occasion when carving tools have to be stored for a length of time, perhaps several months. Above all, protect them from damp: wipe the blades with the same sort of oil used for sharpening, or better still wrap them in oily rags. Protect them from damage by rolling them up in rags or in their own tool rolls. Finally, keep them in a polythene bag in a dry place.

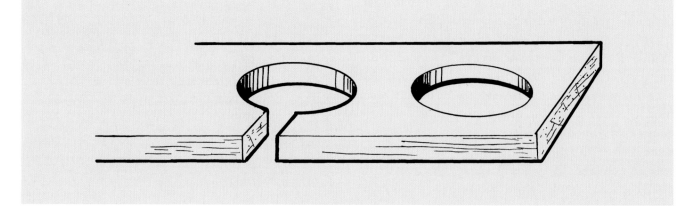

Fig 7.6 *A simple rack with holes and notches for storing tools*

BENCH DISCIPLINE

Previous chapters dealt with carefully selecting your carving tools; Part II discusses working your tools up to their most efficient and sharp condition. Caring for your tools before and after use has been dealt with above. However, the discipline of looking after them also involves the time when they are actually used. Again, some basic practices will help.

DURING CARVING

- Avoid levering or prising wood chips away with the chisel or gouge, as this can break an edge – cut the wood cleanly instead.

- Avoid scraping the edge across the cut wood as the tool leaves it; this action will dull the edge.

- When a delicate tool such as a skew has entered the wood, do not rock it from side to side. There is a real danger of breaking the corner and leaving it buried in the wood.

- Use a mallet only when the tool is strong enough to take it, and be particularly careful with shoulderless tools.

WHEN THE TOOLS ARE ON THE BENCH

The danger is that the carefully sharpened edges may be chipped through knocking up against each other or other metal objects. So to help guard against this:

Line up the tools parallel to one another, with all the blades in the same direction

The tools should be lined up at the back of the bench, or out of the immediate working area. They will look a little like a series of piano keys, which is not a bad way to regard them. It is better if the edges point forwards, as the tools can be recognized more easily from this direction (Figs 7.8 and 7.9). This is an excellent habit to get into right from the start of your carving career. The discipline of always putting down your tools in a row not only protects them from each other but, by making the tools easier to find, speeds up the

Fig 7.7 *Reversing every other tool in a full drawer will safely fit more in*

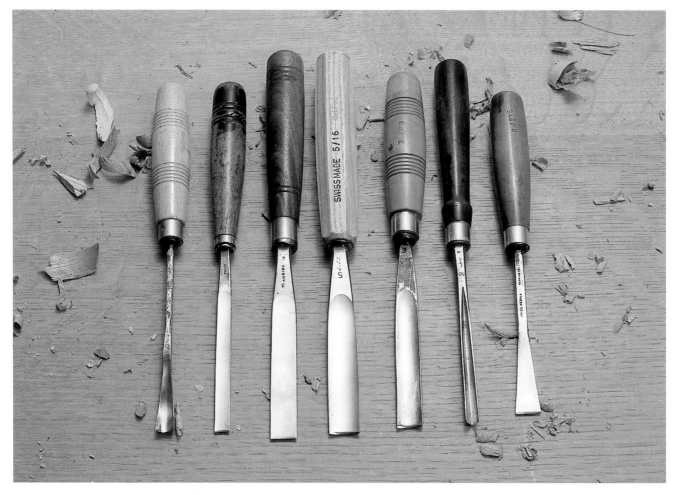

Fig 7.8 *Lining up the tools in use keeps their edges from knocking against each other and makes them easier to recognize*

carving process and adds enormously to the overall awareness and 'flow' of what you are doing.

Try not to have too many tools on the bench

If a lot of carving tools are needed on a particular job, try to organize them so that the tools that are least frequently used are out of the way and lined up towards the back of the bench. Bring forward the ones needed for the immediate tasks.

Periodically clear the bench

Repeating a point made above: make a habit of clearing the work area of surplus tools and putting them away, after first making sure they are sharp. Also clear the bench of wood chips and other bits and pieces occasionally – this can coincide well with natural breaks for brewing up.

Keep tool edges away from anything metal

Quite a few metal objects can be on the bench: clamps, holdfast heads, compasses, metal rulers and so on (Fig 7.10). The sharpened edges of woodcarving tools only have to touch these things, or each other, to damage the edge sufficiently to leave scratch lines. A wooden block placed beneath the jaw of a clamp will help to prevent contact with the cutting edge, as well as protecting the work or the bench top from bruising. Don't forget any metal objects embedded in the wood itself, such as carvers' screws.

Beware of the dangers to carving tools when moving around and adjusting work

This is the time when – because the attention is elsewhere – tools can be rolled about against each other, or knocked to the floor.

Fig 7.9 *Careless placing of tools on the bench will cost time in damaged edges*

Touch up any damage to edges straight away

If an edge does get chipped or damaged accidentally, make a point of dealing with it as soon as possible. If you wait until you need the tool again, it will be when you want to carve, not sharpen.

Fig 7.10 *Delicate edge versus the cast-iron foot of a clamp – an unequal contest. Clamps are commonly used by carvers. Be aware that they are an easy source of damage to cutting edges which have taken time and effort to achieve*

SUMMARY

- Looking after your woodcarving tools from the moment you first get them, through their sharpening, while they are being used, to when they are stored, involves a degree of discipline. Discipline can be seen as developing good working habits – efficient methods of going about things that not only save time and energy, but also facilitate carving itself.

- If you understand and care for your woodcarving tools, in themselves and for what they can do, there is less to get in the way of carving itself. Tools are not ends in themselves – when it comes to actually carving, the heart and mind always play the principal part. Discipline and care can nevertheless be seen as making a very important contribution to the same end.

PART II

SHARPENING
WOODCARVING
TOOLS

Aims of Part II

- To emphasize the importance and benefit of having sharp woodcarving tools

- To make clear what 'sharpness' is, and what factors contribute to a sharp cutting edge

- To describe the sharpening process in general terms and, in detail, how specific types of woodcarving tools are sharpened

- To describe the equipment needed to sharpen woodcarving tools, and how to use and care for it

- To advise on how to maintain sharpness with the least effort

- To compare the merits of traditional sharpening stones and more recent alternatives

- To look at the problems and benefits of electrical sharpening methods

- To promote, through being at ease with the sharpening process, more confidence with woodcarving itself

Each of these aims in turn will now be considered in a little more detail.

The importance and benefit of having sharp woodcarving tools

When you obtain a new carving tool you must first put it into commission; in other words, bring it into full service. This means examining the tool along the lines already discussed: checking the handle for comfort, the shoulder, shank and blade for size and alignment, and so on. These checks you need only do once. Then, of course, check the cutting edge and bevel; this is the working part of the tool.

The view of many newcomers – still maintained by others who have been carving a while – is that sharpening is a chore which has to be tolerated in order to get on with the carving itself. The marketing of pre-sharpened tools caters to these feelings – but unfortunately the spontaneously self-sharpening woodcarving tool has yet to be invented, and the task of sharpening tools will remain, as it always has been, something every carver must undertake.

Even though there is hardly a book on carving that does not start with some information on the subject of sharpening, and information is also given out by tool manufacturers themselves, students at carving classes still turn up with badly sharpened tools – or even tools so useless that no sharpening could reclaim them. The reason is twofold: firstly, the student does not feel or comprehend why sharpness is important; and secondly, the information on sharpening is still inadequate or unclear.

What is needed is a change of attitude to some extent. Carving tools should not be seen as separate from the woodcarving itself. Sharpening is not the bane and penance of the carver but part of the process – a process that involves your-self, working with your design, the wood, your carving tools and the high quality of their cutting edges. All these factors support each other as the whole process moves towards a satisfying end (Chapter 8).

Sharpening woodcarving tools is not a particularly difficult skill to learn and exercise, and can be enjoyable in itself. Its real importance only becomes obvious with experience, so a beginner has to be convinced of the advantages to be had from really sharp carving tools, in order to put in the effort needed to learn the skills of sharpening. These chapters will try to help with learning such skills and getting a feel for their importance.

What 'sharpness' is, and what factors contribute to a sharp cutting edge

As with carving itself, knowing what you are looking for is halfway to finding it. What, then, is this magical sharpness? Is it always the same, for all carving tools, at all times, for all woods?

The theme of these chapters follows the old axiom: 'To give someone a fish is to feed them for a day. To teach someone to fish is to feed them for the rest of their life.' Those who have been given a set of unprepared carving tools as a present must face the problem of sharpening them first. Without proper instruction, this can lead to a frustrating experience – ending, not uncommonly, in the whole notion of carving being abandoned before you have even started.

With a gift of pre-sharpened carving tools, at least one gets to carve wood for the day. But without the necessary sharpening skills the tools dull, begin to cut less well, and dissatisfaction and frustration arise.

The sharpening process in general, and how specific types of woodcarving tools are sharpened

There is a method, basic to the sharpening of all woodcarving tools, that can be taught and learned. The key approach given in these chapters will be adapted for different shapes, sweeps and sizes of blade to allow you to achieve what you want in a particular case, and in the quickest and most straightforward way.

Some of the techniques of sharpening may seem awkward at first – and cer-tainly there are some tools that need more care than others – but they are well within the capabilities of anyone dextrous enough to carve (Chapter 9).

The equipment needed to sharpen woodcarving tools, and how to use and take care of it

If sharpness and carving tools are inseparable, acquiring carving tools means acquiring the means to sharpen them. Once you invest money in carving tools, you need to invest a little more on the sharpening equipment, and learn to use it. There are various options in sharpening, including electrical help. But at the basic level you do not need much in the way of kit, so the cost can be less than that of a few carving tools. And, in the same way that good-quality carving tools last a lifetime, so, as a rule, will good-quality sharpening stones.

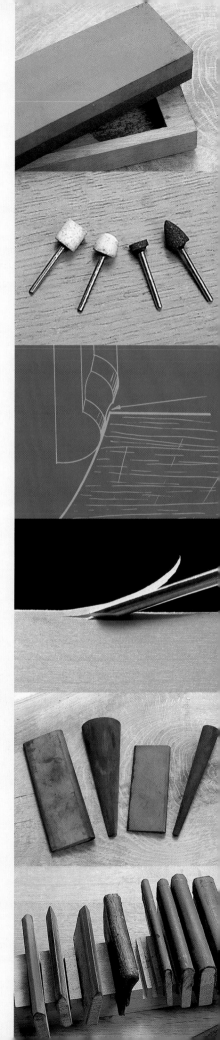

Chapters 10 and 11 explain what equipment you need, why you need it and how to use it, as well as how to look after the various bits and pieces so that they last a long time.

How to maintain sharpness with the least effort

Sharpening tools, and maintaining their sharpness, is essential to the woodcarver. It needs to be accepted, and not seen as a chore or an interruption to the work. The meditative quality of sharpening can be enjoyed, as can the self-respect and joy in achieving and using a beautifully sharpened blade. There is also the opportunity to take stock of how the carving is progressing.

While fostering this attitude, ways can be found to minimize the effort of sharpening and maintaining the cutting edges – creating routines, rather than big events that stand out for their tediousness (Chapter 12). If you have a resistance to the discipline of sharpening, then the chances are you will have problems with the discipline of carving itself.

Traditional sharpening stones and more recent alternatives

Sharpening 'stones' are now available in a wide range of materials, from true stone taken directly out of the earth to substances made with all the guile of high technology. They may be given 'grit' designations in order to make a comparison with conventional stones, but they are not at all the same: their behaviour, cutting properties and feel differ considerably.

Chapter 13 takes an overview of the various 'stones' available, assessing their strengths and weaknesses and how they fare compared with the well-tried

A habit of regular stropping will maintain the keenness of the cutting edge, and help to make sharpening a pleasant routine rather than a major event

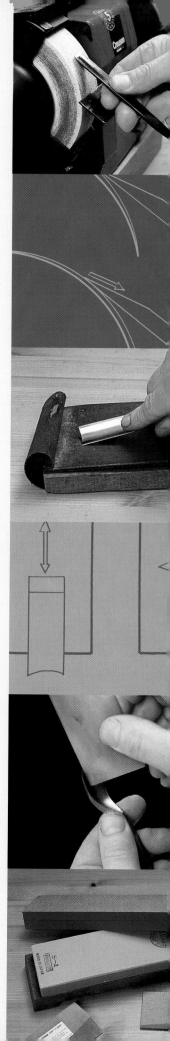

Arkansas oilstone – which I have taken as a rough benchmark, and assumed as standard in my description of sharpening technique.

The problems and benefits of electrical sharpening methods

More and more, electrical sharpening methods are augmenting, even replacing, the traditional use of benchstones, slipstones and strops. When power sharpeners produce the correct qualities of shape and sharpness, safely and easily – and much of the result depends on the expertise of the user – then they soon become essential additions to the workshop of any busy carver.

However, the electrical devices available today have both benefits and drawbacks. They are helpful in some areas but can cause problems in others. It is not simple, and sometimes not even possible, to achieve the shape and quality you aim for using electrical methods. The use of electrical sharpening or honing machines therefore needs careful consideration (Chapter 14).

Promoting, through being at ease with the sharpening process, more confidence with woodcarving itself

Throughout this book I take the attitude that the carving tools should not get in the way of the carver's intention. Tools can get in the way both physically – by being, for example, poorly shaped – and mentally, as when frustration arises from not being able to sharpen a particular tool adequately or to achieve the effect or surface finish that is wanted.

The answer to these sorts of problems lies largely in the idea of discipline: self-imposed habit patterns and approaches to tools, sharpening, and carving itself. Such disciplines ease the way towards what the carver wants to achieve, and command over woodcarving tools and their sharpness removes one of the major barriers between the carver and the carving.

Based on a German woodcut of 1470

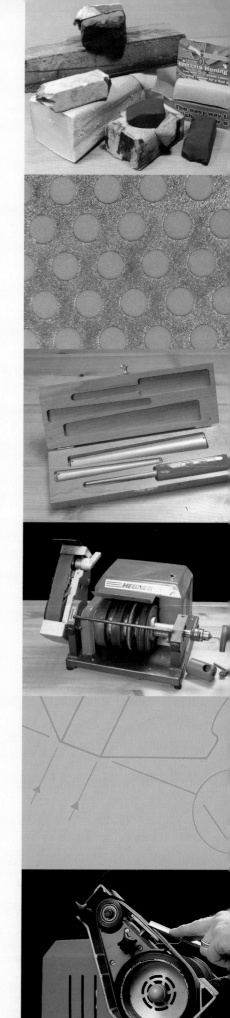

CHAPTER EIGHT

WHY CARVING TOOLS MUST BE SHARP

AIMS

- To emphasize the benefits of having truly sharp woodcarving tools

- To encourage carvers to see sharpening as a useful and pleasant exercise rather than an irksome chore

Apart from carving itself, sharpening and looking after woodcarving tools is the main task undertaken by carvers. A master woodcarver once told me that when costing a piece of work, he would allow up to one third of the allotted time for sharpening and maintaining his tools. This is a stunning bit of information for newcomers to take in, as it was for me at the time. After all, the carving beckons – who wants to spend hours sharpening?

When woodcarving tools are compared with the tools used in woodturning, one difference quickly becomes obvious: turning tools can be used straight from the grinding wheel. This is far from the case with carving tools.

There is nothing to stop you attempting to carve straight from the grinding wheel, if that gives you the effect you are after. But carving tools normally undergo a far more involved process of sharpening before they are ready for use on the wood and the would-be carver can get down to work. Without doubt, this need to sharpen carving tools has caused many a potential carver to become a woodturner instead.

The reason turning tools can be used in such a comparatively rough state has to do with the high surface speed of the wood revolving beneath the cutting edge – which requires short, tough bevels (Figs 8.1 and 8.2) – and the peculiar application of the cutting edge to the wood. Woodturners regularly supplement cutting by finishing the turned shapes with sandpaper to exploit the natural beauty of the wood.

Fig 8.1 *The nose of a woodturner's spindle gouge: both the steep bevel and the rounded end make this an unsuitable shape for a carving tool*

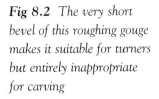

Fig 8.2 *The very short bevel of this roughing gouge makes it suitable for turners but entirely inappropriate for carving*

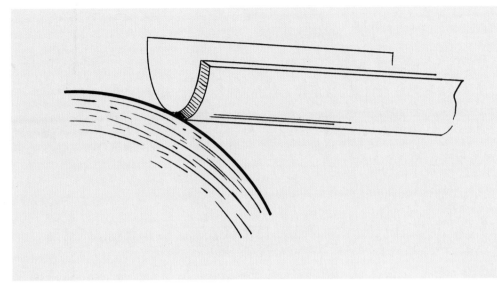

In carving, especially when carving realistic forms, the cuts of the tools can be left as a surface finish in their own right – but this means producing cuts worth leaving (Fig 8.3). Carving involves many more (and more complicated and delicate) shapes of tools than those used in turning, and requires a much more involved approach to sharpening than could be achieved from a grinding wheel alone.

Until quite recently, there was no such thing as 'ready-sharpened' woodcarving tools. Tools came with a bevel roughly ground, or **set**, by the factory. It was taken for granted that a carver would sharpen them exactly as he or she wanted. Although pre-sharpening has its advantages, carvers need to sharpen different tools in different ways for different purposes. This is what the makers would have expected when they sent out tools 'set but not sharpened'.

In this book, the emphasis is on the set carving tool which requires sharpening, and possibly even resetting. Unless stated otherwise, these are the sort of tools that are being referred to. Pre-sharpened tools (Fig 8.4) can easily be dealt with by the same method when it becomes necessary or appropriate to resharpen them. The various advantages, disadvantages and

peculiarities of pre-sharpened tools are considered later, on pages 210–11.

The skill of sharpening the cutting edge 'just so' – and keeping it sharp – is a skill which, for the

Fig 8.3 *Figures from* The Assumption *by Egid Quirin Asam (completed 1750) at Rohr, Germany. The strong changes of plane are the hallmarks of the 'glyptic' (carving) process beneath the gesso covering, and show the traces left by the carving tools themselves*

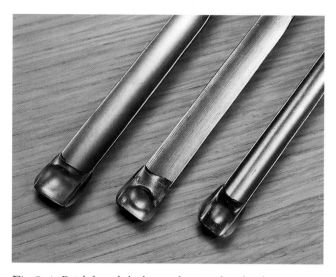

Fig 8.4 Brightly polished, pre-sharpened tools, their tips protected by dipping in a rubbery gel

EFFORT

The cutting edge of a woodcarving blade is nothing more than a wedge of steel – a fine wedge, cutting and prising the wood fibres apart. The angle of the wedge is the angle at which the bevel of the carving tool is set, and this can vary under different conditions. The bevel also needs to be the correct shape, which will be dealt with in more detail in the next chapter (pages 128–40).

If you find that cutting through wood is harder work than it need be, one of the most likely reasons is the incorrect setting of the bevel angle as a preliminary stage to sharpening (Fig 8.5). As soon as this is improved, the amount of effort needed to cut the wood will decrease.

A microscope applied to the very edge of a carving tool shows a crystalline structure. The cutting edge is a wall of molecules making up a crystal lattice. When the blade cuts, this wonderful crystal edge is pushed into a similar microscopic world of wood fibres, prising it apart. When a tool is sharpened, the thickness of this crystal edge is refined down to the most slender state possible – the minimum thickness, given the angle of bevel, that will separate the wood molecules and fibres (Fig 8.6). Eventually this resistance will start to erode the microscopic structure of the steel, and from a thin peak of crystal, a thicker, rounded and broken edge will form (Fig 8.7). Forcing

woodcarver, comes before everything else. Without it, all other skills of design and artistry will be compromised and the execution of the work will suffer. And, as a skill, it must be learnt. Its value cannot be overestimated.

To put in the effort to learn and practise this skill, motivation is needed – the effort must be seen to be worthwhile in terms of results. So what exactly are the advantages that tool sharpness gives to the carver, and why is such a high degree of sharpness needed? The following are some answers, but not in order of importance.

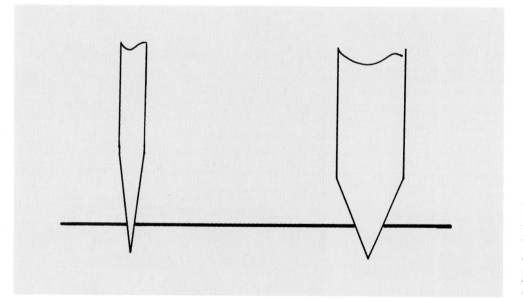

Fig 8.5 It is an obvious principle that the thickness of a wedge relates to the amount of effort required to push it into the same material

Fig 8.6 *Sharpening refines the crystal lattice of a cutting edge to a level which cannot be seen by the naked eye*

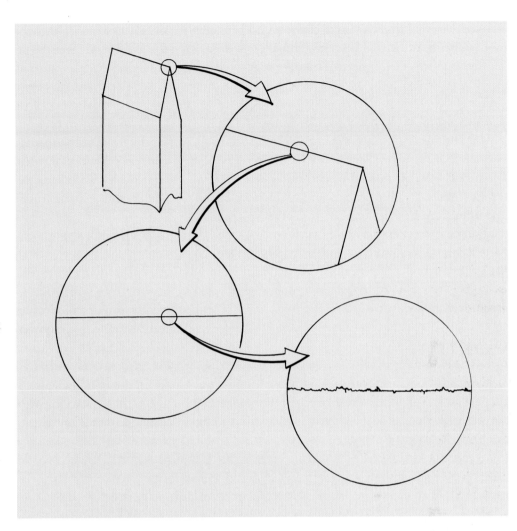

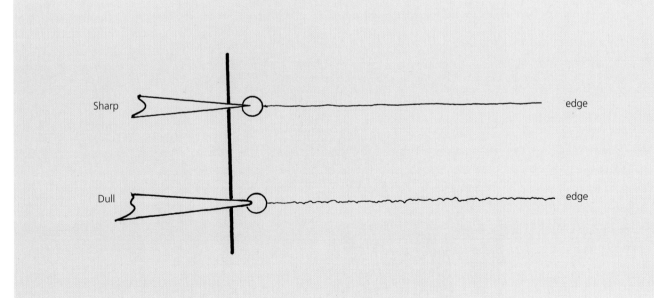

Fig 8.7 *As the crystal lattice of the edge wears down, so more effort is needed to push it through the wood fibres*

a passage against the resistance of the wood becomes more difficult as the tool becomes blunt.

The amount of effort needed to carve is affected by:

• the angle of the bevel

• the refining of the bevel edge by further sharpening.

When less effort is needed to cut, the speed of carving increases, in turn enhancing efficiency. Speed and efficiency also depend on the carver's approach to the work: the method and how the tools are used. Nevertheless, sharpness is indispensably linked to the swiftness and effectiveness with which a work is executed. So, less effort means quicker work and greater efficiency.

CONTROL

With most woods, and correctly sharpened tools, cutting across the grain need not be much different from cutting with the grain. It is even possible, with some woods and the right technique, to cut cleanly *against* the grain if necessary – providing your tools are sharp enough. Because sharpness makes all directions of cut available, sharp carving tools will help you achieve and control whatever form you are seeking.

As a corollary, blunt tools will be inhibiting. They inhibit you mechanically (because of the difficulty in cutting with them), mentally (because blunt tools continually intrude on your intention) and emotionally (because of the frustration that arises).

APPEARANCE

As well as giving control over the form, a really sharp carving tool will leave a beautiful, polished facet as it cuts away a wood chip. The bevel follows behind the cutting edge and burnishes the wood. This effect is best seen when the wood is cut with the grain, but also occurs with cross-cutting using the **slicing** technique. Such clean cutting may be all the surface finish that a carving needs in order to arrive at its finished state (Fig 8.8).

Fig 8.8 A detail of The Banquet at Simon's (1490–2) by Riemenschneider. Light toolwork on the peak of the hat suggests fur, and therefore status; plain surfaces balance with strong areas of tool cuts; and a V-tool was probably used to draw in details in the background

Blunt tools, however, tend to tear wood fibres rather than cut them, and leave scratchy lines – although this can also be the result of bad carving technique. This is when rasps, files and sandpaper will be resorted to as expedients.

Tool cuts in the wood have been called the 'finger-prints of the carver'; they are unique in a way that a sanded surface is not. A sanded carving looks, and feels, very different from one left straight from the chisel. The freshness of cutting, with crisp lines and edges, will all too easily be removed by sanding. The definite changes of plane that makes carving look different from modelling will be smoothed and rounded over. The effect of injudicious sanding can be to make a piece of carved work look as if it has been sucked a while, like a boiled sweet.

Using tools with sharp cutting edges, accompanied by good technique, at least gives you the *option* of a surface finish left straight from the chisel. Many carvers have never experienced this option because their tools are not really sharp. They may have to resort to sandpaper for the finish, whatever the cost in loss of detail or deviation from the original intention. Once really sharp tools have been used, an entirely new range of options is often seen.

Sanding is never an enjoyable task, and the less time and effort spent on sanding, the better. Even if a sanded finish is wanted from the start – say, to show off the natural colour and beauty of the grain – it is still worth working towards the final surface with sharp cutting edges. Odd scratches in otherwise cleanly cut facets of wood can be ignored, as these will be taken out with the sanding. Bear in mind that using tools on a sanded surface will blunt them, so carving must be completed before sanding begins. *Choosing* a smooth sanded finish is not the same as having to finish with a sanded surface because you are incapable of sharpening your tools properly, or have a poor carving technique (Fig 8.9).

SAFETY

This may seem contrary to what is expected, but blunt carving tools are actually more dangerous than sharp ones. Encouraging youngsters in schools to work with blunter tools, in the hope that this will lead to fewer mishaps, is a mistake.

Putting aside hazardous techniques and habits of carving – such as putting parts of your body in the way of the blade – a blunt tool needs more effort

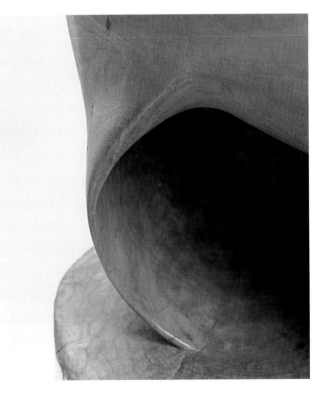

Fig 8.9 *A smooth surface makes a different kind of beauty available to the carver*

125

behind it to force it through its cut. When the blade eventually reaches fresh air again, it is still being propelled by this excessive force, so it tends to leap out of the cut in an uncontrolled manner. It is far better to take easier cuts, with less effort, and in a controlled way, than to be continually jerking a blunt tool out of the wood.

ENJOYMENT

One of the most tangible pleasures of teaching woodcarving is to see the joy and recognition on the face of someone who uses correctly and truly sharpened tools for the first time. Some people may have been working away – possibly for years – with effectively blunt tools, even though they have tried their best to sharpen them.

This is the real case for sharpness: working with blunt tools is a chore, and rarely appreciated for the burden it is until sharp tools are used. Sharpening carving tools is less tedious than working with blunt, badly, even wrongly sharpened tools.

On the other hand, sharpening itself can be a worthwhile use of time. A break from carving to touch up an edge can give you time to stop and think, assess what you are doing and consider the next step. Without wanting to create too romantic a vision, I find that sharpening on a stone can be soothing – a quiet, healing sort of activity that contrasts with the energy often found in the actual cutting.

Finally there is the sheer joy to be felt when a fine edge of steel slices through a good piece of wood. In a silent workshop it makes a noise, a sort of sliding, whispering, as the shaving comes away. The simplicity of the action and the feel of control and command, even when striking the tool with a mallet, is part of the reason why many people carve. All this is facilitated by really sharp carving tools (Fig 8.10).

Fig 8.10 *Sharp tools are a real pleasure to use*

CHAPTER NINE

PRINCIPLES OF SHARPENING

AIMS

- To define the factors which contribute to a sharp and correctly shaped cutting edge

- To give an overview of the sharpening process

FUNDAMENTALS

What is sharpness, and how do we measure it? Is there a difference between 'sharp', 'sharp enough' and 'really sharp'? The answer to these questions lies largely in what we wish to achieve, but also in our attitude.

The meaning of the word 'sharp' includes such connotations as 'keen', 'fine' and 'clear', as well as 'biting', 'piercing' and 'acute'. The word refers to wit and temper, as much as to the cutting edge of a carving tool. Woodcarvers certainly need their tools and wit to have these qualities, if not their temper. There is also the carver's adage to be borne in mind: 'Dull tools make dull work.'

The essential characteristics of a sharp carving tool are these:

- The edge will cut through wood more easily than a dull one with the same angle of bevel.

- It will leave a shiny, polished facet, without scratch marks.

- The surface left from clean toolwork may be regarded as finished, giving a particular clean and sparkling quality to the work.

- The carving tool cuts more or less as nicely across the grain as with it; the sharpness makes negotiating curves easier, where one side of the curve will be against the grain.

- A sharp edge, properly shaped – for example, with its corners retained – works as efficiently as possible.

- Grooves and cuts can be laid down next to each other without tearing up or crumbling the ridges of wood in between (Fig 9.1).

- Using a sharp carving tool is less of a physical effort than using a blunt one.

- Without doubt, such tools are more of an aesthetic pleasure to use than dull ones.

Some wood sculptors, working on large sculpture with the intention of using files and rasps afterwards, can afford to ignore scratches on the surface of the wood

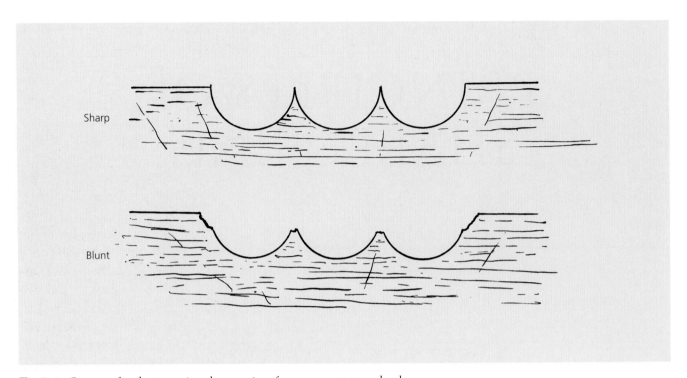

Fig 9.1 *One test for sharpness is to lay a series of grooves next to each other*

or torn grain from tools which are a bit dull, as these marks will eventually be removed. As a conscious decision this may be justified on the grounds of expediency – a case of 'sharp enough', with less 'down time'. More often than not, however, it is a case of the sculptor not knowing – not having been taught – or not bothering to maintain the cutting edges.

What matters is the cutting of the tool in the wood, and whether it achieves what you want it to. With experience you will become acutely sensitive to the feel of the tool as it is working. You will also *see* what is happening from the path of the gouge or chisel, and will know how to make equally sensitive adjustments to the edge.

BEVELS AND CUTTING ANGLES

FUNCTION

The bevel is the shape taken by the thick, supporting metal of the blade as it thins down to the fine cutting edge which actually penetrates the wood. It can be flat, rounded or hollowed along its length, and there may be a bevel on one or both sides of the **cutting edge**, the sum of which gives the **overall bevel angle**.

The bevel on a woodcarving tool is in effect a wedge which cuts and prises fibres apart against resistance (Figs 9.2 and 9.3). As wood fibres from different

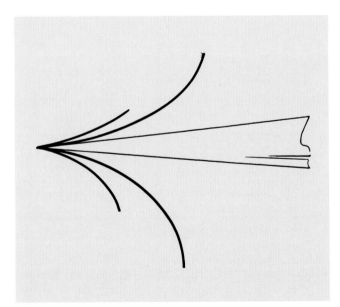

Fig 9.2 *It is helpful to regard the bevel as nothing other than a very refined wedge, cleaving the material*

Fig 9.3 The wedge-like action of the bevel is evident here, causing the wood to split in advance of the cutting edge

species of tree bind together in different densities and strengths, differences in the wedge-shape of the bevel are required to deal with this resistance efficiently.

In the same way that carving proceeds from the main masses and forms through to the final details, sharpening a carving tool is a process of refining the underlying bevel. The importance of the bevel is often neglected by beginners, who tend to sharpen the very edge only, producing a **secondary bevel** that gradually thickens in size (Fig 9.4). Getting the bevel the right shape is a major part of sharpening correctly.

THE SET OF THE BEVEL

The **set** of a carving tool is the angle at which the bevel has been ground on the blade; to put it another way, how long or short the bevel appears. Carvers usually talk about 'longer' or 'shorter' bevels, rather than naming an actual angle, because this is how they appear. When the outer bevel is flat, the bevel angle is more or less the **cutting angle**: the angle between blade and wood when the tool starts to cut. In a V-tool, the cutting angle is taken from the keel bevel, as the apex begins to bite. The cutting angle is an important concept, as we shall see in the discussion of hollow, round and flat bevels (pages 132–6).

Invariably, a bevel will have been set on a carving tool when it leaves the maker, whether it has been sharpened further or not. The grinding of the bevel may be part of an automated process in some factories, or it may involve a skilled person using an industrial grinding wheel. But this bevel angle, preset by the manufacturer, is not necessarily the one that is

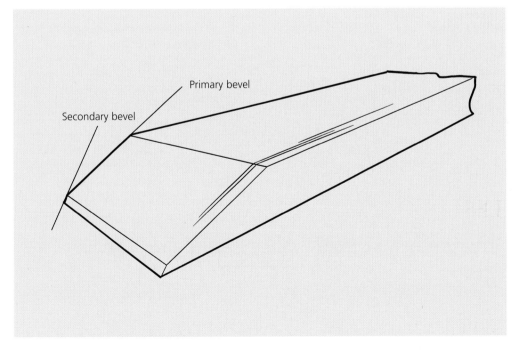

Fig 9.4 Sharpening with a secondary bevel (shown here on a carpentry chisel, where it is common practice) is not the best option for carving tools

Primary bevel

Secondary bevel

wanted by the carver (Fig 9.5). There are various circumstances in which a different angle – a longer or shorter bevel – may be needed.

One problem with pre-sharpened tools is that, while the bevel may indeed be set at a useful angle, it may not be the most useful working angle for the

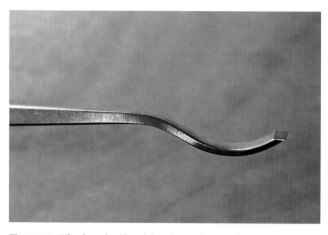

Fig 9.5 *The bevel offered by the maker of this tool is about 45°. It may never occur to a newcomer to carving that this can be, and needs to be, changed*

needs of the individual carver. Someone buying a woodcarving tool for the first time may assume that the shape of the bevel found on the blade is the correct angle for the tool and can not be altered. It *may* be the correct set of bevel, but then again, it may not.

If the angle of bevel you need is different from the one which has been ground on the tool, then you will have to begin by resetting the bevel. This usually involves regrinding.

SHARPNESS VERSUS STRENGTH

There are two factors working against each other in the set of the bevel. As the bevel becomes longer and the wedge effect sharper, the tool, in theory at least, is able to work its way through the fibres of the wood with less effort. But the cost is in loss of strength – there is less metal to buttress the cutting edge (Fig 9.6). As the bevel becomes longer, the cutting edge becomes weaker, until the fibres of the wood may be hard enough to damage the cutting edge before being cut themselves.

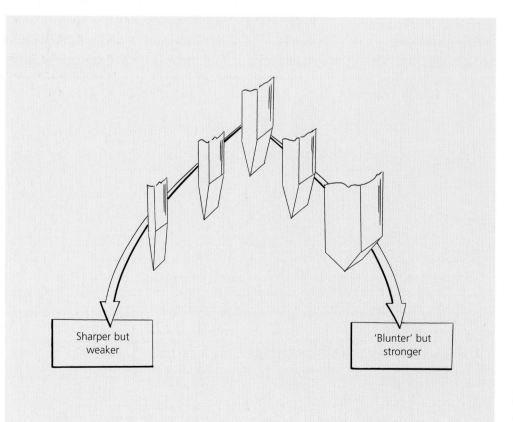

Sharper but weaker

'Blunter' but stronger

Fig 9.6 *The relationship between sharpness and strength*

130

BEVEL ANGLE

Correctly assessing the bevel angle (or length) comes as a matter of experience. The *overall* angle – that of the inner and outer bevels combined – usually varies between 20° and 30° (Fig 9.7). Remember, however, that blades are of different thicknesses, and this will affect how long the bevel appears.

What bevel angles are needed, and under what circumstances? The determining factor is the hardness of the wood fibres.

Wood varies between soft (such as pine) at one end of the range and very hard (such as boxwood) at the other, with medium degrees of hardness (such as lime or basswood) in between. The terms 'soft' and 'hard' in this context are functional ones, and should not be confused with the biological terms **softwood** and **hardwood** as defined in Volume 2, Chapter 6.

The most common woods used for carving fall into a middle range of hardness, and an outer bevel of around 20°, as found on most newly manufactured tools, is appropriate for these. The woods in this middle range of hardness include lime (basswood), walnut, oak and mahogany – but even these woods vary in density and hardness depending on the circumstances in which they were grown, whether there are any hard knots in them, and so on. An outer bevel set at 20° will be suitable for most situations in medium-hardness material. It looks about twice as long as the thickness of the blade, when there is a bevel on one side only.

Soft woods include pines such as northern pine and yellow pine. These timbers were extensively used in the past, especially during the Regency period, for carvings on fire surrounds and panels. To reproduce these pieces and effects today, top-quality pine may still be used.

Many people assume that the softer a wood is, the more easily it can be cut. But what actually happens is that the softer fibres buckle before the advancing wedge of metal (Fig 9.8). The fibres may not resist – stay still long enough – to be cut cleanly, and so they tend to tear. What is needed for carving these soft types of wood is a longer bevel, effectively a sharper edge, than might be expected. The keenness divides the fibres before they crumble, giving proper clean cuts.

However, with a longer bevel, the strength of the cutting edge is reduced. If a carving tool with a longer bevel, suitable for pine, is used on a harder wood such as oak, the cutting edge will disintegrate and produce a scratched and torn surface. It was not unusual in the past for a carver to have more than one set of carving tools: a special set of tools with extra-long bevels was kept solely for work on these very soft woods. Conversely, some exotic woods available

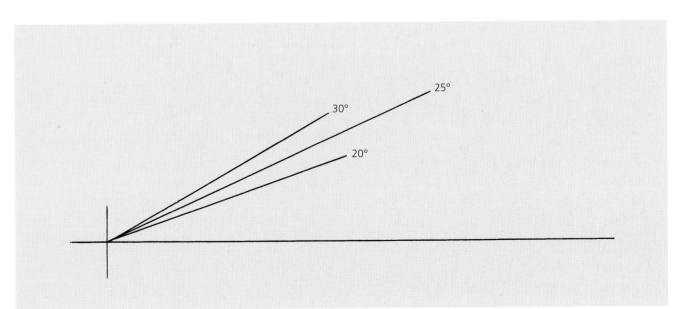

Fig 9.7 *What some different bevel angles look like*

131

Fig 9.8 *Different bevel angles are needed to deal with different resistances of wood fibres*

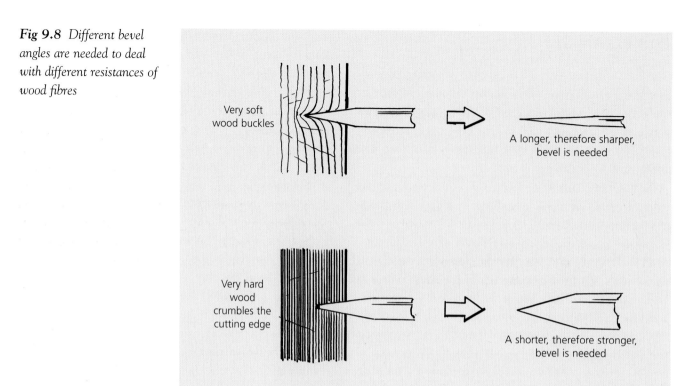

today, such as lignum vitae, are extremely hard. The bevels for these woods need to be shorter for cutting edges to survive.

If a carving tool is not cutting easily or satisfactorily, even though the edge appears to be as sharp as possible, it may be that the bevel needs adjusting to be a little longer or shorter. What is being sought at the end of the day is the longest, and therefore sharpest, bevel compatible with strength.

FLATNESS

The bevel can have three different contours from the heel to the edge (Fig 9.9):

- hollow (concave)

- rounded (convex)

- flat.

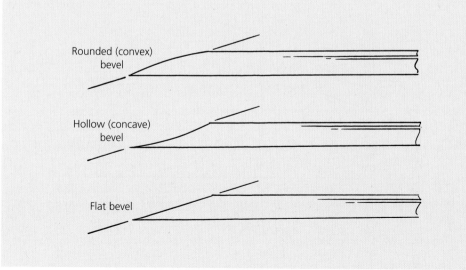

Fig 9.9 *Three types of bevel profile*

In the previous discussion about the bevel angle, the assumption was made that the bevel was simply flat between heel and edge, without any secondary bevels. This is the correct shape, and there are several good reasons why this is the best option. Let us consider the alternatives:

HOLLOW BEVELS

A hollowed contour comes from applying the bevel to a circular grinding wheel, which grinds its own shape into the metal. From the grinding wheel the tool may then be sharpened on flat benchstones, but not enough to remove the hollowness completely (Fig 9.10). A hollow in the bevel continues to exist between the two flat surfaces produced on the benchstones (Fig 9.11).

It might be thought that a slightly hollow-ground bevel is a better option than a truly flat one, as the blade is more free to follow the cutting edge. With this benefit, however, come two disadvantages. The first is the inherent weakness in a hollow bevel. As the hollowness encroaches on the cutting edge, the amount of material buttressing the edge is reduced. The edge becomes effectively sharper, but weaker.

Secondly, a hollowed bevel rides up on the edge of a cut, say when setting in, and working feels awkward and inaccurate compared with a truly flat bevel (Fig 9.12). This relates to the so-called 'self-jigging' action that will be discussed later (page 137).

Fig 9.10 *A hollow-ground bevel with secondary bevels at heel and edge*

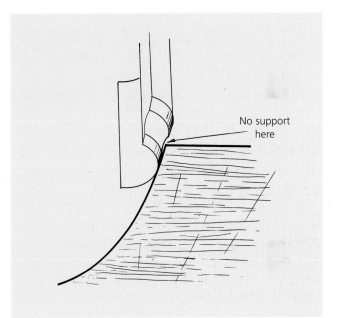

Fig 9.12 *It is difficult for a hollow-ground bevel to 'self-jig'*

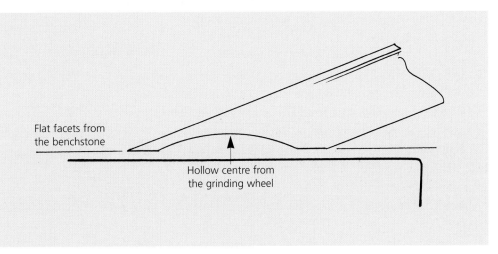

Fig 9.11 *The effect of honing a hollow bevel (exaggerated)*

Fig 9.13 A carving tool bought with the bevel set but not sharpened usually has a flat bevel because of the large diameter of industrial grinding wheels. The bevel may also be quite even and a good size, like this one

Leaving a hollow bevel is not necessarily a quicker way of sharpening a carving tool, either. With correct grinding, it takes no longer to flatten across the whole bevel – so making the edge stronger and lining up more accurate – than sharpening from heel to edge.

New tools are sometimes supplied straight from the grinding wheel, but, because the wheels used by manufacturers are very large, the hollowing is imperceptible (Fig 9.13).

ROUNDED BEVELS

Some hollowness, or concavity, towards the centre of the bevel is preferable to a rounded or convex bevel. A rounded bevel is produced by lifting or lowering the handle during grinding or honing, thereby altering the angle at which the blade is presented to the grinding wheel or benchstone.

At the cutting edge, the rounded bevel has an obtuse profile – the opposite to that of a hollow-ground tool – with two results. In the first place, a

thicker wedge of steel has to be pushed into the wood, requiring more effort (Fig 9.14). Secondly, the carving tool will not start to cut the surface of the wood until its handle is positioned higher than would be the case with a flat bevel. In other words, a rounded bevel gives a higher cutting angle (Fig 9.15). The angle at which the tool cuts affects your ability to control it. The lower the angle, the more control you have when cutting – your hands rest on the wood and work more surely. The higher the cutting angle, the more awkward and uncontrolled the cutting becomes.

Rounding the bevels of woodcarving tools is a frequent and major cause of their handling and cutting badly, with unnecessary effort. It is a more common fault than a bevel which is flat but with an incorrect angle. A seemingly small change from round to flat bevels makes an enormous difference to the quality and control of cutting.

The exceptions to this rule are the longbent and shortbent chisels and gouges. A slight rounding of the bevel is acceptable here as an extension of the bent or rounded shape of these tools, helping to jig the edge through its hollow cut.

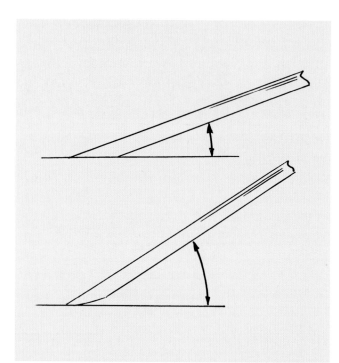

Fig 9.14 Although the edge may look sharp, the cutting edge of a rounded bevel gives a thicker point of contact with the wood than a flat one, and a higher cutting angle

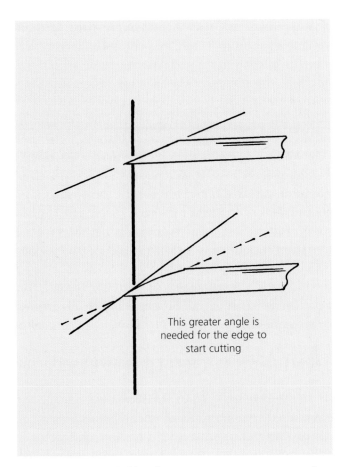

This greater angle is needed for the edge to start cutting

Fig 9.15 A rounded bevel requires a steeper cutting angle

Fig 9.16 A shallow, flat bevel; note the relief grinding on the heel

FLAT BEVELS

Flat bevels cut most efficiently and contribute the greatest amount of strength to the edge for a given degree of sharpness, compared with hollowed or rounded bevels. The cutting angle can be accurate and low (Fig 9.16); and the bevel will self-jig (see page 137) along the face the edge is cutting. It is no more trouble to sharpen a flat bevel than any of the other shapes so far discussed. The practicalities of producing accurate, flat bevels are dealt with in Chapter 12.

One final point about V-tools: the keel – the line of metal at the angle where the two sides join – is the main part of the bevel that is rubbing the wood during its cut. As such, it should be like the bevels of other straight tools – flat from the cutting point to the heel. However, the keel is slightly softened by rounding it from side to side, and is not kept as a knife-like angle (Fig 9.17). This helps the blade slide along its groove and cut curving lines more easily.

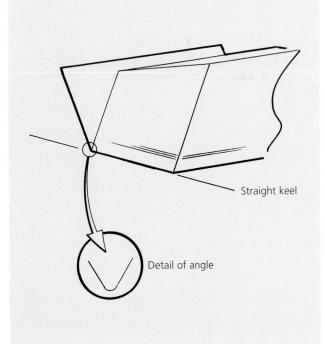

Straight keel

Detail of angle

Fig 9.17 The actual angle or apex of a V-tool, along the keel, is slightly rounded; the keel remains straight throughout its length

SECONDARY BEVELS

There are three things which increase the cutting angle and make you feel less in control of the tool:

- sharpening at too steep an angle in the first place

- rounding the bevel

- including a secondary bevel.

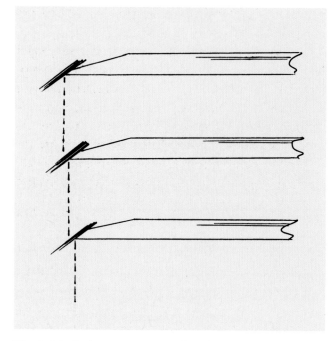

Fig 9.18 *Resharpening a secondary bevel increases the thickness of material behind the cutting edge and therefore the effort needed to cut wood; the tool will need regrinding at some point*

Some carvers sharpen only the very edge of their carving tools, producing a small secondary bevel. This in effect thickens the wedge of metal, as the angle of the secondary bevel must be greater than that of the primary one. The secondary bevel gets longer with each sharpening, which gives much the same effect as increasing the cutting angle of the tool (Fig 9.18). Eventually the tool will need regrinding.

Sharpening a secondary bevel is more often than not an ill-directed habit. It takes the same amount of time and effort to present the bevel flat to the bench-stone and produce a continuous, flat bevel from heel to edge at the outset, as it does to produce a secondary bevel. A blade with a flat bevel will only need regrinding if, say, a corner is broken, not because the bevel angle has changed. So secondary bevels cannot be recommended.

INNER AND OUTER BEVELS

If you compare a carpenter's chisel with the flat firmer chisel used by a woodcarver, one difference is immediately apparent: while the carpentry chisel has a bevel on one side only, the firmer chisel has a bevel on both sides. An echo of this occurs in carving gouges, where a second bevel is usually found on the inside (Figs 9.19 and 9.20).

A lot of books on woodcarving neglect the inner bevel altogether. Although there are instances where an inside bevel is not needed, or may even be undesirable, the practice in the woodcarving trade has always been to sharpen an inside bevel on straight

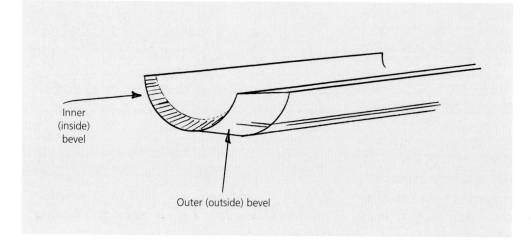

Inner (inside) bevel

Outer (outside) bevel

Fig 9.19 *Inner and outer bevels on a carving gouge*

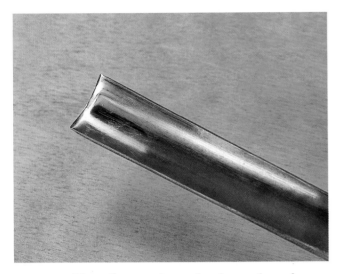

Fig 9.20 The well-stropped inner bevel, seen from above

gouges for the several advantages it gives. It may be helpful to summarize these advantages. An inner bevel on a straight carving gouge:

- eases away the wood chip or shaving from the blade as it cuts, allowing the cutting edge to proceed through the wood with less effort

- facilitates using the gouge in a reversed ('upside-down') position

- shares the overall bevel angle between the inner and outer bevels, which allows the outer bevel to be longer, lowering the cutting angle and giving greater tool control

- strengthens the cutting edge by placing it more towards the centre of the steel, where it is buttressed on both sides.

It is only fair to say that these points are debatable. It is worth looking into the reasoning behind the use of inner bevels a little further. The difference between the single-bevelled carpentry chisel and the carver's double-bevelled firmer chisel can be used to illustrate some important aspects of how woodcarving tools and bevels work.

Carpentry chisels are used mainly to make woodworking joints, such as mortise and tenon joints, and to pare accurate, flat surfaces prior to gluing up. The flat face causes the tool to be **self-jigging**: as the edge enters the wood, the flat underside of the chisel rests

on the cut surface, which then acts as a guide, or jig, for the rest of the blade. The chisel will cut accurately in a straight line, provided it is pushed sympathetically (Fig 9.21).

There is no equivalent flat face to a carving chisel – the flat bevel may have *some* self-jigging quality but, being so short a surface, the effect is negligible. Although carved surfaces can look very flat, on close inspection they have usually only been worked smooth enough to *appear* flat to the eye. Often a finger can detect shallow facets where the surface has been finished with a flat (no. 3) gouge.

In normal use, woodcarving chisels and gouges enter and leave the wood continuously in a fluid procedure which is not aimed at creating surfaces for exact, functional purposes. The self-jigging action is not, therefore, appropriate. Having said this, carvers often have a few carpentry chisels in their kit for those occasions when true flatness *is* required. Also, some carving procedures – such as the rounding over

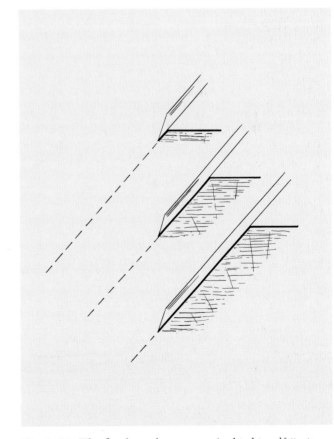

Fig 9.21 The flat face of a carpenter's chisel is self-jigging and runs along the line of its own cut

of berry (pea) mouldings – may work better without the inside bevel; but these are more the exception than the rule.

As a practical exercise, take a carpentry chisel and, with the unbevelled side of the blade down, cut a flat face across the edge of a piece of softwood. The jigging action can be observed, helping the blade to line up. Now try to lift the blade out of the wood, while continuing to cut, by lowering the handle. You will find this difficult, if not impossible, to do cleanly: the edge tends to snatch and break out the wood in front of the blade.

Now turn the chisel upside down so the bevel is towards the wood, and repeat the exercise. You will see how much more difficult it is to cut a truly flat face, while at the same time how much easier it is to cut out of the wood by lowering the handle (Fig 9.22).

When the bevel is down, the heel end of the bevel acts as a fulcrum, lifting the edge to bring it out of the wood. This ability of carving chisels and gouges to

pivot around the heel and remove wood chips and shavings is essential to the act of carving.

Many beginners fail to understand that shavings of wood can only be removed cleanly *while the cutting edge is moving through the wood*. It is not enough to cut into the wood with a gouge and lever down on the handle to prise a wood chip away – this only blunts the edge, and might actually break it. The edge can only work with the heel in the way described, and the chip or shaving can only be cut cleanly, if the edge is actually being pushed forwards through the wood.

If you take a long shaving with a double-bevelled chisel or gouge, you will find that the shaving curls up and away from the blade and does not remain straight; a similar curling effect is seen in a carpentry plane (Fig 9.23). This curling is the result of the shaving being forced upwards by the top bevel (against the cap iron or chipbreaker in a plane). The underside of the shaving is broken but the top remains intact and compressed. The different tensions curl and clear the shaving away from the blade as it is cut.

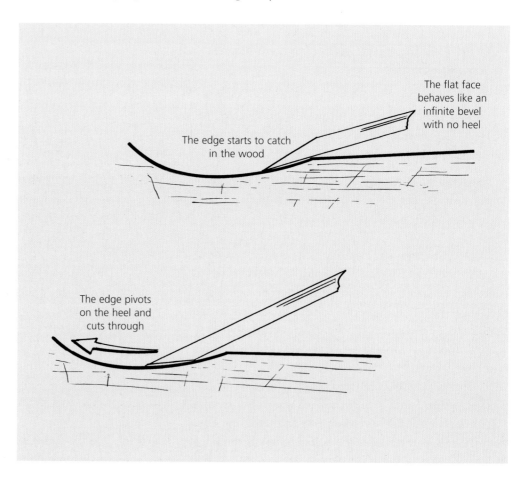

The flat face behaves like an infinite bevel with no heel

The edge starts to catch in the wood

The edge pivots on the heel and cuts through

Fig 9.22 *The effect of turning a carpenter's (single-bevel) chisel upside down is to allow the cut to pivot on the heel of the bevel; try this*

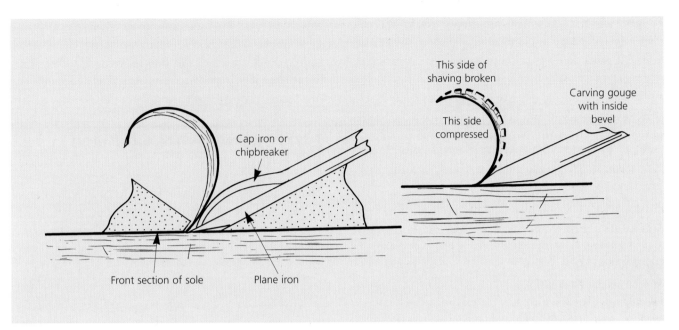

Fig 9.23 The inside bevel helps to curl the shavings up and away from the cut, in the same way as a joiner's plane

Putting an inner bevel (in-cannel) on carving gouges imitates the effect of a carver's double-bevelled firmer chisel and, as the inside bevel curls the shaving away, the edge cuts through the wood more easily (Fig 9.24).

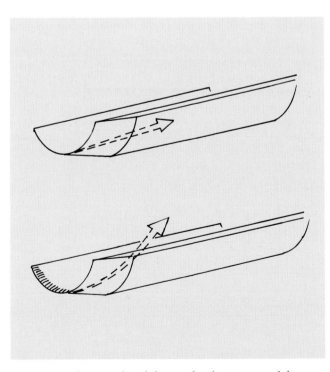

Fig 9.24 The inner bevel directs the shaving out of the mouth of the gouge, easing the passage of the tool

Another occasion where an inner bevel is an advantage occurs when a gouge is used upside down, with the mouth (the concave side) to the surface of the wood. In this position, a gouge will shape rounded forms: beads, reeds and so on; the inner bevel enables the edge to negotiate and leave the cut more easily. Being at such a shallow angle, the inside bevel normally lacks a true heel, and tends to merge with the cannel, but it helps nevertheless.

The actual amount of bevel on the inside varies. It tends to be longer on a flattish gouge, and can be as much as one third of the length of the outer bevel. The quicker the gouge, the shorter the inner bevel is likely to be. The deepest, U-shaped gouges (nos. 10 and 11) are not used upside down and will have very short, tight bevels, serving only to direct the shaving up and out of the narrow cannel better.

A low cutting angle – the angle at which the tool has to be offered to the wood in order for it to start cutting – gives greater tool control. A low cutting angle is caused by a smaller outer bevel angle as it rests on the wood. But, as we have seen, this means a weaker edge. An inner bevel keeps the cutting angle low while making the edge stronger, throwing the cutting edge towards the centre of the metal and effectively buttressing it from both sides. Being short, the inner bevel offers less resistance than a single bevel with the same overall angle would do (Fig 9.25). This is one good reason for having an inner bevel: *it gains you a lower cutting angle while maintaining toughness.*

When considering the strength of the edge, it is important to remember that when the edge rocks out of the cut on the heel, quite a lot of pressure is exerted on it by the wood chip. The cutting edge of a blade with a single bevel is only supported by the steel on one side. With an inner bevel as well, the cutting edge is moved towards the centre of the blade, and is now buttressed by the steel on both sides,

which braces and strengthens it. Carvers tackling very hard woods may consider placing the cutting edge quite far towards the centre of the blade by sharing the total angle of bevel more equally between the inside and outside.

DIFFERENCES IN CUTTING PROFILE

The configuration of the **cutting profile** – the longitudinal section through the cutting edge (Fig 9.26) – varies between tools. Not all tools have the same

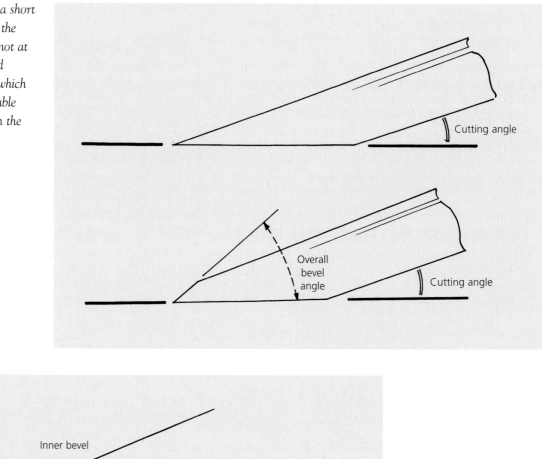

Fig 9.25 Although a short inner bevel increases the overall angle, this is not at all the same as a solid wedge of this angle, which would need considerable effort to push through the wood

Fig 9.26 The ideal cutting profile for most carving gouges throws the cutting edge towards the centre

thickness of metal, or the same angle or disposition of inner and outer bevels, for example.

- U-shaped gouges (fluters and veiners) and V-tools, which are not used in the reversed or upside-down position, tend to have a significantly shorter inner bevel.

- The flatter the gouge, the longer the inner bevel is; cutting in the reversed position is a principal function of these gouges.

- Inner bevels are not normally put on the curved and bent gouges. The curve of the blade itself directs the edge through the cut, and these tools are never used upside down.

Not all carvers decide to add an inner bevel to their gouges, but there are enough good reasons and advantages to make this practice worthwhile.

THE CUTTING EDGE

If you examine the metal of a blade's cutting edge under a microscope, a crystalline structure can be seen. The carbon and iron, together with any other additions making up the steel, form themselves into tense crystal lattices. These lattices are the 'grain' in the metal, formed by the forging and heat treatment, which give it strength and resilience.

This wonderful edge is a refinement of the bevel. But, in addition to the flatness of the bevel, the best cut, feel and efficiency is only gained from the carving tool when a certain form is given to the cutting edge and bevel as a whole. This form includes:

- edges at right angles to the blade

- straight edges

- sharp corners

- even thickness.

These particular features need to be borne in mind while sharpening. They can be regarded as standards at which to aim.

SQUARENESS

Carving tools, with the exception of skew chisels, are sharpened with the cutting edge at right angles (90°) to their longitudinal axis (Fig 9.27). Apart from the skew chisel, it is not necessary to give carving tools skewed edges, although there are some skewed gouges that have appeared on the market fairly recently. This point needs exploring further, as it relates to useful ideas about the actual technique of carving.

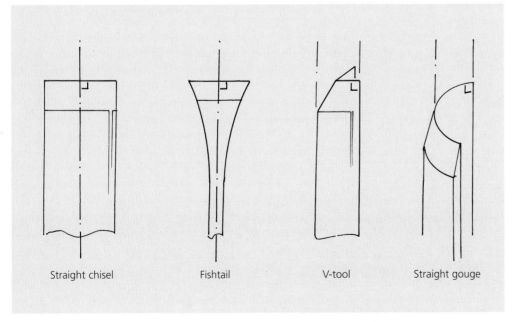

Straight chisel   Fishtail   V-tool   Straight gouge

Fig 9.27 *Cutting edges at right angles (90°) to the longitudinal axis*

Skewed fishtail chisels go back a long way. Etchings depicting carvers at work from the late Gothic–Renaissance period (around 1480–1530), which includes the work of such pre-eminent names as Tilman Riemenschneider, depict such tools in use (Fig 9.28) – but not skewed gouges. The Science Museum in South Kensington, London has an example of a Chinese skewed fishtail chisel with a socket instead of a tang, dating from around 1850, in its collection (inventory no. 1875-53); it is illustrated in Volume 2, Chapter 3.

Skewed gouges have never been in the standard kit of the carver anywhere. That skewed *chisels* have a long history reflects the general usefulness of the skew chisel to the carver. The corollary can also be made: the reason that skewed gouges have never appeared as standard reflects their comparative lack of usefulness, even though carvers might feel the need for a skewed edge under some circumstances. The recent introduction of skew gouges seems to me to answer a need which is not really present, at the same time sacrificing other useful qualities that right-angled edges have. On the other hand, some carvers do find such refinements useful (see Chapter 6, pages 101–2).

One point given in favour of such gouges is that their oblique edge slices the wood in a similar fashion to a guillotine. However, this effect can be achieved more simply by an appropriate cutting action with an ordinary gouge. A gouge can be pushed dead straight along the wood, or it can be given a winding, slicing action by rotating the wrist of the pushing hand as the tool advances. The gouge is thus rotated or 'rocked' through its cut, slicing the wood (Fig 9.29).

Fig 9.28 *From an engraving by Hans Burgkmair, around 1500; illustrations of this period often show skew chisels in use*

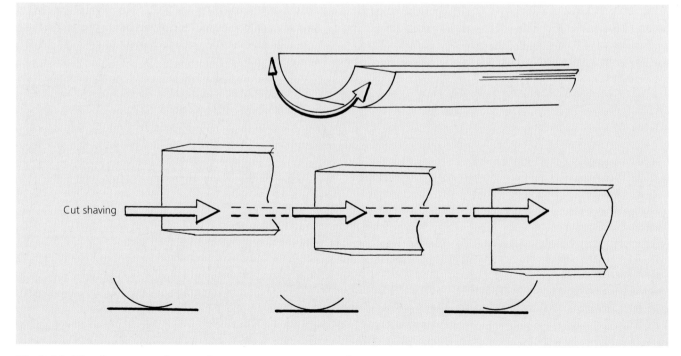

Cut shaving

Fig 9.29 *The slicing cut: a basic and very important carving technique*

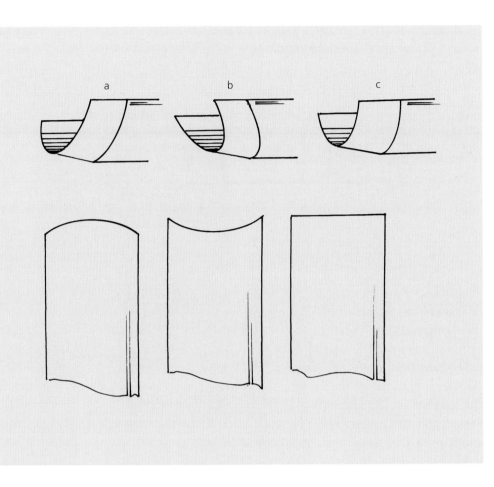

Fig 9.30 *Three profiles of cutting edges: (a) pointed or nosed; (b) winged; and (c) straight*

This slicing cut can be made to the left or the right, and to a greater or lesser degree as needed. Such a slicing cut is a very basic and important carving technique, which beginners need to master as early as possible. There is no need to skew the edge of a gouge to achieve this particular effect.

The only gouges with which this slicing cut is not possible are those based on a U-shape (nos. 10 and 11). Since the sweeps of all other gouges are based on arcs of circles, the edges can be applied with a winding stroke. Firmers can also be used with a slicing action.

The 'square-on' orientation of a cutting edge is also essential for clean setting in, allowing the tool to be lined up accurately and easily in the wood. A skewed edge makes setting in more difficult. Again, for all practical purposes, almost any corner can be cleaned easily with a small range of straight and shortbent skew chisels. It is not necessary to skew a gouge to produce a long corner for this sort of purpose.

STRAIGHTNESS

The cutting edges of carving gouges and chisels can have one of three profiles (Fig 9.30):

- The central part of the edge may protrude beyond the corners to some extent – it is said to be **nosed** or **bullnosed**.

- The central part of the edge may recede behind the corners – the corners protrude and can be described as **winged**.

- The central part of the edge may form a straight line with the corners, in addition to being at right angles as discussed above.

Each option gives rise to different effects as the tool is used:

NOSED EDGES

A woodcarving tool bought 'set but not sharpened' (that is, with the bevel ground to a rough shape)

Fig 9.31 *Setting in cleanly to the next plane is difficult with a nosed edge, which tends to leave cut marks*

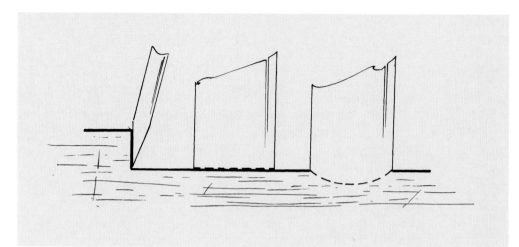

quite often has a nosed or 'lady's finger' profile: the centre of the edge protrudes beyond the corners to form a rounded point. The effect may also be called 'pointed'. V-tools may sometimes appear this way, with the angle pushed forward, sometimes quite far beyond the corners. These shapes are a product of the forging, with the shape perpetuated in the grinding. Beginners often assume, wrongly, that this must be the correct shape for the tool, whereas the manufacturers assume that the carver will be altering it.

This pointed state of the cutting edge is the least useful of all the three options, for several reasons. In the first place, setting in – the purpose of which is to relieve one plane of the design from another – looks best when the planes purposely and cleanly meet. It is difficult, if not impossible, to get an exactly straight bottom to the cut when a bullnosed gouge enters the wood, as the projecting centre will always tend to leave a stab mark (Fig 9.31). The round end is the wrong shape to set in crisply and cleanly, except for very particular conditions where some feature of a carving, such as a moulding, calls for it.

The second reason why a nosed gouge or chisel is a poor option is that, with this profile, the useful corners are lost. This is dealt with in more detail in the next section.

The final, and least important, reason for not having a nose on gouges or V-tools involves the way in which these tools like to cut wood (Fig 9.32). With the centre of the cutting edge leading and cutting the wood before the sides enter, the central part of the shaving advances prematurely up the cannel, creating

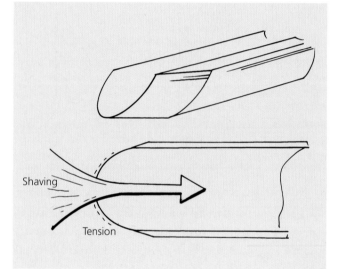

Fig 9.32 *A bullnosed gouge tends to tear the wood towards the sides of its cut*

tension with the sides. Even if the wood towards the sides of the cut is not actually torn, there is still a tendency to produce a less clean surface. This effect is increased in proportion to the extent of nosing. To some extent, a build-up of tension like this must happen with a straight-edged gouge also, but tension is always quickly and adequately relieved as the surface is cut before the wood underneath.

Having said that, nosed gouges do occasionally have specific uses. An example might be the common gouge-cut ornament shown in Fig 9.33. Here, setting in with a nosed gouge gives you a vertical cut which neatly matches the sweep of the second, horizontal cut as it meets to remove the chip.

144

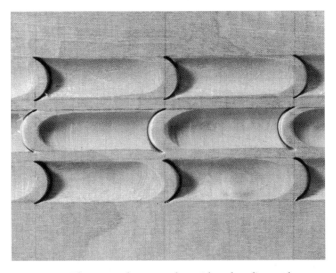

Fig 9.33 *The vertical cuts in these 'thumbnail' motifs can be made more neatly with a nosed gouge than a square one*

Fig 9.35 *A winged V-tool or deep gouge will make good, clean running cuts, though less useful in other contexts*

WINGED EDGES

Going to the other extreme, a cutting edge with the corners advanced gives rise to similar problems of setting in as a nosed gouge (Fig 9.34). However, there is a particular instance where this shape does score over the straight-across edge: running grooves with the deep U-shaped gouges (Fig 9.35). Because the wood at the surface of the groove is cut *before* the wood in the centre, the shaving will always come away cleanly, even on a side which is cutting against the grain, as when rounding a curve. The disadvantage is that it is impossible to run the grooves into vertical walls, or to use the same tool for setting in.

For general carving, I advise keeping all gouges square across: unless there is a compelling reason to do otherwise, square is the most useful shape. But if you are carving a lot of flutes or grooves with deep gouges – in the veins of acanthus foliage, or example, or in hair – then consider having a selection of deep gouges raked forward at the corners, and kept expressly for this purpose.

STRAIGHT EDGES

Straight edges give the best of all worlds: clean setting in, useful corners and clean cuts. For general purposes, sharpen all gouges, chisels and V-tools, straight or

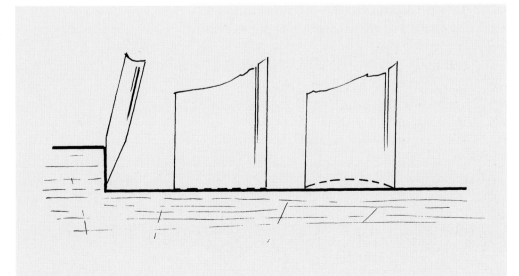

Fig 9.34 *Setting in cleanly to the next plane is difficult with a winged tool, as the corners tend to cut further than intended*

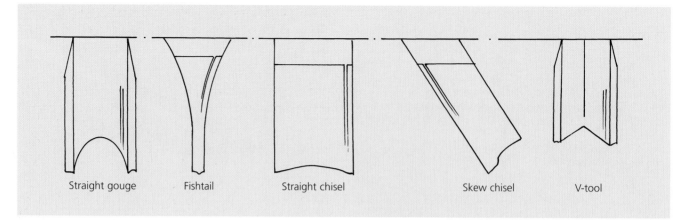

Fig 9.36 *Straight edges*

bent, with the cutting edge in a straight line from corner to corner and at 90° to the longitudinal axis (Fig 9.36). This makes possible accurate setting in and full use of the edge.

A wavy or notched edge is usually not acceptable – depending on the degree of irregularity and whether it has any effect on the work. If care is taken, sharpening the edge to such a shape can be avoided.

CORNERS

The importance of maintaining the full width and shape of a woodcarving tool, right into the corners, needs stressing (Figs 9.37 and 9.38). Beginners in particular do not appreciate, or make full use of, the corners of gouges or chisels. It is all too easy to oversharpen the corners and reduce a tool's usefulness.

Corners are singled out for use continuously in the routine of carving: for joining surfaces or planes neatly

Fig 9.37 *The corners must be considered an extremely important part of the cutting edge*

and accurately; setting in; cleaning into angles and corners; and so on. Corners are often used more in the fashion of knives. A tool such as the skew chisel is really only a glorified corner; and a skew with its long pointed corner missing is effectively crippled. Fishtail

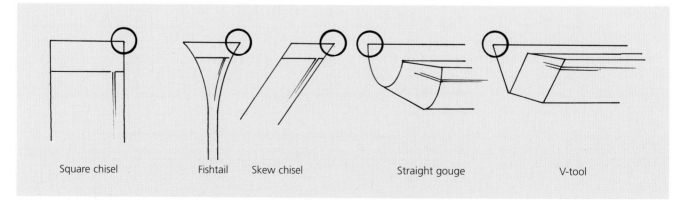

Fig 9.38 *Corners are important working parts of carving tools and should be kept*

tools also have emphasized corners for getting into awkward recesses. Paying attention to the corners of all carving tools is an important aspect of sharpening.

EVEN THICKNESS

The steel of which a carving blade consists ought to be of even thickness across its width, and this uniformity should be maintained along its length, even though the blade may thicken towards the shoulder. An uneven thickness can mean some parts are weaker than others.

Uneven wall thickness can become a real problem in the V-tool. If the two sides are not of equal shape and thickness, with the cannel lined up truly down the centre, the tool can be impossible to sharpen correctly (Fig 9.39). The condition needs to be assessed first, and corrected where possible, before time is wasted on sharpening.

With an even wall, and a flat bevel shaped evenly from side to side, the heel will lie parallel to the cutting edge (Fig 9.40).

Fig 9.39 *Uneven wall thickness in a V-tool may sooner or later cause difficulty in sharpening*

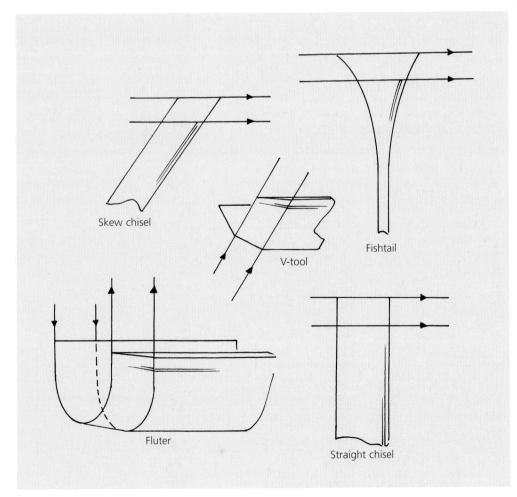

Skew chisel

V-tool

Fishtail

Fluter

Straight chisel

Fig 9.40 *Edges and heels should be parallel*

THE HEEL

The heel is the angle formed as the bevel meets the blade proper – one can imagine the cutting edge to be the 'toe'. The importance of the heel in the carving stroke has already been mentioned, but a couple of further points need to be added.

Firstly, a flat bevel will make the angle of the heel quite sharp and well defined. When the bevel and

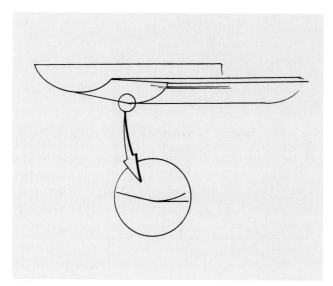

Fig 9.41 *Slightly softening the heel smooths its passage over the wood*

heel follow after the cutting edge, they rub the surface of the wood and burnish it, which adds tremendously to the appearance of the work. However, if the heel is too keen a ridge, it will roughen or score the surface of the cut as it passes, rather than smooth it. To avoid this effect, the heel needs to be *slightly* rounded over, smoothed and polished; but *only* the heel – keep the rest of the bevel flat (Fig 9.41).

The best way of smoothing the heel is on a fine benchstone, not on the grinding wheel. Leave it until the blade, with its flat bevel, is completely sharp, and then soften the definition of the heel as a final act.

This softening also applies to the heels of the V-tool – the two proper heels, as well as the point at the base of the keel where it meets the main body of metal. Slightly rounding the keel itself prevents a sharp angle scoring the bottom of the groove. It also helps the tool slide round and navigate corners more easily. The keel itself should be kept flat and straight.

One further refinement involves removing facets towards the sides of the heel; thinning the metal here allows the corners to get into tighter recesses (Fig 9.42). The facets can be produced on the fine grinding wheel, after the tool has been sharpened; take care not to remove metal from the corners of the cutting edge. Although this feature can be useful on any carving tool (see Fig 2.15), it can weaken the edge. Do it to a particular tool when circumstances require.

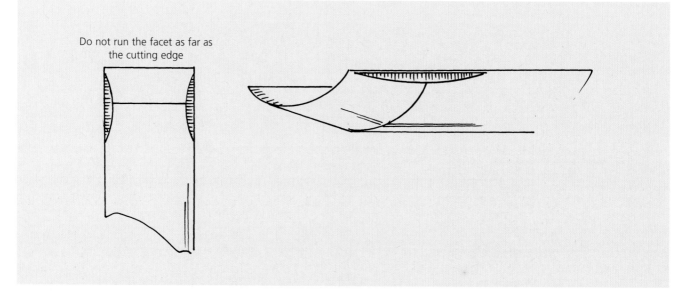

Do not run the facet as far as the cutting edge

Fig 9.42 *Facets in the side of the bevel allow the corners to get into tight recesses more easily*

IN BRIEF

Sharpening a carving tool for the first time is a matter of aiming to do the best you can, but it must be attempted in the right way. There is no point in spending an equal amount of time sharpening the tool wrongly.

All the points so far discussed – the bevel with its appropriate angle and shape; the cutting edge and its profile; the heel and so on – may seem a little much for a beginner to take in all at once. Some tools are not so easy to sharpen, and it may be that you concede a little on the shape. But do the best you can. Then each time the edge needs touching up, improve it a little further until the tool arrives at as perfect a shape and sharpness as you can give it (Fig 9.43).

I have tried to make the information arise logically out of how carving tools work for the carver, and what can be expected from them. The following summary gathers these points together for reference and gives an overview of what you are looking for.

- Keep the bevel flat from edge to heel, with an even thickness from side to side and no secondary bevel.

- The angle (length) of bevel needs to be adjusted according to the hardness of the material to be carved. Overall angles vary from 15° to 30°, with 20–25° being suitable for most purposes.

- There are many advantages to working an inside bevel on straight gouges and throwing the cutting edge towards the centre, especially in those tools that will be used in the reversed or upside-down position.

- The cutting edge, with the exception of skew chisels, should be square-on to the longitudinal axis of the tool.

- Keep the corners.

- Make the cutting edge straight from corner to corner and parallel to the heel.

- Slightly round over and polish the heel after sharpening.

THE SECRET OF SUCCESS

There is a particularly straightforward approach to sharpening carving tools which, if followed rigorously, is more or less guaranteed to lead to the cutting profile and edge that is wanted.

Look at the end of any unsharpened gouge, which has only been set by a manufacturer. The very blunt edge can easily be seen reflecting light, and appears as a thick, shiny line (Fig 9.44). This is called the **white line** or **line of light**. These terms will be used synonymously to refer to the visible edge.

Fig 9.43 *A tool with a straight edge, corners present, and flat, polished bevels inside and out*

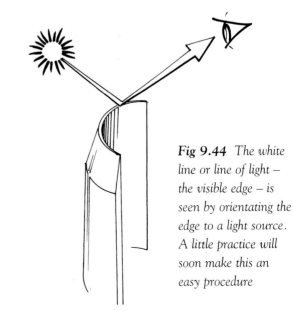

Fig 9.44 *The white line or line of light – the visible edge – is seen by orientating the edge to a light source. A little practice will soon make this an easy procedure*

This line of light is your primary guide to the state of the cutting edge. By constantly checking the thickness and distribution of this visible line while sharpening, the quality of the potential cutting edge is monitored (Fig 9.45). The thicker the line of light, the thicker the edge of steel, and vice versa. As the tool is sharpened, the line gets thinner and thinner. When the edge reaches 'sharp', the line of light will have disappeared. The crystalline structure of the edge has been made so thin as to be no longer visible to the naked eye.

To reflect the light, the edge of the carving tool must be orientated to the light source in a way that displays the white line. You may think the white line is gone, only to have it reappear when the blade is turned around a little.

When the edge is approaching sharpness, the line of light attenuates and can be a little difficult to see. Sometimes a magnifying glass is useful for having a really close look at the line, helping to decide what state the edge is in. Pushing the edge into a piece of medium-hard waste wood will also toughen and emphasize the edge to reveal any remaining white line or speck (Fig 9.46).

An uneven line of light indicates that some parts of the edge are thicker than others. Continuing to sharpen in the same way will produce an uneven, wavy cutting edge, perhaps with missing corners. Small spots or areas of light along the edge will be echoed in scratches to the surface of the wood as it is cut.

This line of light is the first indicator of the state of sharpness of the cutting edge. Returning to the unsharpened carving tool, look at the bevel, where scratch marks – probably quite coarse – will be seen (Fig 9.47). These marks result from the grinding-wheel abrasives which were used to set the bevel. The scratches will change in appearance as the bevel is sharpened on progressively finer grades of stone (Fig 9.48). From these marks, information about the state of the bevel can be gained: its flatness, evenness, how it is being applied to the stone, and so on (Fig 9.49).

So there are two indicators we can use to assess how the sharpening is coming along:

- the white line of light

- the condition of the bevel surface.

Both the line of light and the bevel scratches show where metal is to be removed and – equally important – where metal is *not* to be removed.

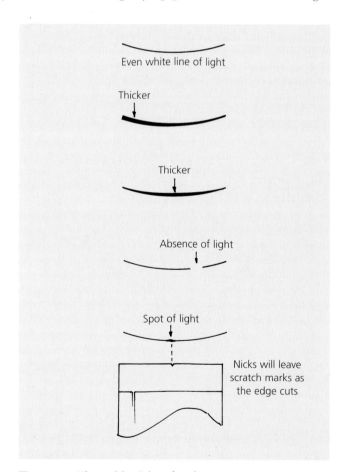

Fig 9.45 *The width of the white line reveals the thickness of metal along the cutting edge*

Fig 9.46 *The white line of light is getting thinner and more uniform, but is still clearly visible all along the edge*

Fig 9.47 *Coarse scratches on a bevel which has been ground but not honed; you will need to orientate the blade to examine them clearly*

Fig 9.49 *The scratches towards the heel, as well as the polished metal towards the edge, would suggest that the bevel is rounded and not flat*

The key word in using these two indicators is *evenness*. Sharpening involves a balance between removing metal from the bevel and leaving it on; and you need to proceed in an even, regular way (Fig 9.50). The secret of successful sharpening is constantly to allow

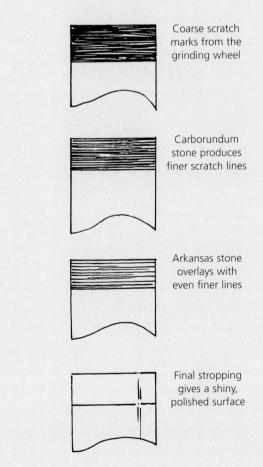

Coarse scratch marks from the grinding wheel

Carborundum stone produces finer scratch lines

Arkansas stone overlays with even finer lines

Final stropping gives a shiny, polished surface

Fig 9.48 *Different patterns of scratch marks on the bevel result from the action of specific abrasive stones*

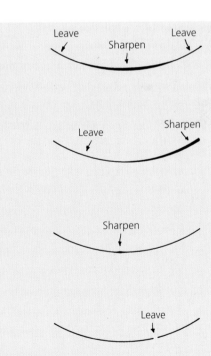

Leave · Sharpen · Leave

Leave · Sharpen

Sharpen

Leave

Fig 9.50 *The state of the white line of light indicates the next step in sharpening. Always strive for evenness. In the bottom example, it might be best to return the whole edge to a visible line first – missing points such as this are tricky to deal with*

the line of light and the surface of the bevel to guide the next step, maintaining an even appearance from start to finish.

Where part of the white line is thicker than another part along the edge, this part must be worked on specifically – whatever stage in sharpening you are at – to bring the line back to a uniform thickness. It is important to put this same point the other way round: where the line is found to be thinner, this part of the edge needs to be left alone and consciously avoided until the rest of the metal has been brought to the same state of thinness.

As the abrasives used to sharpen the blade get finer and finer, so do the scratch marks in the metal of the bevel. The scratches of finer abrasives overlay and hide those of the previous ones until a final polished surface is achieved. These marks can be observed on the bevel at any stage in the sharpening process, and the position at which the blade is offered to the sharpening stones should be adjusted accordingly (Fig 9.51).

For example, say a firmer chisel is put from the grinding wheel to a flat benchstone. If the handle is inadvertently raised, the part of the bevel towards the cutting edge will be worked on more than the rest. The line of light will show the edge thinning – it may even disappear, and the tool will be thought sharp. Indeed, this is often an expedient with beginners, who try to move the sharpening process on more

quickly by raising the handle and working more on the edge. But the result will be a rounded or secondary bevel.

What has happened will immediately be obvious if the scratch marks are looked at occasionally – they will not be evenly distributed across the face of the bevel. By checking the bevel in this way, the handle can be lowered appropriately and the flatness of the bevel re-established.

SUMMARY

Starting with the grinding, through to the final sharpening, retain an even white line of light, right up to its final disappearance. Continually check this and the bevel surface, maintaining a uniform appearance to both. The main points, therefore, are:

- the line of light
- the surface of the bevel
- evenness from start to finish.

If this advice is followed, there is no reason not to achieve straight, acutely sharp cutting edges, with intact corners and flat bevels.

Fig 9.51 Finer and coarser marks on the bevel may indicate that the handle has been raised during honing, which makes the line of light disappear sooner, and creates a rounded bevel

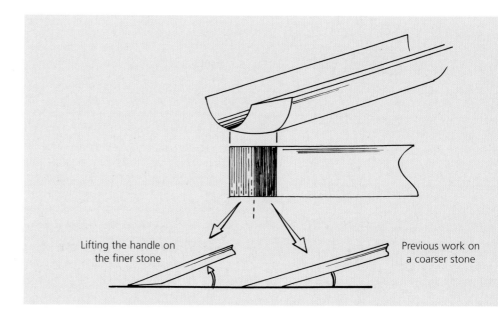

Lifting the handle on the finer stone

Previous work on a coarser stone

CHAPTER TEN

EQUIPMENT: GRINDERS

AIMS

- To give a brief overview of the sharpening process and the equipment required

- To consider in detail the equipment needed for the grinding stage of the process

OVERVIEW

The equipment needed to sharpen woodcarving tools is relatively straightforward. It consists entirely of an assortment of abrasives which remove unwanted metal from the blade. There is no trickery in it. These abrasives can be thought of as a scale, or range. At one end there are very coarse abrasives – represented by the grinding wheel – for removing metal quickly. At the other end are finely dressed strops, the cut of which polishes the metal. Between these two extremes lies a spectrum of artificial and natural stones with graded abrasive qualities (Fig 10.1).

A blade moves along this scale from coarse to ever finer abrasives in the sequence of shaping and sharpening its cutting edge. Not all the elements in the scale are necessary or appropriate on any particular

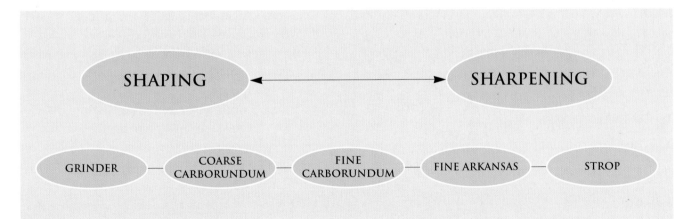

Fig 10.1 *Sharpening is a process which starts with initially shaping the cutting part of the blade and setting the cutting angle (commonly adding an inner bevel), and moves through a spectrum of abrasives to the final, sharp cutting edge. On later resharpening only the later stages may be required, depending upon what the edge needs to return it to a correct state of sharpness*

occasion. With practice, the carver can skip stages and feel free to move around the scale, up or down, according to what is needed at that moment.

A few terms need clarifying. Technically, the terms **grinding wheel** or **grindstone** refer to the abrasive wheel itself and not the machine. In practice, the wheel is inseparable from the machine, which is termed either a **grinder** or a **bench grinder**.

Too all intents and purposes, **benchstone**, **whetstone** and **honing stone** all mean the same thing. **Oilstones** are still the commonest sharpening stones used by carvers, though nowadays there are a number of alternatives (see Chapter 13). The word *hone* comes from an Old English word for a stone, so 'honing' means 'stoning'. And *whet* derives from the Old English *hwæt*, meaning 'quick' or 'active'; so a whetstone was a sharp, active stone, to be differentiated from ordinary ones. **Whetting, honing,** and **stoning** synonymously describe the act of sharpening a tool on a benchstone. All these words are in common usage and have become a little confused.

A point that was made about woodcarving tools themselves also needs to be made about the equipment needed to sharpen them: it is false economy to buy an inferior quality of either. As with carving tools, the expense is really an investment in personal satisfaction as well as time and money. Good-quality sharpening stones will last at least the lifetime of the carving tools themselves. As long as they are looked after properly, they only need to be bought once. You could say that buying a better stone is tantamount to upgrading your whole tool collection in one go.

The sequence of sharpening a carving tool involves working along the range of abrasives in the following order:

- the grinding wheel

- coarse benchstones (and slipstones)

- fine benchstones (and slipstones)

- strops.

The bench grinder sets the bevel and squares the edge; then the benchstones and slips refine and sharpen this shape, and the strops polish it to produce the final working edge.

In the following chapters we will first look at the equipment in a little detail, then consider in general terms how to use and care for it (Chapters 10 and 11). Next, points related to working the individual shapes of tools will be dealt with (Chapter 12). The emphasis in these chapters will be on the traditional method of sharpening with oilstones and strops. Finally we shall consider some more recent innovations which some carvers may like to try: other types of sharpening stone (Chapter 13), and electrical sharpening systems (Chapter 14).

BENCH GRINDERS

Whether a bench grinder is really needed or not depends largely on the sizes and numbers of carving tools to be managed. A carver with only a few, small tools may find that a coarse benchstone will adequately do the job of a grinder. A sculptor, on the other hand, with only a few but nevertheless large gouges would find it laborious to use only benchstones; a bench grinder would save a lot of time, especially as some sculptors tend to use their carving tools ruthlessly. A grinding wheel at the coarsest end of the abrasive spectrum removes the most metal, most quickly.

If you are new to carving and do not know whether you are going to be hooked on the craft or not, you should probably leave the grinder to start with. Working with flat bevels as recommended in the last chapter, tools only need regrinding when they become damaged. It may be sufficient to have access to a grinder, rather than actually owning one. But a grinder, while not essential to begin with, can save a lot of time, especially where there is serious blunting or breaking to the edge of a tool. Most carvers end up with one.

TYPES

Modern grinders are electrically driven. There must be some treadle- or hand-operated wheels out there – not without their advantages – but they are very unusual today. Some parts of the following discussion are applicable to them, but note that working arrangements that allow both hands to be kept free for controlling the tool on the wheel are the best. Although hand grinders are slower and more 'friendly' than electric machines, less control over the tool is possible because one hand is always occupied turning the wheel.

Electrically driven grinding wheels can be **dry** (fast-running) or **wet** (slow-running). On some dry grinders an abrasive belt may replace one of the wheels.

Whichever type of machine is chosen, proper eye protection must always be worn.

DRY BENCH GRINDERS

Dry bench grinders with two abrasive wheels are the cheapest option (Fig 10.2). An abrasive belt, as an alternative to one wheel, is worth having: you can get a flat finish on the bevel quite easily and the blade tends to keep cooler. Machines fitted with belts are more expensive.

The wheels are mounted directly on either end of the motor shaft, and so turn at the same speed as the motor – somewhere around 2,900rpm. There are protective guards around the wheel, as well as in front, since high-speed cutting throws off particles and sparks quite violently. However, properly used, a good-quality machine is quite safe, and, being about the simplest machine in the workshop, it will last a long time.

The motor size of dry bench grinders varies between ¼ and ½hp, the smaller size being quite

Fig 10.2 *A typical dry bench grinder*

adequate for the needs of the carver. There are many excellent and reliable makes on the market, as well as cheap imports. The wheels and bearings of the latter tend to be inferior and wear quickly. The two wheels will be of different grits but the same size, and positioned at either end of the motor shaft. Diameters vary between about 5 and 8in (125 and 200mm); for our purposes a wheel of at least 6in (150mm) diameter is required.

The wheels themselves are made of artificial stone, usually based on vitrified aluminium oxide or silicon carbide. 'White' wheels designed for use on high-speed steel (as used for woodturning tools) can also be used on carbon steel, though a fine grit is not usually available. Because there are two wheels to choose from, the machine is normally supplied with both a coarse and a fine grit of stone. It is useful if these grits correspond to those of your (artificial) benchstones.

Replacement wheels in a variety of grits can be easily obtained from engineering suppliers. The size of wheel should remain the same on either end of the motor spindle, to keep the machine balanced and prevent undue strain on the bearings. Always follow the manufacturer's instructions when changing wheels.

When one or both wheels are replaced or removed from the grinder, for whatever reason, they will need balancing on the machine – rather like motor-car tyres need balancing. There is often some spot on the wheel denser than another and, revolving at high speed, the centrifugal force of this imbalance can create unpleasant vibration as well as stressing the bearings.

To balance the wheels of a high-speed dry grinder, follow these steps:

❶ Unplug the machine and remove the wheel guards from both sides.

❷ Remove one wheel completely. Note that the two wheels have opposite-handed threads to prevent them unscrewing in use.

❸ Spin the remaining wheel freely, and when it comes to rest, mark the lowest point on the rim of the wheel with a pencil. Repeat this a couple of times and you should be able to locate any 'heavy' spots, as gravity will pull these consistently to the low point of the free-swinging wheel.

④ Remove this wheel and fit the other one to the opposite side.

⑤ Mark the second wheel similarly to the first.

⑥ Now replace both wheels, lining up the pencil marks to *opposite* sides, so that the heaviest point of each wheel counterbalances the other when the machine runs.

⑦ Tighten the wheels according to the manufacturer's instructions and replace the guards.

WET BENCH GRINDERS

The motor of a wet grinder usually has the same standard rating as a dry grinder, but the speed of the wheel itself is decreased by some kind of reducing drive. This makes them a little more complicated and larger, although both wet and dry machines need space to work around. The wheel speed will be around 50–100rpm, which is slow enough not to fling water out of the trough in which it revolves. The water constantly flushes over the wheel, washing away particles and cooling the blade, but obscuring what is going on.

There is usually only one, larger-sized grinding wheel on a wet grinding machine; the wheel is approximately 8–10in diameter by 1½–2in thick (200–250 x 40–50mm). A separate buffing wheel may also be included in the arrangement (Fig 10.3). These wet grinders can be significantly more expensive than the commoner dry-running bench grinders. Their advantages are that they eliminate the danger of tool overheating; they do not fling out sparks; and they generally operate in a gentler way. The Swedish Tormek range are regarded as good-quality and reliable machines.

ALTERNATIVES

Cheaper options for grinding include using an electric drill attachment or a small high-speed motor unit (Fig 10.4). These are inexpensive alternatives, but suitable when only a small amount of light grinding is wanted, or as a temporary expedient. A bench grinder is a better alternative for the busy carver.

Quite small grinding wheels are available for drills and flexible shafts. These can be useful for some preliminary shaping – for example, putting an inner

Fig 10.3 *A wet grinder, showing the large, slow wheel in its trough on the right and a buffing wheel on the left*

Fig 10.4 *This sort of inexpensive unit is now widely available. Besides small abrasive wheels, it can be fitted with burrs and cutters for working directly on wood*

bevel on a large gouge, while the blade is gripped in a vice. However, they do not have the same safety arrangements as bench-mounted grinders and extra care needs to be taken in their use – choose the slowest drill speed and wear proper eye protection.

SPEED AND FRICTION

Dry grinders are designed to remove metal quickly: the wheels are coarse and the speed is high, and sparks of white-hot metal shoot off dramatically into the air. While this may seem fun, it can create two problems.

First, it is very easy to over-grind – to grind off more metal than you intended. Sometimes it is better to use a coarse benchstone and take a little longer to set the shape precisely, rather than risk over-grinding and destroying the shape.

The second problem lies in the heat generated by friction between the fast-moving surface of the wheel and the tool. Overheating and 'blueing' the cutting edge – turning the surface blue – seriously damages the steel. A short foray into the world of physics is relevant here: by understanding how the heat is actually generated, steps can be taken to minimize it.

The difference between heat and temperature, while not often appreciated, is of real, practical importance to the carver. Simply put, *temperature* is what is measured by thermometers, whereas *heat* is the combination of this temperature with the mass of an object. To take a common example: a dinner plate may have a lower temperature, but more heat, than a spark. So a spark landing on the skin may hardly be felt – its mass is very small and the heat disperses rapidly into the skin. But a dinner plate at a lower temperature has a much greater reservoir of heat available to raise the temperature of the skin.

Referring back to carving tools, two principles arise:

- The larger a chisel or gouge, the slower its increase in temperature on a grinding wheel.

- The thinnest parts of the blade – the parts with the least mass – will increase in temperature faster than the thicker parts.

In other words, the tools which are most susceptible to overheating are the smaller ones, and the most vulnerable parts of any tool are the corners and edges – for example, the point of a skew chisel and the corners of fishtail gouges.

The hardness and toughness of carving-tool steel is brought about by specific heat treatment, a process which can be undone by reheating the blade. Above a certain temperature – around 235°C (455°F) – the metal starts to anneal, softening towards its original unhardened state. When a blade turns blue on a grinding wheel, the temperature will have reached somewhere around 300°C (572°F). It now loses its ability to hold a cutting edge, and dulls rapidly. Blueing usually starts in one spot on the edge, or at a corner. It is all too easily done, and it happens very quickly.

Unfortunately the loss of hardness in the blued cutting edge cannot be rescinded, and further heat treatment is needed to restore the temper. This is dealt with in Volume 2, Chapter 3, but normally it is simpler to regrind the blade back to an unaffected part without further blueing. This is obviously a great waste of time and steel; it needs to be avoided from the start by understanding the causes of excess heat production.

The amount of heat is related to the amount of friction, which is a product of two things:

- the speed of the wheel surface

- the pressure with which the tool is applied.

So the following three things should be borne in mind while grinding a carving tool:

THE MASS OF METAL

The effect of the amount of metal being offered to the wheel on how quickly the temperature rises has already been mentioned. Grinding with a fast, dry grinder should not be taken beyond a certain thinness of metal – not only because of possible overheating, but also because metal needs to be left for the finer abrasives to work on.

PRESSURE

A light pressure, enough to steady and direct the tool, is all that should be applied, allowing the wheel to do the work. The faster the wheel, the lighter the pressure. Even though these dry grinders work quickly, many users still get impatient and apply the bevel too arduously and for too long. At fast speeds, events happen quickly.

A small point is that the coarse wheels, with a more open grain structure, cut away more material but actually create less friction than the finer stones. Blueing therefore tends to happen more often on the finer stone – also, in part, because the metal is thinner at this stage.

SURFACE SPEED OF THE WHEEL

The speed of the motor on a commercial grinder is fixed, but what actually matters is the surface speed of the rotating wheel itself. The surface speed of larger wheels is proportionately faster than smaller ones – motor speeds between grinders being similar. An 8in (200mm) wheel generates a quarter more heat than a 6in (150mm) one at the same rpm, other things being equal.

A serviceable low-speed bench grinder is not hard to make. Slow surface speeds enormously reduce the heat generated by friction. Some notes and guidance for making a low-speed grinder follow.

BELT GRINDERS

The abrasive surface of a **belt grinder** moves at a much greater speed than that of a wheel. Although a thin belt dissipates heat faster than a solid wheel, the effect is offset by the speed. One advantage of these machines is that the grinding takes place on a flat surface, so producing a flat bevel more easily. They are less common than double-ended wheel grinders, but are worth considering. Remember to check that the toolrests are adequate.

MAKING A LOW-SPEED GRINDER

For many years I used a low-speed dry grinder which I made myself (Fig 10.5). A machine of this type has several advantages:

- It provides lower speeds that are otherwise unavailable.

- The size and grit of the wheels are of my own choosing.

SUMMARY

Overheating a carving tool on a dry grinder – blueing the steel – is more likely with:

- faster motor speeds

- larger-diameter wheels

- finer-grit wheels

- thinner metal

- smaller tools

- increased pressure

- longer periods of contact.

So, to prevent overheating the metal:

- Bear the above principles and points in mind while working with the grinder.

- Constantly monitor the temperature of the blade with your fingers on its back; never let the metal get warmer than can be comfortably handled.

- Always keep a container with cold water next to the grinder; dip the blades in as often as necessary to keep them cool.

If these points are remembered and the advice is always followed, using a dry grinder need never be a problem.

Wet grinders eliminate the problem of heat generation by revolving at a slow speed and constantly flushing the blade with water. Even with a lot of pressure you could never blue the edge and, in this respect, they are excellent and safe machines.

Disadvantages of wet grinders include the following:

- Water washing over the edge of the tool makes the edge less easy to scrutinize, so more of a sense of 'feel' is needed.

- The wheels tend to be softer and wear more quickly than their dry counterparts.

- The wheel should not be left standing unused in the water trough for a long time, as water soaks into the wheel and unbalances it.

- Wet grinders are usually larger machines than dry ones, and the cost must certainly be a consideration.

- The cost proved to be much less than that of buying a new high-speed machine.

About 400rpm produces a surface speed on a 6in (150mm) wheel of about 3ft (1m) per second. This speed, about one-seventh that of a similar-sized commercial grinder, reduces the generation of heat drastically – in fact, by the same ratio. The possibility of over-shaping and overheating becomes much less, although the wheel still revolves at an efficiently useful speed.

Making a low-speed grinder is a straightforward project for anyone who has the practical skills to be woodcarving already. It mostly involves the assembly of parts – with a little improvisation – rather than clever metalwork.

The motor from a washing machine, pump, etc. can be picked up cheaply from a second-hand tool shop or a scrap yard. Look for the information plate giving the power rating and speed: you need a motor of ¼–½ hp (185–370W), single-phase and in good condition, with mounting lugs. Make sure all the electrics are safe and appropriately earthed.

The bearings, spindles and matching grinding wheels can be bought new. It is also possible to fit a useful chuck at one end of the spindle. Always get the best-quality stone, at least 1in (25mm) wide. A car fan belt (not your own!) links the pulleys and is tensioned by the weight of the motor, hinged beneath the table on which the wheel assembly is mounted. It is then a matter of fashioning and assembling the toolrests, belt guard, etc. to suit. The grinding wheels should rotate *towards* the user.

The speed of the motor, which is specified on the information plate, is reduced by the pulleys so that the wheel rotates at a slow surface speed. The basic formula for relating the speeds and the pulley diameters is:

$$G \times S = M \times D \quad \text{where}$$

G = the speed of the grinding wheel (rpm)

S = the diameter of the spindle pulley

M = the speed of the motor (rpm)

D = the diameter of the drive pulley (on the motor).

Fig 10.5 *The parts of a simple home-made low-speed grinder*

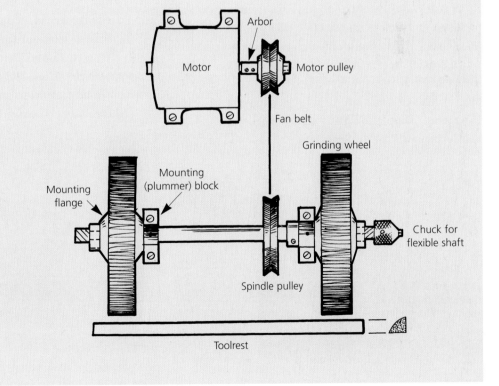

The slow speed of a home-made wheel makes it much safer than a high-speed machine, but nevertheless it is still fast enough for accidents to happen. When improvising, the onus of responsibility for safety rests on the improviser and an attitude of thoughtful caution is needed. All moving parts which do not need to be exposed – the fan belt and pulleys especially – should be enclosed. The fastenings, such as bolts, and the motor, spindle and grinding wheels should be secure, and inspected at intervals. With these precautions, and observing the normal safety rules described in the next section, there is no reason why such a low-speed grinder should not prove to be a great asset in shaping and sharpening woodcarving tools.

SAFETY AND CARE OF GRINDERS

When you buy a grinder, whether wet or dry, read and observe the manufacturer's advice. This is usually well thought-out, and is as much for the user's benefit as the manufacturer's own protection.

Manufacturers often advise the 'running in' of new stones. This means running them on the machine for several minutes before applying a tool; the idea is that any flaw or crack in the stone – enough to cause it to fly apart – is given a chance to reveal itself. Always tap a wheel before mounting it: a dull sound may indicate a hairline crack; although well tested in the factory, these stones are brittle and may get knocked in transit. Keep the wheel running true and use all the surface uniformly.

The following points need to be emphasized:

- Keep wiring from any machine neatly out of the way, not trailing over the floor or work surfaces. Do not allow water from the cooling jar to drip over the motor, electrical connections or plug.

- Guards, rests, etc. should be properly adjusted and used. *Face or eye protection is necessary, as grit and sparks are quite capable of penetrating the eyeball.* Face masks are also advisable, as the dust produced by silicon-carbide or aluminium-oxide wheels or by ground metal cannot be 'user-friendly'.

- Tie back long hair and do not wear loose clothing such as cuffs and ties; serious injury can be caused if these are caught in a wheel.

- Never stab at the wheel, which can lead to 'digging in'. Approach the surface positively but gently, working as much as possible from the fixed toolrests. The side of the wheel can be used, but *very lightly*; they should never be worn away.

- The surface of the wheel will need dressing occasionally to keep it flat and true. A **dressing stone** (sometimes called a **devil stone**) or **dressing wheel**, is drawn carefully across the spinning stone to level it (Figs 10.6 and 10.7). This is a simple but particularly dusty operation, *for which the use of a face mask and eye protection is imperative.* A strategically placed vacuum nozzle should also be considered.

Fig 10.6 *Dressing stone (left) and dressing wheel*

Fig 10.7 *The wheel has hammer-like projections that spin on the surface of the grinding wheel and break it down, producing a fine, level surface*

CHAPTER ELEVEN

EQUIPMENT: OILSTONES AND STROPS

AIMS

- To review the equipment needed for the traditional method of sharpening carving tools using oilstones and strops.

- To advise on the care and maintenance of this equipment.

When I began woodcarving in the mid-1970s there were only two sorts of sharpening stone available: artificial Carborundum and natural Arkansas. Both are **oilstones** – they must be used with light oil. When this book was first published, there was still little else to be had in the UK, or elsewhere. However, since then there have been many changes, with water, diamond and ceramic stones now appearing strongly in the market – stones which are used with water rather than oil, or even with nothing at all.

In this book I use my Carborundum and Arkansas oilstones as the paradigm for describing the sharpening process, and as a standard of comparison for the other types of stone. The methods and approaches have not changed, even if the type of stone has, and the combination of Carborundum and Arkansas is one that remains common with many woodcarvers and other woodworkers; it is still my favourite. Alternative stones are considered separately in Chapter 13, where they are compared and contrasted with what I am presenting here.

I strongly advise that you work through the instructions in this chapter, even if you intend sharpening with a different sort of stone – just pretend you have mine for the moment. Then turn to Chapter 13 to see what variations or additional considerations there may be when other stones are used.

BENCHSTONES

There are two sources of benchstone: artificial and natural. For the traditional method of sharpening you will need both.

Generally the artificial stones are coarser than the natural ones, and follow the grinding wheel in the sharpening process, refining the shape and starting the sharpening proper. The natural stones can cut extremely finely, removing hardly any metal at all, and it is these which put the keen cutting edge to carving tools, after which the leather strop imparts the last degree of sharpness.

161

ARTIFICIAL STONES

TYPES

Artificial stones are commonly referred to as **Carborundum** stones. This is actually a trade name for vitrified silicon carbide that has entered general circulation. There are three grades available – coarse, medium and fine – having different sizes of cutting crystals or **grit**. The speed at which they remove metal from the blade varies: the coarser the grit, the greater the quantity of metal removed and the faster the cut.

It is common to leave out the middle grade, passing straight from the coarse stone to the fine one. This is reflected in the fact that a **combination stone** is available, with one side coarse and the other fine (Fig 11.1). Such a combination stone is the most economic option for the carver. Buy the largest surface size available, 8 x 2in (200 x 50mm), which is easy to use and can sharpen a wide range of tools.

OILS

The Carborundum and Arkansas oilstones must be used with oil. The oil is not being used as a lubricant; its purpose is to float away the abraded particles of stone grit and metal. So really the oil is a rinsing agent, a wash. Without the wash of oil, the gaps or pores between the cutting crystals fill and the stone

Fig 11.2 *Reflections from a glazed oilstone (left) indicate that the pores are clogged with stone and metal particles*

glazes over (Fig 11.2) so the metal of the blade slides without being cut. It follows that it is possible to use too little oil, but not too much. Although experience will tell you when a balance has been struck, do not be mean with the oil.

After a while the oil becomes a fine, black pulp. Regularly wipe off this slurry of oil, metal and grit with a cotton rag, and replace it with fresh oil.

The best oil is the readily available, light lubricating oil used for bicycles, sewing machines, etc. Some oils, such as linseed oil, dry in contact with the air and would rapidly clog the stone; such oils, and thick motor oil (designed for a different purpose), should not be used.

At a pinch, water will do the job of washing away the ground-off grit and steel pulp from the pores of the stone. It will soak in more quickly than oil and will disappear more easily; it also evaporates. However, it is an expedient that will do no harm when the can of oil suddenly runs out.

If the oil is diluted with paraffin (kerosene), it produces a keener cut on the stone – as does the water. Proprietary honing oils are premium-quality light oils, but in practice are of no apparent advantage over the commercial light oil already mentioned.

It is easy to get oily fingers from sharpening carving tools, and equally easy to transfer the oil to your carving (Fig 11.3). Hang a kitchen roll and a cotton rag near the benchstones. You may need to wash your

Fig 11.1 *Combination stones are a laminate of coarse and fine Carborundum grits*

Fig 11.3 *Oil stains on a bench top; clean habits are needed to avoid stains on the workpiece itself. The oil on the stone will slowly soak through the wooden box, which is a point in favour of having a separate sharpening area*

hands with soap and warm water, especially if you are undertaking finishing cuts.

CARE OF OILSTONES

Sharpening stones are brittle and will crack or damage easily if you drop them on a hard surface. Keep them in boxes, bought or made, and cover them up when not using them (Fig 11.4). Grit or dirt in the oil, which interferes with the way the blade travels on the stone surface, should always be removed. Wipe off the black slurry after using the benchstone and never let it dry on the surface, as this clogs it.

Wash the stone periodically in paraffin oil (kerosene), petrol or warm, dilute sodium bicarbonate solution. Scrubbing with these liquids will loosen and clean a clogged stone.

A new stone soaks up oil like a sponge unless it has been previously impregnated with oil by the manufacturer. If it has not, you need to 'prime' the stone by soaking it in light oil, diluted with a little paraffin, for a few hours (or overnight) before use.

Fig 11.4 *Keep your oilstones in a box, and covered when not in use*

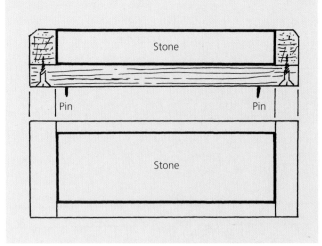

Fig 11.5 A useful way of mounting a benchstone. The nipped-off pins are shown overlength: in reality they need only protrude a small amount

If a box to fit the benchstone is not available, mount the stone between wooden end blocks (Fig 11.5). With the endpieces of wood made level with the abrasive surface, the possibility of damaging the edge of a tool by running it off the stone is eliminated. Screwed from beneath, the glued-on end pieces can be trimmed down as the stone wears and gets re-dressed.

To stop the stone, in its box or mounting board, from moving around when sharpening is underway, tap panel pins into the corners underneath and nip them off short (Fig 11.6). The pin stubs will project

enough to anchor the board or box to the bench, however it is placed.

DRESSING WORN STONES

It is not just metal that is removed during honing – crystals of stone are abraded as well. After a while the stone will no longer be flat, and a concave shape starts to interfere with sharpening. At this point the surface of the stone needs **dressing**, or flattening, once more.

You can delay this process by sharpening evenly over the whole surface as much as possible. Even so, the stone normally erodes towards the centre, as the parts nearer the edges are naturally treated with caution (Figs 11.7 and 11.8). If you are using separate

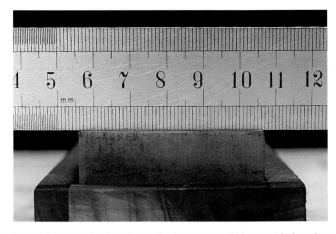

Fig 11.7 Typically, the end of a stone will be avoided and remain reasonably flat . . .

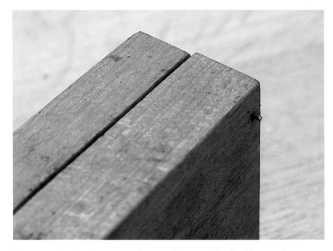

Fig 11.6 A close-up of one of the pinched-off pins that prevent the box from moving during use

Fig 11.8 . . . but the centre will wear down. After a while this affects sharpening, and the surface then needs levelling

Fig 11.9 *An extremely hard cast alloy block meant for dressing stones*

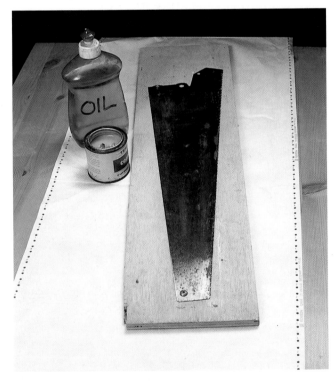

Fig 11.10 *An old saw blade, with the handle removed and the teeth rendered flat and safe, is mounted on a board (preferably with a wipe-clean surface). This, together with light oil and an abrasive grit, is a simple means of flattening a benchstone*

coarse and fine stones rather than a combination stone, these can be turned over to work on a second flat face before having a 'levelling session' for both sides. It is a good idea to dress all sharpening stones at the same time, as the procedure is a bit messy, although less time-consuming and more straightforward than is generally thought.

To level a benchstone you need:

- another hard, flat surface, such as thick (plate) glass, a stone or slate slab, or a metal sheet, such as an old saw blade mounted on a piece of wood (Figs 11.9 and 11.10).

- an abrasive to cut back the stone, such as Carborundum grit (say 400), valve-grinding paste or even fine sharp sand (using a fine grit gives a smooth finished surface to the stone)

- an oil (one part) and paraffin (four parts) mix which will wash the particles around and maintain the cutting action of the abrasive

- a straightedge such as a metal ruler

- newspaper and polythene to keep the table or bench clean.

Method

❶ Make a slurry of the abrasive and liquid on whatever flat surface you are using (Fig 11.11).

❷ Set the face of the stone on to it and rub it backwards and forwards and in a circular motion (Fig 11.12). Be methodical, and lean your weight on the stone a little.

❸ After a while, wipe the straightedge across the surface, scraping off the sludge. You will see the extent of the worn depression in the stone clearly (see Fig 11.13).

❹ Continue rubbing the stone, reversing the grip and, if necessary, topping up the abrasive or oil.

Keep checking the surface of the stone with your straightedge – eventually no depression will appear in the middle, which shows the surface to be truly flat (Fig 11.14).

❺ Rinse the stone in fresh oil and paraffin, and it is ready for use again.

ALTERNATIVE WAYS OF FLATTENING STONES

- Instead of the saw blade and oil, wet-and-dry abrasive paper can be fixed to a plate of glass with spray-on adhesive – or you can use one of the versions of this paper which are adhesive-backed already.

Fig 11.11 Mix some oil and grit on the flat surface . . .

Fig 11.12 . . . rub the stone firmly backwards and forwards for a while . . .

Fig 11.13 . . . and wipe with a metal straightedge. The new flat surface will be seen encroaching on the hollow, sludge-filled centre

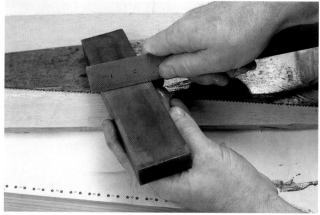

Fig 11.14 It does not take long before the surface of the stone is truly flat

- Diamond benchstones or lapping plates can be used to flatten other sharpening stones, as well as for sharpening carving tools themselves.

- The belt grinder is a very quick method, but not without its hazards. In particular, a lot of dust will be flung into the air; this dust is bound to be harmful, as the crystals of stone will be sharp and will contain silicon and other toxic chemicals. You must do this outside and away from everyone else, fully protecting your lungs with an adequate dust mask or filter, and your eyes with a face shield or goggles. In addition you must take care to keep a grip on the stone which, being brittle, will break if it strikes the ground.

NATURAL OILSTONES

TYPES

Before the days of industrially made whetstones, natural stones were all that was available. These stones have some evocative names: Charnley Forest, Shammy, Dalmore and Turkey stone. Originally they were quarried from specific rock seams, which perhaps no longer exist; today they can sometimes be found in second-hand tool shops. The hardness and cutting quality vary between different types of stone, and even within one type, depending on where in the seam of rock it was taken from.

Two natural stones still readily obtainable are the Arkansas and the Washita. They are available as benchstones and **slipstones** (see below), are fairly consistent in quality and are much more expensive than manufactured stones. However, they are essential for honing the keen edges needed by the carver.

Arkansas and Washita stones are types of what is geologically known as **novaculite**. Today, most of this material is quarried from limited seams in Arkansas, USA by the Smith family business. They have quarried the stone and prepared it for commercial use since 1885 – although before then it was used by the native Americans to make spear and arrow heads. Novaculite as a name derives from the Latin *novacula*, 'a razor', in recognition of the cutting qualities of these fine-grained stones. Novaculite is graded according to its hardness: the softer the stone, the coarser its cut, and vice versa.

Washita is the softest grade, with a cut approximately equivalent to that of a fine Carborundum stone. In fact, Washita has little advantage over the cheaper artificial stone. The Washita is really a medium grade of Arkansas, and has a mottled appearance (Fig 11.15). It makes useful slipstones, but its softness makes the stone less capable of holding a thin-edged shape or a fine angle.

The next variety, harder than the Washita, is the **white Arkansas** that sometimes appears translucent, especially when wet (Figs 11.16 and 11.17). Three grades of the white Arkansas can be distinguished: soft white, hard white and translucent. Unequivocally, it is the translucent Arkansas that gives the perfect

Fig 11.15 (Left to right:) Washita, hard white Arkansas, translucent Arkansas

Fig 11.16 The white Arkansas benchstone appears white when new, going grey with oiling. The one with white mottling on grey has been newly dressed

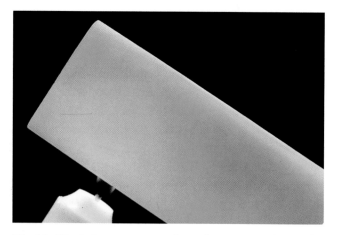

Fig 11.17 *A demonstration of translucency in a fine grade of white Arkansas*

cutting edge to carving tools. It follows on from the coarse (or fine) Carborundum in the sharpening process, and it is the only one that I recommend students to buy. The quality of Arkansas stone has, in my opinion, deteriorated over the last few years, apparently as the best seams are being quarried out; so the cost of the best-quality stones has risen and the size (thickness) that you get for your money has decreased. Nevertheless, the translucent Arkansas is the only one for woodcarvers.

The hardest grade of novaculite is the **black Arkansas** – always the most expensive stone and, luckily, not much use to the average woodcarver (Fig 11.18). These stones cut so finely that it amounts to

polishing the blade, which carvers more usually undertake by stropping.

So the translucent stone is the most useful to the carver. The hard white needs heavy stropping – as do the ceramic and diamond stones considered in Chapter 13 – to get the required edge; and the black is too fine. Buy a translucent stone in the largest surface size possible.

The cost of a natural translucent benchstone may seem exorbitant to the newcomer to carving, but the expense is relative. A good-quality stone is an investment – they will never get cheaper – a pleasure to use, and it does its job efficiently and well. Think about how many meals or golf balls you could buy for the same amount. Perhaps, too, there is also a little magic in the knowledge that these stones have been wrested directly from the earth, each one unique and irreplaceable.

OILS, CARE AND DRESSING

The same advice applies to natural stones as to the artificial ones: keep them in a box (Fig 11.19) or mounted. As they will both clog and break more easily, perhaps a little more care is needed.

Fig 11.19 *The boxes supplied with standard-size stones are often significantly bigger than the stones. Some slips of wood packed around the edge of the stone will keep it stationary in the box*

Fig 11.18 *The black Arkansas stone, which is very black in appearance, is too hard for general purposes*

SLIPSTONES

TYPES

Slipstones (or slips) are the small, specifically shaped stones that work the insides of gouges and V-tools. The word *slip* describes these stones well. Coming from Middle Low German, it retains the original connotations of being small and strip-like ('a slip of paper'), sliding ('slip up'), and letting loose from ('let slip'). These stones do not lie passively on the bench but are actively applied by the fingers.

Slips are available in both artificial and natural stone, and in a large number of shapes and sizes (Fig 11.20). You will need both large and small Carborundum stones for heavy sharpening or reshaping (Figs 11.21 and 11.22), and the finer natural stones for the final honing (Fig 11.23). The small cylindrical, triangular or square ones shown in Fig 11.22 are sometimes known as **stone files**.

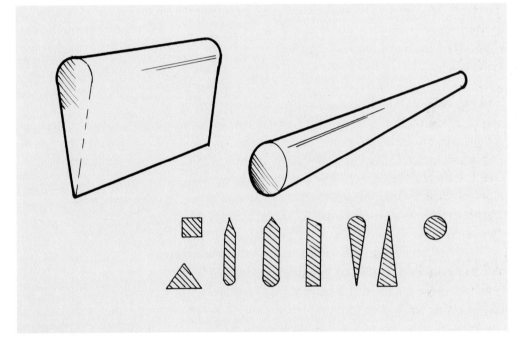

Fig 11.20 *Some slipstone shapes and profiles*

Fig 11.21 *Larger Carborundum slipstones are useful for larger sculpture tools: (left to right) standard wedge shape; 'kidney' or half-conical; standard; conical*

Fig 11.22 *Small Carborundum slipstones: (left to right) large and small triangular; rectangular with bevelled edge; large and small cylindrical*

Fig 11.23 *Translucent Arkansas slipstones, about 2½in (65mm) long*

It is the edges of slipstones which are used for shaping: rounded edges (flatter or quicker) shape the inner sweeps of gouges, whereas angled edges suit the V-tool and other angled tools. Conical shapes are also very useful. It is not necessary to have large numbers of slipstones – as with carving tools themselves, it is best to start with an essential few and build up numbers as they are needed, or as they become available.

A slip is worked up and down the inside of a gouge and if necessary from side to side, creating an inside bevel – a process known as 'opening the mouth' (Fig 11.24) – or they may simply be used to clean away any burr left from sharpening the outside bevel.

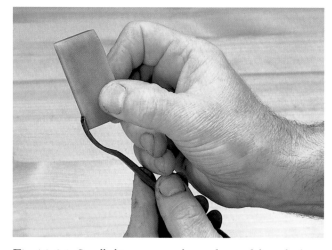

Fig 11.24 *Small slipstones can be used very delicately for specific and exact sharpening*

A slip that is smaller and of quicker sweep than a particular gouge can still be used, but one that is flatter tends to dig its corners into the metal (Fig 11.25). Where possible match the exact shape to the sweep of the blade, but, with dextrous use, a few slipstones can be made to go a long way. A small set of Arkansas slipstones is available (Fig 11.26); this, together with a larger round-edge slip, will cover most of what is needed.

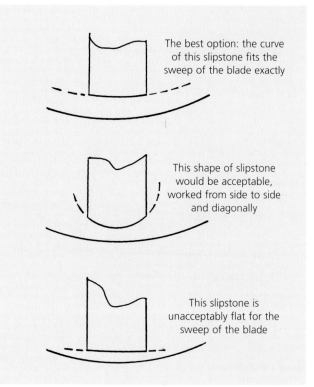

The best option: the curve of this slipstone fits the sweep of the blade exactly

This shape of slipstone would be acceptable, worked from side to side and diagonally

This slipstone is unacceptably flat for the sweep of the blade

Fig 11.25 *The shape of the slipstone needs to be carefully matched to the cross section of the blade*

Fig 11.26 *A very useful set of four small Arkansas slips with different profiles and (above) a triangular slipstone*

Fig 11.27 *The edge of this Arkansas slipstone has been given a flatter curvature at one end than the other, making it far more versatile than before*

ALTERING THE SHAPE

This is easily done and often necessary: the number of available stones is far less than the range of cannels they need to fit. You can alter the shape of a slipstone to suit a particular use with the grinding wheel, benchstones or even a file and sandpaper. With the larger slipstones, one half can be given a rounder profile and the other a flatter one – saving on the cost of two (Fig 11.27). Leave the surface of the slip, after shaping it, as finely finished as the sides, using, for example, fine sandpaper.

CARE

Slipstones, like benchstones, are brittle and easily damaged. They are best kept covered in a box

Fig 11.28 *Small slipstones are quite brittle and easily chipped or broken. A rack like this will stop them damaging one another*

and separate from the rest of the mess on the workbench; better still if some means can be found to prevent them knocking against one another (Fig 11.28). Slips need preparing before use, keeping clean of grit and, in the same way as benchstones, occasionally reshaping.

STROPS

Strop is an older form of the word *strap*, meaning 'a strip of leather'. The strop is used, impregnated with a fine abrasive, to give a final, finishing sharpness to the microscopic cutting edge of a carving tool while simultaneously polishing the bevel. ('Stroppy' people often exhibit an abrasive quality.)

Strops take the form of **benchstrops**, for use on the outside bevel, and **slipstrops**, for working the inside. They are a very important part of the carver's kit, and both types are used regularly to brighten up a dulling edge and maintain its sharpness. Most commercially made benchstrops are too small. It is not difficult to make a good one (Fig 11.29).

MAKING A BENCHSTROP

LEATHER
Strops are best made from the tight-grained, harder type of leather used for saddles, harnesses, belts

Fig 11.29 *A benchstrop with its cover tucked back and ready for use. Also shown are some dressing compounds: a proprietary stropping paste (left), a home-made mixture of tallow and fine abrasive, and a block of crocus abrasive*

and briefcases. This is mostly vegetable-tanned cowhide. If too soft a leather is used, the surface curls up as the tool passes, rounding the cutting edge (more will be said about this effect later: see page 208). The firmer the leather, the better. Leather may also stretch or ruck if it is too thin, so a minimum thickness of ⅛in (3mm) is needed. A local saddler or hand leather-worker will normally have suitable offcuts.

A good size for a strop is 10–12in (250–300mm) long by 3–4in (75–100mm) wide. The leather surface should be untreated so that the pores are still available to take the abrasive. Use a wire brush to cut back finishes that have been applied to the leather. The leather can also be used with the grain side (the outer or hair side) down.

MOUNTING THE STROP

Mount the leather on a block of wood which is a little oversize, fixing it at the top end only. Do not glue it down, as a free lower edge can be bent to form a slipstrop. A cover of thinner leather or canvas-like material will keep the strop dust- and grit-free when not in use. Nipped-off panel pins in the underside of the mounting board, as with the benchstones, will hold the strop on the bench (Fig 11.30).

ABRASIVES

The strop can be dressed with almost any very fine abrasive. Some alternatives which are suitable include:

- crocus powder
- Carborundum powder (at least 400 grit)
- finest emery powder
- finest valve-grinding paste
- jewellers' rouge
- tripoli wax
- diamantine (aluminium oxide)
- proprietary metal polishes such as Brasso
- proprietary strop paste.

These can be obtained from any of the major mail-order tool suppliers.

The abrasive is held to the leather with tallow (preferably), Vaseline, lard or light oil – being very fine, these powders tend to get everywhere. Some of these abrasives are available in blocks, already made up with wax or tallow.

Do remember to wipe tools after stropping to prevent these greasy compounds from transferring to the wood.

DRESSING THE STROP

1 Sprinkle some of the abrasive powder on to the leather, leaving a ½in (13mm) margin around the edges.

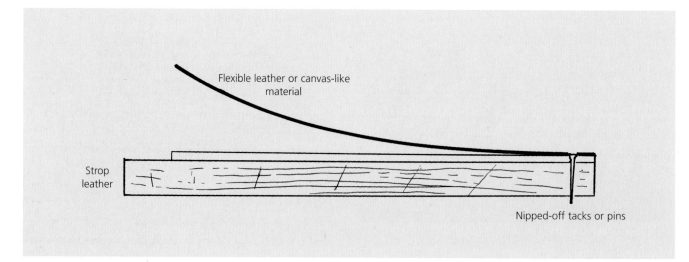

Flexible leather or canvas-like material

Strop leather

Nipped-off tacks or pins

Fig 11.30 The benchstrop

❷ Use a finger to rub some tallow into the powder.

❸ Repeat a few times by sprinkling on a little more of the powder and working in more tallow to get a uniform colour and consistency. If the abrasive comes as a paste or block, work it straight into the leather.

❹ Place the strop in a warm oven or under a grill for just long enough to melt the tallow, which then soaks further into the leather, binding the abrasive to the surface better.

❺ When cool, beat the strop with a large chisel or something similar, dragging the strokes towards you. This works the dressing in and removes surplus; keep any surplus for re-dressing.

For a while, excess dressing may come off the strop and on to the gouges; these will need wiping before use. Although the strop will settle down quickly, blades still need wiping after using it and before carving. Leave a rag by the strop, and always wipe *away from* the cutting edge.

CARE

Cover the strop when not in use, keeping it free from grit and dirt.

A strop is always used by dragging the cutting edge *towards* you so as not cut the soft leather. The technique is described in greater detail in the next chapter (pages 189–92). It is easy to nick the strop with a casual forward stroke. Gashes or nicks can usually be filled with dressing or smoothed by stropping over the area. Over a period of time, the dressing will start to work its way to the near end of the strop; reversing the orientation of the strop now and then, to strop in the opposite direction, will inhibit this effect.

If you are moving to the strop from the benchstones, do not wipe the oil from the blade but allow it to work into the strop; it will keep the leather supple and fresh.

SLIPSTROPS

Slipstrops work the inner bevel of a gouge or V-tool, and resemble the shapes of slipstones. There are several ways of making them:

- Simply fold over another, smaller piece of the benchstrop leather and dress the fold as described above. A piece 6 x 4in (150 x 100mm), folded on the longer edge, produces a size big enough to keep the fingers clear of the tool's cutting edge (Fig 11.31). Push the folded part into the cannel, where it flexes to fit the inside bevel. This type of slipstrop is particularly good for the larger gouges.

Fig 11.31 *For larger tools a piece of folded and dressed leather is the simplest slipstrop. Be sure to make it of an adequate size to keep the leather flexible where the abrasive covers it, and to keep your fingers clear of the blade*

Fig 11.32 *Slipstrops made from thin leather on a wooden core*

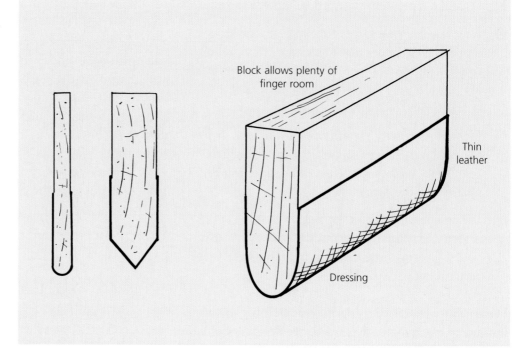

- Glue thin leather to appropriately shaped pieces of softwood and dress the part which fits the carving tool (Figs 11.32 and 11.33). Profile the wood with the gouge (or V-tool) that will be stropped; create the shape by inverting the tool and cutting along (that is, with) the grain. Be sure to leave enough wood for a safe grip with the fingers, well clear of the passing tool edge.

Fig 11.33 *A slip of wood shaped specifically and covered with thin leather makes an excellent slipstrop*

Such slipstrops are good for medium-sized gouges and V-tools.

- Use hardwood in a similar way, but without the leather, and dressing the abrasive straight on to the wood.

- For the smallest tools, a leather pad constructed like the benchstrop works well. Deeply scored lines of varying widths take the corners of a gouge as its edge is pulled along the leather (Fig 11.34*a*). Score the lines with a knife, using lightly scored lines from the corners of the tool itself as a guide. A leather thong is an alternative.

- Small strips of wood, without leather but dressed with abrasive, can be stuck onto a board or into a shallow box (Fig 11.34*b*). Cut the necessary profiles with the appropriate tools.

- The lower edge of the main benchstrop – or a large, folded slipstrop – can be dressed with abrasive for use on the insides of small gouges. You can also pare the edge to a bevel to fit inside a small V-tool. (You might like to know that the technical term for paring leather is *skiving*.)

Fig 11.34 *Two methods of making slipstrops for small tools*

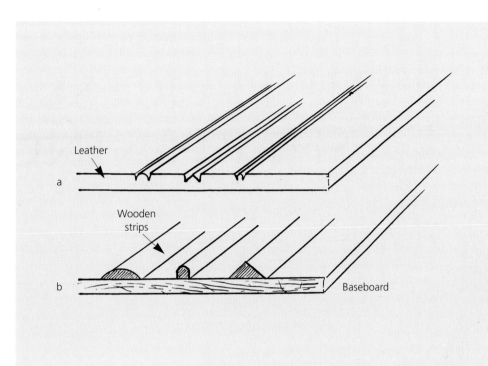

As with slipstones, a few shapes can be made to go a long way.

Care of slipstrops is similar to that of benchstrops. Keep them with the main strop on the bench, free from dirt or grit; a simple rack will keep them in order (Fig 11.35). Move the leather *away from* the cutting edge and re-dress notches if they occur. Again, a little oil will keep suppleness in the leather.

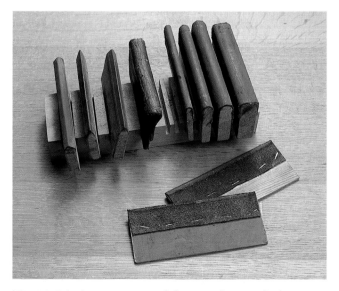

Fig 11.35 *An assortment of slipstrops kept ready for use in a purpose-made rack*

SUMMARY

Here is a list of the basic equipment needed by the woodcarver to sharpen and look after carving tools:

- bench grinder (optional)

- coarse Carborundum benchstone

- fine Carborundum benchstone

- white or (preferably) translucent Arkansas benchstone

- slipstones: large round-edge slips, and conical and smaller slipstones of varying shapes, matching the benchstones in composition

- benchstrop

- slipstrops

- light oil

- abrasive dressing for the strops.

CHAPTER TWELVE

THE PROCESS OF SHARPENING

AIMS

- To describe in detail the whole process of sharpening, from initial grinding to final stropping

- To draw attention to the specific problems posed by particular tools

- To advise how to keep tools sharp

- To consider the layout of the sharpening area of the workshop

SHAPING AND SHARPENING

Here is an overview of what happens when you sharpen a carving tool. I am going to use the oilstones (Carborundum and Arkansas) as my model for benchstone sharpening. If you are using waterstones, ceramic stones or the like, you will need to allow for differences in grit: if they are coarser or much finer than the Arkansas stones, more stropping (by hand or power) may be needed. These other types of stone are considered in the next chapter; use the advice given there in addition to what is discussed here. (Power stropping is covered in Chapter 14.)

It is helpful to conceive of a preliminary stage of **shaping** a carving tool, before the sharpening proper. At this shaping stage:

- The overall contours and profile of the blade are formed, using the grinding wheel and the coarse benchstone and slipstones.

- Edges are squared off and the corners made true.

- Inside and outside bevels are set.

- Adjustments are made to get the line of light neat and even; at this stage it should be about the thickness of a line drawn with a ball-point pen.

After preparatory shaping comes the actual sharpening. Slipstones for the inner bevel, and benchstones for the outer one, gradually thin the visible edge while maintaining a flat bevel, a straight edge and so on. The white line attenuates to a hair's thickness, then disappears altogether. If the honing has been true and even, the whole of the line disappears at the same time. If not, a little more honing in specific places will remove any white specks or areas.

If you end up with a poorly shaped edge – through over-enthusiasm or inattention – it must be levelled off square again. Present the tool dead upright to the Arkansas stone and gently draw it over the surface a few times. The amount of white line showing and the state of the bevel then dictate the next stage: what coarseness of benchstone or slipstone is needed to resume sharpening.

When the white line has disappeared, it might be thought that the tool is sharp. However, pushing the cutting edge into a piece of scrap wood may cause the line of light to reappear in whole or in part. This is because a **wire edge** (or **burr**) – a feather-edge of metal – occurs where the sharpening of the inner and outer bevels meet, and hides the white line. Pushing the cutting edge into the scrap wood removes the wire edge at the same time as toughening up the metal and revealing the white line. A few more strokes of careful honing will eliminate the white line. Once more the edge is pushed into the wood, and touched up on the fine stones again if the line returns.

When the white light does not reappear, try cutting across the grain of another piece of wood, such as a good-quality softwood. The cut surface should be polished and without scratch marks. If scratches occur, a slipstone can be applied to the corresponding tell-tale spot of light, with a final touch-up on the benchstone. Try the cut again. When a clean, sharp cut has been satisfactorily made, the bevel and edge can be slicked up on the strop.

CUTTING PROFILES

Although there seems to be a large variety of shapes for woodcarving tools, there are in fact only two general profiles across the cutting edge – flat and curved – with a few combinations. Carving tools divide into these profiles in the following ways:

Flat profiles

- firmer chisels
- skew chisels
- V-tools and macaroni tools

Curved profiles

- straight gouges
- fishtail and other tapered gouges
- longbent gouges
- shortbent gouges
- backbent gouges

Combinations

- deep gouges (nos. 10 and 11).

Different approaches, but all using the basic procedures outlined above, will allow you to master all these different profiles.

The following sections deal with how to use the various pieces of equipment to work these profiles correctly; the specific needs of individual tools then follow.

BASIC PROCEDURES

Carvers differ in the way they use grinding wheels, benchstones and so on; they differ also in what final shapes and bevel angles they want. Beginners, too, will eventually develop their own preferences. The methods given here work successfully and are consistent with all that has previously been said regarding cutting profiles and angles.

GRINDING

Grinding wheels shape the carving tools initially, setting the bevel and edge. They may also be used to repair broken or damaged edges.

The grinding wheel should always turn *towards* the operator. This is a debatable point: it is sometimes recommended that the wheel should turn away from the operator. The reasons for recommending a direction of rotation towards the operator therefore need to be considered in some detail, since different directions of the wheel have differing effects on the tool edge.

With the wheel turning towards the user, metal is peeled back from the edge and towards the handle, leaving a small burr and a strong edge. A wheel turning in the opposite direction tends to draw the metal forward, producing more burr – which then tends to crumble off – and an edge which is less strong (Fig 12.1). The difference can be seen by comparing edges after pushing them into a piece of wood; this removes the wire edge and allows the stronger metal underneath to be seen.

A second point is that the surface of the wheel rotating towards the user bites into the metal more effectively than one turning away, which tends to bounce the tool more and give a less efficient cut. Wheels rotating away from the user may feel safer because, certainly, the edge cannot 'dig in' – but the correct presentation of the blade to the wheel never causes this result in any case.

Whichever way the wheel rotates, a carving tool can be presented to it in several ways, each of which serves a different purpose (Fig 12.2):

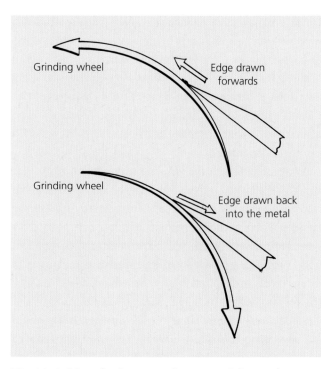

Fig 12.1 *How the direction of rotation of the grinding wheel affects the wire edge*

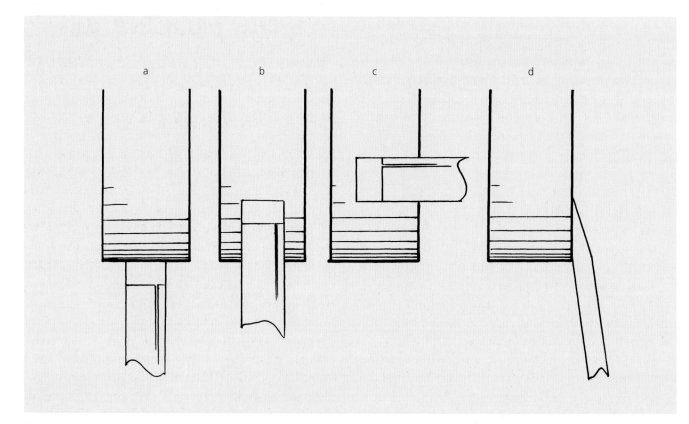

Fig 12.2 *Four ways of presenting a carving tool to the grinder: (a) perpendicular to the rotating wheel; (b) in line with the rotation; (c) square-on to the rotation; (d) to the side of the wheel*

Perpendicular to the cutting surface of the wheel

Tools are presented in this way (Fig 12.3) as part of the preliminary shaping – straightening or flattening the cutting edge from corner to corner. Be gentle and precise. Use the whole surface of the wheel where possible, and use the toolrests. Always wear eye protection.

Fig 12.3 *Perpendicular presentation (for clarity the grinder's perspex guards are swung up)*

In line with the rotation of the wheel

This is the usual method for setting the angle of the bevel. When a tool is offered in line with the grinding wheel (Fig 12.4), the bevel tends to pick up the circular shape of the wheel, producing the hollow grind mentioned earlier. The smaller the wheel, the more hollow the bevel. This hollowness can be removed on the benchstone.

Fig 12.4 *In-line presentation, with fingers on toolrest*

Square-on to the rotation

Offering the gouge square-on (at right angles) to the wheel (Fig 12.5), and rotating it from corner to corner while keeping the same angle of presentation, will produce a flat bevel. This operation involves holding the tool in your hands and steadying your hands in turn on the grinder's toolrest. It is not a difficult technique and, if a firm but gentle approach is taken, it is quite safe.

Fig 12.5 *Square-on presentation*

Touched to the side of the wheel

The quickest method of grinding flat bevels on a gouge or chisel is to start with the normal (in-line) presentation to the wheel and remove most of the unwanted metal from the bevel. Then make a final few passes with the tool presented square-on, removing any hollowness. You must rotate a gouge across the *whole* of its bevel surface, whatever the orientation to the wheel. Aim to grind smoothly, with any rotating coming from your wrist at the handle; try to produce a clean bevel with no facets.

For a chisel or V-tool, flatten the bevel by touching it *carefully and gently* to the side of the wheel, using the grinder's toolrest (Fig 12.6). Use only the lightest touch, as these wheels are not really designed to take sideways pressure. Look at the scratch marks on the bevel and let them guide your positioning of the tool.

Fig 12.6 *Touching the carving tool to the side of the grinding wheel; only the lightest touch is permissible*

Even though a grinder removes metal quickly, impatience may still lead to two unwanted consequences:

Overheating

With a fast, dry wheel, check the temperature of the blade frequently and never allow it to rise above hand-warm. This means adopting a rhythm of short bursts of light grinding, dipping the blade in cold water between times.

Over-grinding

The same regular approach will help prevent over-grinding – a pitfall to be aware of from the beginning. Try not to take too much metal off at a time, but work evenly. Take the white line of light at the edge continuously as your guide. Keep looking at its thickness and the scratch marks on the bevel to be sure of exactly where you are removing metal, and how much. Bear in mind the shape you are aiming at. If the edge loses its shape, you may need to level it off by presenting the tool perpendicularly and starting the process again.

METHOD

❶ Start by setting the cutting edge, from corner to corner, at right angles to the longitudinal axis, as shown already in Fig 12.3. Smooth and clean up this straight edge right at the start on the Arkansas stone.

❷ For gouges, set the outside bevel by grinding in line with the wheel, rocking the gouge from corner to corner (Fig 12.7) and making a

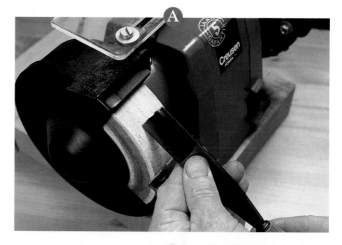

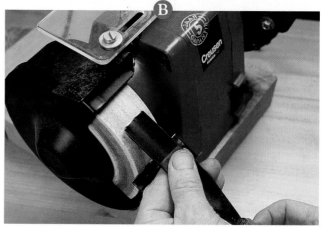

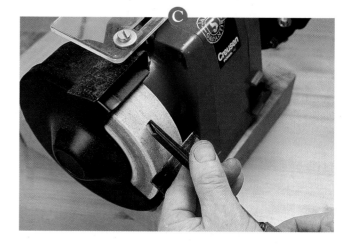

Fig 12.7 *After the edge has been straightened, set the bevel of the gouge on the grinding wheel by smoothly rotating it at the correct angle from corner to corner. Keep checking the result. (For clarity the grinder's perspex guards are swung up)*

uniform line of light with the heel and edge parallel. Finish at right angles to the wheel, flattening the bevel (Fig 12.8).

❸ For large gouges, small grinding wheels in drills or flexible shafts can create an inner bevel

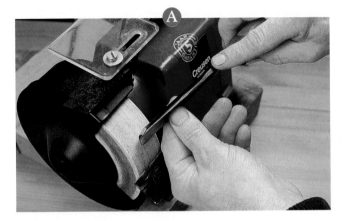

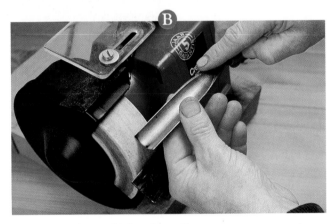

Fig 12.8 Flatten the bevel by offering it square-on to the rotation. Do this lightly and make sure your hand is supported by the toolrest. If preferred, this method can be used for all the bevel shaping

quickly, although coarse slipstones are more often used. The white line will thin down – keep it even and uniform.

❹ For flat chisels, the grinder's toolrests can be used to help set the bevel equally on both sides. Move the tool from side to side, covering the whole stone evenly. If you do not want to use the side of the grinding wheel (or even to grind square-on) to flatten the bevel, use the coarse benchstone.

❺ The tool should now be ready for the benchstones.

STONING (HONING)

Some beginners are unsure at what angle to present their chisel or gouge to the benchstone in order to get the right cutting angle. I'll give you here, right at the beginning, the key: you should simply present the tool to the benchstone *at the angle at which you want to hold it while you are carving wood* – that is, the cutting angle.

Imagine the surface of the benchstone to be wood; pretend to carve it with your gouge. You will see you are at the 15-20°, which is the 'natural', most controlled angle at which to carve. Keep this angle as you sharpen.

The two basic carving-tool profiles – curved and flat – are presented differently to the benchstones for sharpening:

- Flat chisels are presented in line (end-on) with the stone (Fig 12.9).

Fig 12.9 Working along the benchstone with a chisel; the stone is orientated on the bench end-on to the user

Fig 12.10 *Working across the benchstone with a gouge; the stone is orientated on the bench square-on to the user*

- Gouges are presented at right angles (square-on) to the stone (Fig 12.10).

Because of this differing orientation, mount the benchstones so that they can be turned around; do not fix them permanently in position on the bench with cleats.

The following procedures to get a straight edge from corner to corner of your tools apply to all types of benchstone; remember that oilstones must be oiled first.

STRAIGHTENING THE EDGE

For both chisels and gouges, start by holding the blade perpendicular – like a pencil – to the coarse stone and dragging it across the surface a few times (Fig 12.11). This is a more exact alternative to straightening the edge on the grinding wheel. In both cases, finish off the straight edge on the Arkansas stone; this produces a strong, smooth, clean edge with which to start; it also makes the line of light easier to see.

Whenever a cutting edge has become unacceptably wavy – or the corners lost – you can reinstate a fresh white line using this procedure. Try not to do

Fig 12.11 *Cleaning the edge of a carving tool involves offering it in a perpendicular position and pulling it along a flat benchstone. This is necessary each time you move to a finer stone, refining the edge from the coarser grit of the previous one*

this too often, as it is wasteful of material. Perhaps only one pass on the Arkansas stone may be needed to produce a clean edge from which to resharpen.

All other ways of holding the tool for sharpening involve the correct use of the whole body. This is important to achieve the right effect. Carving tools are sharpened from the hips and legs, not the elbows.

HONING THE BEVEL: CHISELS

❶ Position the stone on the bench so that its end points away from you (i.e. end-on).

❷ If you are right-handed, hold the chisel handle in the right hand with the first two fingers of the left hand on the back of the blade, a little behind the bevel – vice versa for the left-handed.

❸ Place the heel of the chisel on the near end of the stone. Try to get a sense of the heel resting on the surface (Fig 12.12). Keep your elbows by your sides.

❹ Raise the handle until the bevel lies flat on the stone, and then a little more to bring in the actual edge. By raising and lowering the handle

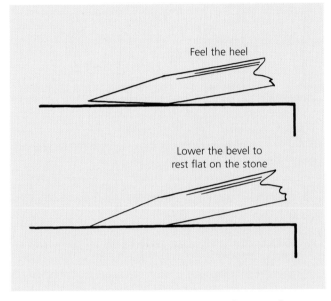

Fig 12.12 *How to get a sense of the bevel resting flat on the surface of the benchstone*

fractionally, learn to feel when the bevel lies truly flat on the surface.

❺ Remember to present the chisel or gouge to the benchstone at the cutting angle – the angle at which you want to hold the tool while you are carving. Move the chisel forwards and backwards along the benchstone, maintaining this angle consistently and keeping the bevel flat. To do this, keep your elbows by your sides and rock your whole body backwards and forwards from relaxed knees. You will need one foot a little in front of the other. If you keep your body still and just push the blade backwards and forwards with your arms, there is a strong tendency to raise and lower the handle, rounding the bevel; this is called 'rolling the edge' (Fig 12.13). Keeping the bevel flat requires this whole-body approach.

❻ Use the whole of the stone's surface, but keep clear of the very edge. Be careful not to pull the chisel off the stone on the back stroke, as this inevitably damages the edge.

❼ After a little while, turn the chisel on to the opposite side and repeat the action. Counting the number of strokes on each side can help you

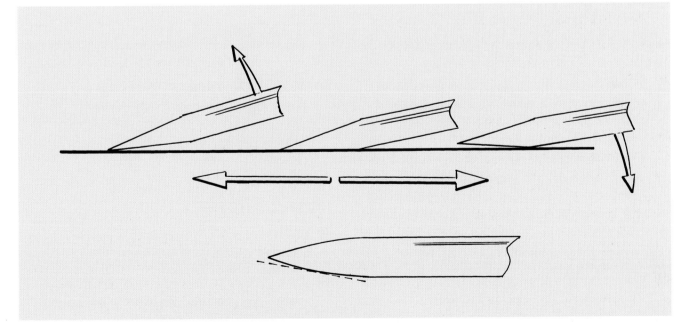

Fig 12.13 *Lowering and raising the handle rolls (or rounds) the bevel*

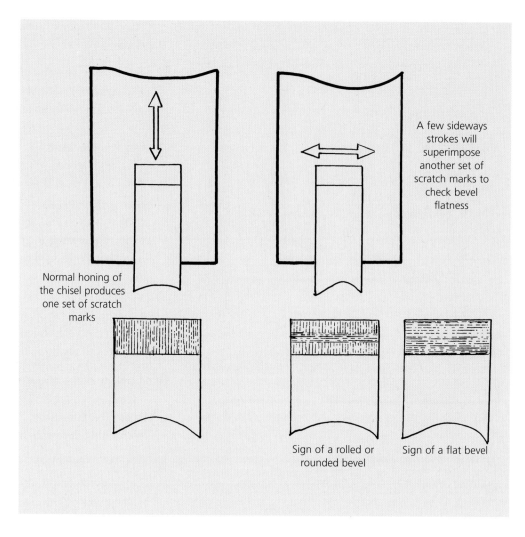

Fig 12.14 *Use the appearance of the bevel surface to monitor the flatness of the bevel*

Normal honing of the chisel produces one set of scratch marks

A few sideways strokes will superimpose another set of scratch marks to check bevel flatness

Sign of a rolled or rounded bevel

Sign of a flat bevel

keep the two bevels equal. Maintain a patient, steady rhythm. Watch the amount of oil on the stone, as the edge tends to push it off.

⑧ Always look at the white line of light, keeping it uniform with sensitive adjustments to the point of contact between stone and metal. Do not be tempted to raise the handle to make the line of light disappear more quickly. If the line is thicker on one side, try not so much to tilt the tool as to *imagine* putting more pressure on that side of the blade. You may find that you have a built-in bias to one side or the other, and have to guard against this.

⑨ Occasionally, still keeping the bevel flat, make a short sideways stroke *across* the stone rather than along it. Examine the scratch marks on the surface of the bevel. If the bevel has been

rounded, a new mark will appear as a line across the middle. If the bevel is flat, the new mark will extend from edge to heel (Fig 12.14).

⑩ Working through the stones in this way, and observing the white line and the bevel scratches, you can maintain an even, flat reduction of the metal to an edge which finally disappears.

HONING THE BEVEL: GOUGES

❶ Position the benchstone so that its side is facing you (i.e. side-on).

❷ Taking a medium-sweep (no. 6) gouge as an example: if you are right-handed, hold the handle in the right hand with the first two fingers of the left hand in the cannel or mouth of the blade, about a finger-joint back from the edge. Vice versa for the left-handed.

3 Place the heel of the outside bevel in the centre of the stone. Keep your elbows by your sides.

4 Start by getting a feel for how the flat bevel rests on the surface of the stone. Raise the handle until the bevel lies flat on the stone, and then raise it a little more on to the actual edge. By raising and lowering the handle a little, learn to feel when the bevel is lying truly flat on the surface. With a little practice you will be able to go straight to resting the bevel flat on the stone.

5 Remember to present the gouge to the benchstone at the cutting angle – the angle at which you want to hold the tool while you are carving. Start on the left of the oilstone with the gouge turned on to its right corner. The mouth of the gouge will be pointing towards the centre of the stone.

6 The gouge must now move to the opposite end of the benchstone. In doing so, you must also rotate the blade so that it comes to rest on its opposite corner, with the mouth pointing once

more towards the centre. This constitutes one sharpening stroke.

7 Without lifting the gouge from the surface, reverse the movement so the gouge comes to rest on its right corner, over on the left of the stone once more (Fig 12.15). This completes a cycle of two strokes. Notice that the direction of rotation goes *against* the direction of travel, efficiently biting the metal into the stone.

8 The gouge is rocked like this, from one end of the benchstone to the other and back again, in regular, even strokes. Use the whole cutting surface, but avoid both a figure-of-eight pattern – which rounds over the bevel – and the very edge of the stone.

9 Present the bevel *flat* all the time. To accomplish this, keep the elbows in, rotating the tool handle from the wrist and forearm. Shift the weight of the body from one leg to the other, keeping your back upright and your knees relaxed and slightly bent. This posture has something of the judo stance and balance about it, and should feel comfortable and unforced. If you work from the elbows only, the bevel will invariably become 'rolled' or rounded.

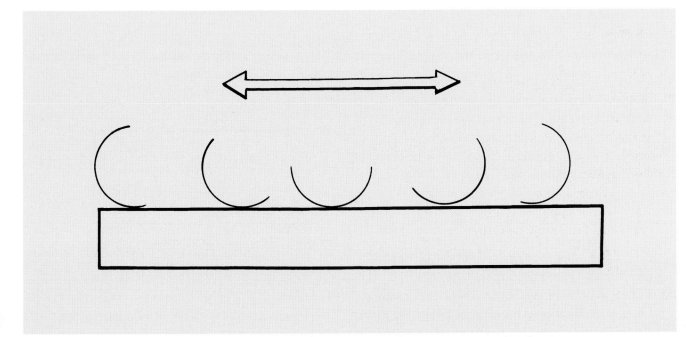

Fig 12.15 *The direction and rotation of a gouge while being sharpened on a benchstone*

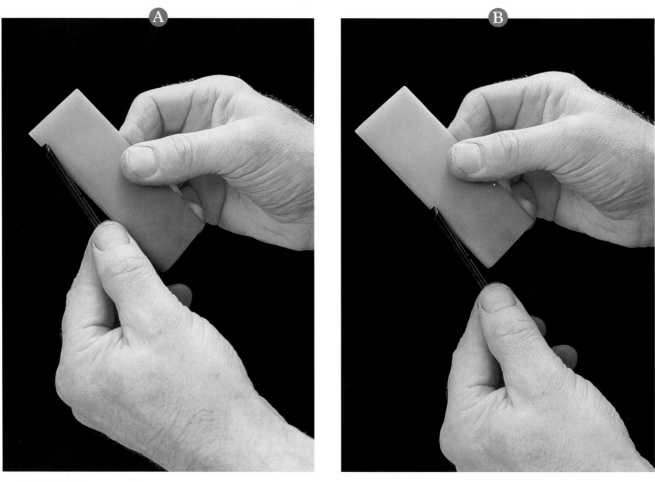

Fig 12.16 *Slipstones are used in a partnership with benchstones, rubbing backwards and forwards while maintaining the same angle to the blade. The upper hand moves, not the lower*

This is the basic technique for gouges, to which some extra points need to be added:

- Use the slipstones with the benchstones to work the inner bevel or remove the wire edge (see pages 187–9). In the sharpening process, the honing of the edge alternates between benchstones and slips (Fig 12.16). Slipstones are often used first, where an inner bevel is required.

- Regularly check the state of the white line. If it becomes thicker in one part compared with another, limit the rotation of the blade for a few strokes and work more specifically on the thicker part. Conversely, if some part of the white line becomes unduly thinner, avoid honing that part of the edge. This may mean you have to divide your honing into two separate strokes – lifting the gouge to avoid the thin part in the

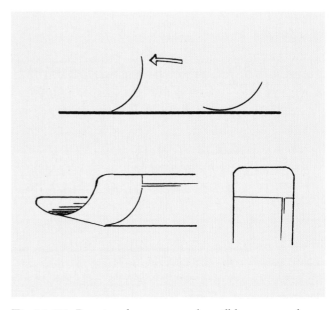

Fig 12.17 *Rotating the gouge too far will hone away the all-important corners*

middle – until the white line is returned to a uniform thickness.

- To sharpen the whole bevel, the corners must be included, but it is very easy to over-rotate the handle and sharpen them away (Fig 12.17). Extra care must be taken with the corners at the end of the stroke, so that the gouge is rotated neither too much nor too little. Additionally, all the finger pressure on the gouge tends to lie on the corners at the point where it changes direction, so pressure needs to be eased a little at this point.

- The amount of rotation that a gouge needs depends on its sweep – the amount of curve it has. Flat gouges require only a slight turn at the wrist; quicker gouges a lot more. If the wrist action becomes uncomfortable, you may have to hone the edges of the quickest gouges in sectors which you then carefully merge. With flexible wrists this is not normally necessary up to the semicircular (no. 9) gouges, but the U-shaped gouges can be more of a problem. They are best dealt with as a combination of flat and curved bevels; details will be given in the section on individual tools (page 204).

- By constantly monitoring the line of light at the edge, and adjusting which parts of the bevel are being honed, a straight, even contour will result. As with the chisels, it is a good idea to make a short stroke with the gouge moving at 90° to the normal direction. The subsequent scratch mark will show you whether the bevel has become rounded or remained flat. As the grade becomes finer, changes in the abrasive marks on the bevel can also be used to monitor the angle at which the bevel is presented.

Some carvers sharpen their gouges by rubbing the bevels on a benchstone in the same direction as that described above for the chisel. As the gouge is moved backwards and forwards it is rotated from one side to the other, often in a figure-of-eight pattern. I have always found it difficult with this method either to produce a straight edge with corners, or a flat bevel; it also wears the stone in the centre more quickly.

SLIPSTONING

As a general rule, use the same type of stone on one side of the edge as on the other. So, when working the outside bevel on the coarse Carborundum benchstone, use a coarse Carborundum slipstone on the inside – matching grade to grade as the abrasive stones get finer.

Match the curves and angles of the slipstones to the curves and angles of the tools as closely as possible. Bear in mind that you can change slipstone shapes, and use smaller slips on larger tools.

METHOD

By way of example, let us put an inner bevel to a medium gouge.

❶ Rest the round back of the blade on the edge of the bench with about 1in (25mm) projecting upwards and at an angle of about 45° away from you.

❷ Using some oil – which can be taken up from the benchstone – place the slip into the mouth of the gouge. Hold it between your fingers and thumb at a shallow angle. *Make sure your fingers clear the sharp corners of the blade*. A right-handed person would normally hold the slip in the right hand.

❸ With firm pressure, rub the stone backwards and forwards; if appropriate, work from side to side and diagonally as well. To keep the angle of the inner bevel flat, avoid rocking the slip up or down (Fig 12.18). Work evenly across the edge and include the corners, but be careful not to over-sharpen them.

❹ Do not let more than half to two thirds of the slipstone project from the blade. To put this another way, always keep a substantial amount of the slipstone in-cannel (Fig 12.19). This means working in short, rapid strokes. If the slipstone projects more than this, there is a danger of its coming off the blade completely.

Fig 12.18 Do not rock the slipstone up or down *as it is moved backwards and forwards*

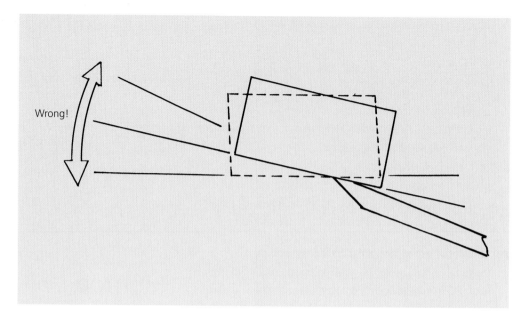

Almost invariably, the sharpening hand starts a return stroke, only to strike the sharp cutting edge of the tool with the slipstone – or with your fingers.

⑤ Work in conjunction with the benchstone: drawing the inner bevel back with the slipstone, cleaning and working with the benchstone, returning to the slip, and so on. The line of light on the cutting edge is, as always, the guide to where the slip needs to be applied.

An alternative is to rest the gouge in one of your hands and not against the bench. For a right-handed person, the gouge would be held in the left. Allow the hand holding the handle of the gouge to relax so that the round back of the blade nestles in the angle between the thumb and first finger – this hand is supported by holding the elbow in to the body. Work the slipstone with the other. This method is more suited to smaller tools and the final, more delicate stages of slipstoning. It allows the work to be held a little closer to the eye.

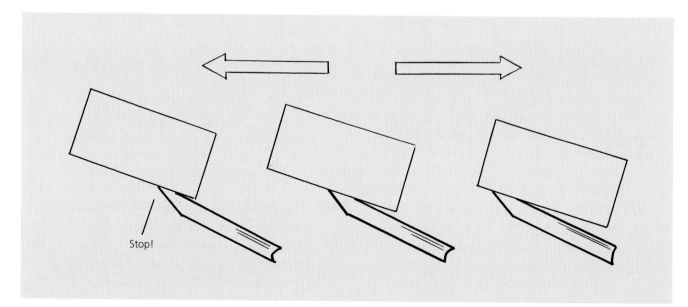

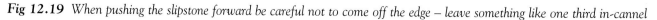

Fig 12.19 When pushing the slipstone forward be careful not to come off the edge – leave something like one third in-cannel

Another approach that suits some carvers is to fix the movement of the stone and rub the gouge over it, rather than the more usual reverse situation. This method is not recommended, as visibility of the edge is not so good.

STROPPING

METHOD: CHISELS

❶ Line up the benchstrop end-on, supporting the near edge with the fingers (of the left hand, for a right-handed person).

❷ The strop is *always* used with the blade being drawn *towards* the user, the edge dragging so as not to cut the leather.

❸ Hold the chisel around the shank with the right hand. The first two fingers extend along the metal, but keep them back from the cutting edge roughly the length of a finger joint.

❹ Place the bevel flat on the furthest part of the leather and, with firm pressure, draw the tool along the strop towards you (Fig 12.20). Try to maintain the angle and work on the *bevel* – not the edge, as that will take care of itself.

❺ At the end of this stroke *lift the chisel clear* and place the bevel flat on the strop at the far end again. Draw the blade towards you for a second stroke.

❻ This action is repeated a few times on one side of the chisel, then the blade is turned over for an equal number of strokes on the other side. You can strop the tool quite vigorously, in which case it makes a slapping sound on the strop as it is placed for each stroke.

METHOD: GOUGES

❶ With the strop end-on, hold the gouge as you did the chisel, with the extended fingers in-cannel.

❷ Start at the far end of the strop with the gouge turned on to one corner. Draw the blade towards you with firm pressure at the same time as rotating the wrist to rock the gouge on to its other corner (Figs 12.21 and 12.22). The gouge arrives at the near end of the strop facing the opposite way. Keep the bevel flat by maintaining the angle of presentation.

❸ Lift the gouge clear of the leather, and return it to the far end for a second stroke. This time start the gouge on the opposite corner and

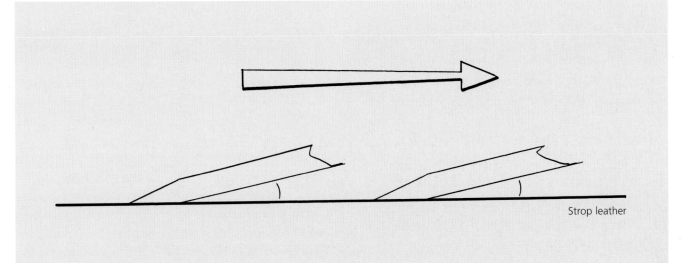

Strop leather

Fig 12.20 *When stropping, maintain the same angle and always* drag *the edge to avoid cutting the leather*

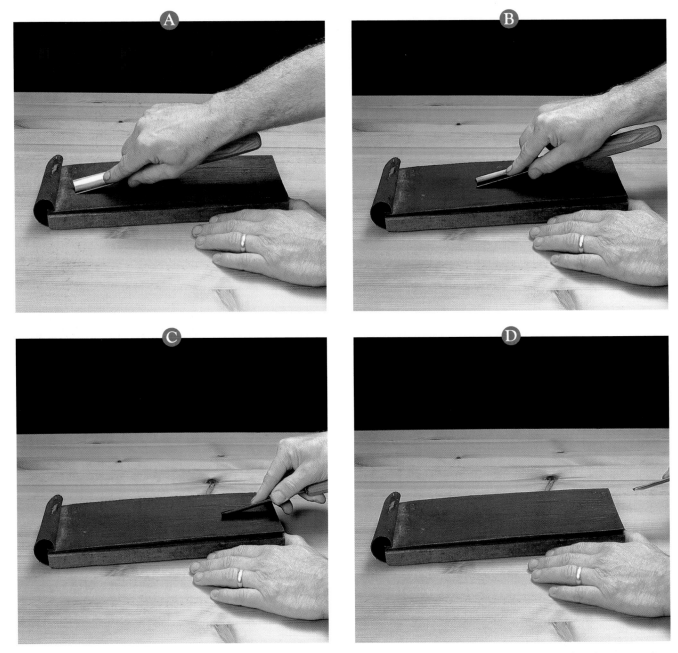

Fig 12.21 *Using the benchstrop involves rotating the gouge as it passes along the leather, while keeping the bevel consistently flat on its surface; lift it off the leather for the return stroke*

repeat the rotating stroke; this completes one cycle.

④ Repeat the cycle several times. Do not land heavily on the corners.

⑤ After a few cycles of stropping, use the slipstrop on the inside.

⑥ Only a few passes are needed to maintain the edge; stropping can be quite a brief business.

SAFETY

There are two dangers in using the benchstrop:

Cutting the leather
Avoid running the tool into the strop by making sure the blade is lifted clear of the leather surface on the return strokes. Develop a habitual action that automatically ensures this.

Fig 12.22 *As the gouge is drawn towards you on the strop, it must be rotated to cover the full surface of the bevel, including both corners. Change the direction of rotation with alternate strokes*

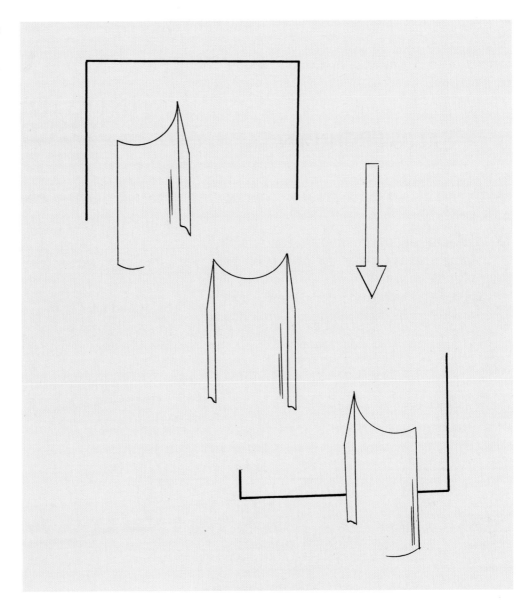

Cutting your hand

There is a danger of cutting the hand that is steadying the strop – the thumb, especially, can be caught by a negligent forward stroke of the carving tool returning through the air (Fig 12.23). Since the edge is now extremely sharp, this danger must be taken seriously.

The strop needs some steadying, since it tends to be pulled towards you as you use it. Pins beneath the mounting board (see page 172) will largely anchor it, and only a light touch of the hand will be needed to steady it. *This steadying hand must be positioned to the side of the working area, out of the path of the blade entirely.* The position can be to one side, at either end of the strop.

Fig 12.23 *The hand that steadies the strop must be kept out of the way of the returning cutting edge*

By experimenting with the safest, yet most relaxed hand position – and by being mindful of the movement of the tool – the danger of cutting yourself can be eliminated.

SLIPSTROPPING

❶ Position the gouge or V-tool as when using slipstones.

❷ Again, the slipstrop must move *away from* the cutting edge. Place it on the inside bevel and push it forward with firm pressure into the air and beyond the edge (Figs 12.24 and 12.25).

❸ Return the slipstrop *clear of the cutting edge* and position it for a second forward stroke.

As with slipstones, be aware of the fingers and the very sharp cutting edge.

INDIVIDUAL TOOLS IN DETAIL

These notes should be read in the context of what has been said previously about:

• the shapes and profiles that carving tools need

• the use of the shaping and sharpening equipment.

Study and refer to this information first. I have tried to avoid repetition as much as possible but, for the sake of clarity, some is unavoidable.

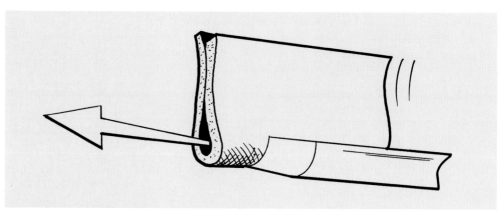

Fig 12.24 *Slipstrops must only be pushed* out *of the cannel, to avoid cutting the leather*

Fig 12.25 *A leather slipstrop will deform to fit the sweep of the gouge as it is pushed forward*

With accurate grinding it is possible to go straight up the scale to the finer stones and save time. The skill of knowing which stones to use, and when, comes with practice.

Decide first on your bevel angle. As a guide, an overall angle (including an inside bevel) of 20–25° is a useful, average one. In practical terms, a length of bevel between two and a half and three times the thickness of the blade would be approximately right.

• Without an inside bevel: all the angle is taken on the outside.

• With an inside bevel: make the inner bevel between one quarter and one third the length of the outer bevel.

- With a carving chisel: the angle and amount of bevel are divided equally between both sides.

It may be helpful in the beginning to make a wooden template of what the sharpening angle looks like in order to get some feel for it. In practice, no experienced carver estimates these angles to accurate degrees; it is done more by feel, and whether the tool cuts as you want.

FLAT CHISELS

1. Grind the edge square and establish the corners. The coarse benchstone may be preferred to the grinder, especially for the finer tools. The white line of light should be unbroken along the whole length of the edge.

2. Make one or two perpendicular passes on the oiled Arkansas stone to clean and refine the white line.

3. Grind the bevel flat to the required angle on both sides of the chisel, with the heel parallel to the cutting edge. The edge should be in the centre of the blade (Fig 12.26). Make the white line an even ½in (1mm) thick at this stage.

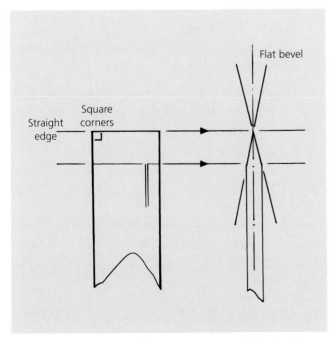

Fig 12.26 *Features of a correctly sharpened flat chisel*

Use the side of the grinding wheel to remove any hollowness in the bevel, or leave this until the next step.

4. Set the oilstone end-on, present the bevel flat and hone both sides. Repeat equally on both sides, regularly checking the white line and bevel scratches.

5. When the line of light reaches hair thickness, push the edge into a piece of clean scrap wood to remove any burr. A little more work may then be necessary on the coarse stone to return the line to uniformly hair-thin.

6. Set the Arkansas stone end-on and proceed in the same way. After every ten strokes on each side, push the blade into scrap wood to emphasize the line of light and strengthen the edge. As the line thins, push the edge into the wood every five, then every couple of strokes. Do not raise the handle to make the line disappear more quickly, but proceed patiently.

7. When the line is no longer visible, and does not reappear when the edge is pushed into the wood, try carving across the grain of a piece of softwood. Look to see if the line returns, or if there are scratch marks on the cut surface, and touch up the edge appropriately on the Arkansas stone.

8. Once a polished, clean cut has been produced, strop both sides equally and then carefully wipe the blade.

SKEW CHISELS

1. Grind the skew angle first: the acute angle at the tip of the blade should be 40–45° for general use, around 30° for more delicate work. Present the end of the blade to the wheel so as to keep a straight line along the edge. This grinding will make the edge look wedge-shaped, narrowing to the long point (Fig 12.27).

2. Make one or two perpendicular passes of the edge on the Arkansas stone to clean and refine the white line.

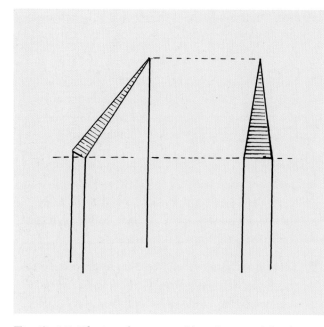

Fig 12.29 When the cutting edge of the skew is moved across the stone, the handle must be angled over the side (for clarity the oil is not shown)

Fig 12.27 The initial setting and lengthening of the skew angle makes the chisel look wedge-shaped

❸ Grind the bevel flat, with the heel parallel to the cutting edge. To do this, position the handle at a corresponding angle to the side of the wheel. Work more on the thicker end of the wedge, and remember that *the point can be overheated very easily*. Keep the cutting edge in the centre of the metal (Fig 12.28).

❹ The skew is offered to the benchstones so that the edge orientates in the same way as the edge of a firmer chisel – across the width of the benchstone. The handle angles out over the side of the stone, to one side for one bevel, the opposite side for the other (Fig 12.29).

❺ Hone the skew in the same way as a firmer chisel: two fingers exerting gentle pressure on the blade, and working on both sides uniformly. Keep an eye on the white line and avoid over-sharpening the long point – so removing the most important part of the tool. Test the white line in scrap wood.

❻ Strop by holding and moving the skew as if it were a firmer chisel – but at an angle, as before – and carefully wipe the blade. Test the edge by slicing across the grain of a piece of softwood.

V-TOOLS

Consider the V-tool or parting tool as two flat chisels, joining to form a cutting angle. There are three bevels to deal with: the central keel, and the chisel on either side. Of the three bevels, it is the keel which is the most important: not only does the keel form the principle cutting angle, but *the way the keel itself is formed* from the thickness of the metal on each side decides how well the tool cuts.

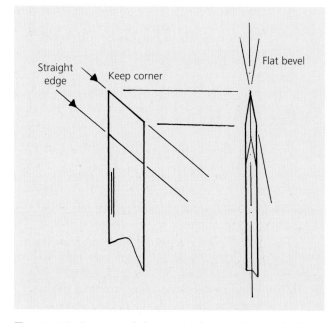

Fig 12.28 Features of a correctly sharpened skew chisel

Straight edge

Keep corner

Flat bevel

You must, of course, have keen cutting edges along the two chisels and at the apex of the V, at the keel. It is crucial that the cutting apex and edges of the V-tool – the parts that leave the finished cut – are properly sharp, otherwise a ragged cut is inevitable.

A lot of problems are caused by faults in the tools themselves: different wall thicknesses on either side, for example. If the sides of the V-tool are of uneven thickness, or the cannel is not lined up accurately, matching the two side bevels can be difficult. If you find that equal matching is impossible, but the bevels are nevertheless flat and the cutting edges straight, then the tool should still be usable. Do check this aspect of your V-tool and make sure it is well made; if you are running into unaccountable problems, this may be the cause.

As has been mentioned before, the apex of the V is not actually a sharp angle but slightly rounded, both inside and out (Fig 12.30). This is not that noticeable unless you examine the groove cut by the V-tool closely. The rounding-over allows the tool to negotiate corners more easily. The keel itself remains straight and at the usual cutting angle of 15–20° (Fig 12.31). Keep the corners: they are used in deeper cuts

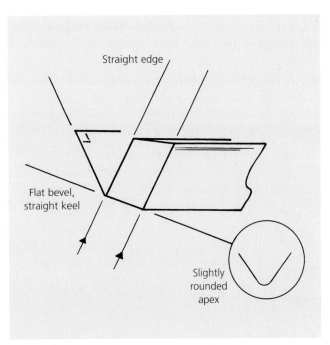

Fig 12.31 *Features of a correctly sharpened V-tool*

sometimes. However, they are the least useful part of the tool; the apex of a V-tool will cut very well despite missing corners.

Specially shaped angle-edged slipstones will clean off the wire edge and work any inner bevel into the angle itself; different stones will be needed to match the different angles of V-tools (Fig 12.32). Only a small inside bevel is needed; it can be worked back every time the tool needs touching up. The slipstone must fit exactly into the angle; it is all too easy to

Fig 12.30 *Close-up of the end of the V-tool; the apex of the V is not a sharp angle but slightly rounded*

Fig 12.32 *The three different V-tool angles will need corresponding angles on the slipstones*

work the slip to one side of the angle rather than in the centre, which creates a notch (Fig 12.33). Most of the problems encountered in sharpening these tools arise from improper shaping at the grinding stage, or inaccurate application of the slipstones.

It is not too difficult to sharpen a V-tool if you proceed step by step:

❶ Grind the edges square, with the V-tool perpendicular to the grinding wheel. If the tool was supplied nosed, the edges will now look like two wedges, thickening to the angle (Fig 12.34a).

❷ Make one or two perpendicular passes on the Arkansas stone to clean and refine the white line.

❸ Set the keel angle by presenting the tool *across* the wheel; an average angle would be a bit less than 20°. Reduce the thickness of the white line at the apex to about ¹⁄₁₆in (1.5mm). The outside corner of the angle will look cut off (Fig 12.34b).

❹ Set the bevel angles on the wheel, treating each side of the tool in turn like a chisel and rendering the white lines to a thickness of about

Fig 12.33 *It is important to align the V-tool slipstone exactly with the apex when working the angle; it is easy to rub to one side and notch the edge*

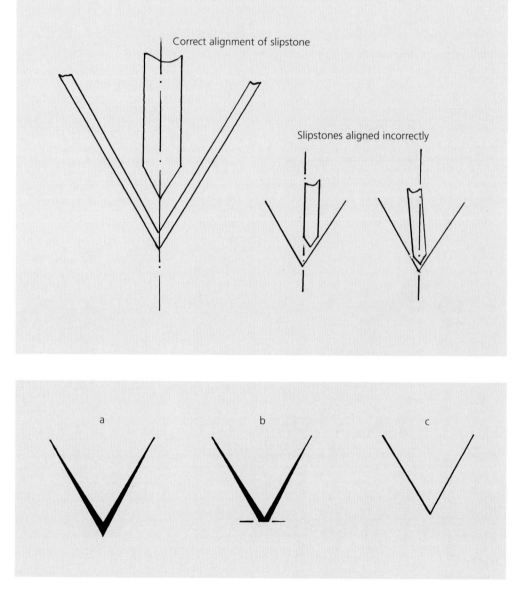

Fig 12.34 *With the edges but not the apex ground, the tip of the V-tool looks like two wedges (a). When the angle of the keel has been set, the apex will look cut off (b). As the bevel is set, the edge is reduced to a uniform thinness (c)*

½in (1mm). The heel should be parallel with the cutting edges and the V apex aligned dead in the centre. End-on, the angle will still look slightly cut off.

⑤ Position the benchstones as for the flat chisel, and select the appropriate angled slipstone for the inside. Taking each side of the V in turn, start reducing the thickness of the edge with the Carborundum, then the Arkansas, stone (Figs 12.35 and 12.36). There is always a tendency to over-sharpen the corners, as they are thinner than the central parts. If the line thins at any point, slightly turn the wrist to exert a little more pressure on the thicker part of the edge and away from the thinner part. Take great care to keep the bevels flat, and check the white line and bevel scratches to make decisions as to exactly how the tool should present to the stone. Push the edge into scrap wood as with the chisel, but do not rock the tool from side to side.

Fig 12.35 *Treat one side of the V-tool like a chisel . . .*

Fig 12.36 *. . . then the other (for clarity the oil is not shown)*

197

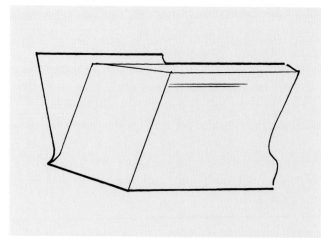

Fig 12.37 *A hook may be left towards the end of sharpening; this is caused by the thicker metal at the angle where the two sides join*

Fig 12.39 *Rounding over the keel of the V-tool by careful rubbing on the benchstone. As always, present the bevel flat and keep checking the edge by its line of light*

6 As the white line attenuates and disappears (Fig 12.34c), a point of light will be left at the apex, probably projecting a little with a hook (Fig 12.37), because the metal is thicker at the junction of the two sides. To remove the hook, turn the Arkansas stone side-on and lay the keel flat on the surface, with the blade at its proper 15–20° cutting angle. Rock the tool, like a gouge, from side to side and very carefully hone the keel until the spot of light has gone (Figs 12.38 and 12.39). Overworking the keel will cause the apex to dip back. Final spots of light can be removed with the slipstone (Fig 12.40).

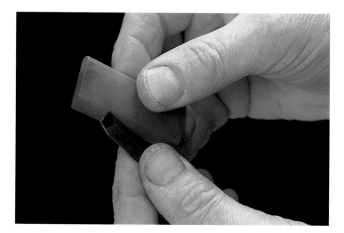

Fig 12.40 *Using an angled slipstone to finish the inside of the V-tool*

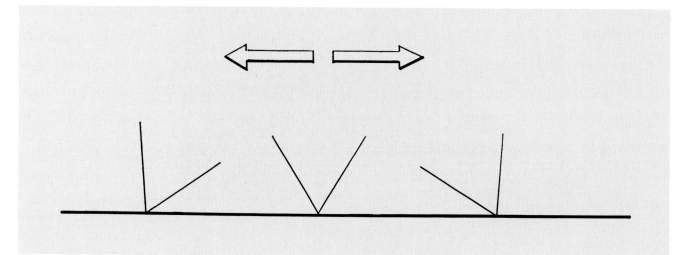

Fig 12.38 *Remove the hook by honing the keel at the correct cutting angle. Keep the keel flat on the stone and check the white line*

Fig 12.41 A specially made V-tool slipstrop. Keep your fingers clear

7 If the V-tool ends up with the edge dipping at the apex, wavy, or in other ways unsuccessfully sharpened, one or two perpendicular strokes of the Arkansas benchstone will cut the edge back and reveal the white light from which to start again.

8 Test the edge by cutting across softwood grain as before; strop inside and out (Fig 12.41) and carefully wipe the blade.

THE KEEL

Now turn the tool upside down to look at the keel; it should be a straight line, of course, but additionally it should be a smooth, narrow line, in line with the axis of the blade. If it is out of line, then the V-tool will tend to veer to one side like a supermarket shopping trolley. This fault is not common, but may arise from uneven wall thickness. A much more common problem, specific to some makers, is a keel which is more of a cone-shape: the point of the cone is at the cutting apex, but as you pass back from the apex the metal thickens.

If you have a narrow keel, you can stop here and enjoy your carving. A conical keel, however, is definitely a problem: its wedge-like shape causes the blade to rise up out of the cut because the radius of the cone is larger than that of the initial groove made by the apex of the V. Shallow cuts require no more effort than with a narrow-keeled V-tool, but it is much harder to sink the conical keel into the wood because it is continually resisting – especially if the metal is thick, or the tool is a large one. The following alteration should bring a very significant improvement:

1 Look again at the conical keel. You will see that there is a pyramidal point on either side at the base of the cone, where the two side walls meet the keel. It is here that you need to remove metal equally on both sides (Fig 12.42).

2 Place these points carefully on a coarse benchstone (or the side of the grindstone) and carefully remove metal, forming a facet at this point. You may find it easier to use the corner or side of the grinding wheel, like a knife. Aim to be neat. Get both sides the same, resulting in a parallel, narrow keel, but *stop short of the cutting edge*, which is already sharp.

3 Quite a lot of metal may need to be drawn back, after which you can merge the facet with the rest of the blade metal on either side.

4 When you have removed the metal and reduced the cones to a narrow keel, check the cut in the wood. Smooth off the facets on the fine stones and make sure the keel is smooth and slightly rounded. Your V-tool should now be ready for use.

Fig 12.42 *Correcting a conical keel: the feel and cutting properties of the V-tool are greatly improved by removing the excess metal in the shaded area*

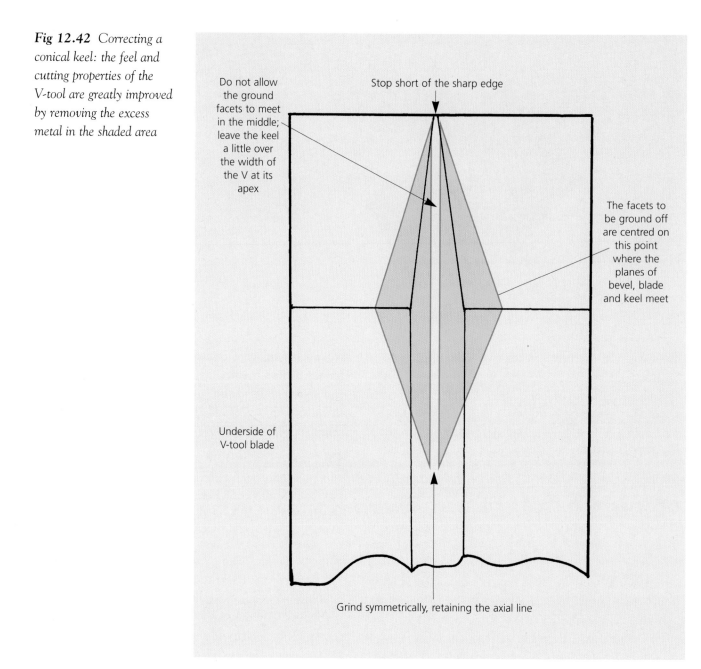

Do not allow the ground facets to meet in the middle; leave the keel a little over the width of the V at its apex

Stop short of the sharp edge

The facets to be ground off are centred on this point where the planes of bevel, blade and keel meet

Underside of V-tool blade

Grind symmetrically, retaining the axial line

Macaroni tools are treated in similar fashion: regard them as three chisels joined at two corners which are very slightly rounded. A matching square-edged slip is needed to work the inside.

BENT CHISELS

Sharpen the edges of bent square-end and skew tools in the same way as the straight versions, but with a main bevel in contact with the wood, and a smaller bevel on the upper side. Although the cutting edge is not absolutely in the centre, it is still thrown towards the middle of the metal. The bent V-tool needs little inside bevel.

The main problem comes in holding these tools so that you can present them to the benchstones correctly. Hold the blade like a pencil to form the main bevel (Fig 12.43). Work the reverse, or upper, bevel by turning the tool over and using the end of the stone (Fig 12.44). Place the stone near the edge of the bench so the tool handle hangs free of the bench surface. A little trial and error may be needed.

Fig 12.43 *A frontbent chisel can be held like a pencil*

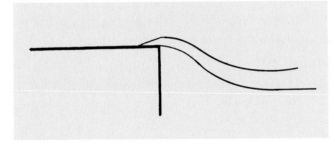

Fig 12.44 *Working the upper surface of a bent chisel*

GOUGES

❶ Grind the cutting edge straight and square, keeping the corners. Leave an even white line of at least ¹⁄₁₆in (2mm), or less if no inside bevel is wanted.

❷ Make one or two perpendicular passes on the Arkansas stone to clean any jaggedness and smooth the white line.

❸ Start by working the inside bevel with a coarse slipstone held at a shallow angle, working it evenly from corner to corner. Do not be afraid of working the inside bevel; aim to throw the cutting edge towards the centre of the blade.

❹ Shape the outside bevel on the grinding wheel.

❺ Position the coarse Carborundum benchstone side-on. Present the bevel flat and sharpen from left to right while rotating the gouge (Fig 12.45), as described on pages 184–7. The amount of

Fig 12.45 *Rotating the gouge from one end of the benchstone to the other. The motion is then repeated in the opposite direction, without lifting the blade from the stone*

rotation will depend on the sweep. Keep an eye on the line of light, reducing its thickness to about ⅓₂in (1mm) (Fig 12.46).

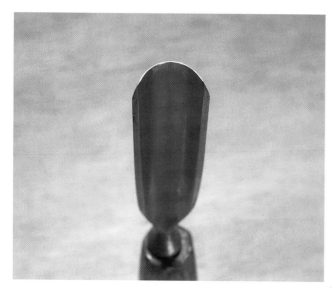

Fig 12.46 *An even and thin line of light is visible when the tool is held at the right angle*

⑥ Go now to the Arkansas benchstone and slipstones. Keeping the bevel flat, work the inside and outside bevels alternately, leaving any part of the edge which is thinner than the rest and specifically removing metal from the thicker parts. Occasionally push the edge into a piece of scrap wood to remove any wire edge.

⑦ As the line starts to attenuate, alternate a few sharpening strokes with pushing the edge into the wood. All the line should disappear more or less at the same time, leaving sharp corners and a straight edge (Fig 12.47).

⑧ Cut some wood across the grain and see how the resulting cut appears. If there are scratches, look for tell-tale spots of light on the cutting edge and remove them with a slip or benchstone as appropriate.

⑨ When a clean, polished cut is produced, strop the inside (Fig 12.48) and outside and carefully wipe the blade.

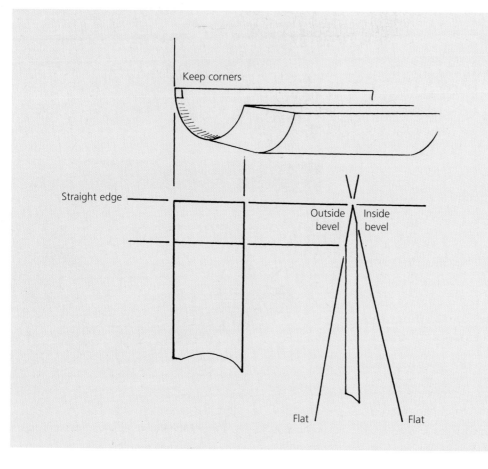

Keep corners

Straight edge

Outside bevel

Inside bevel

Flat

Flat

Fig 12.47 *Features of a correctly sharpened gouge*

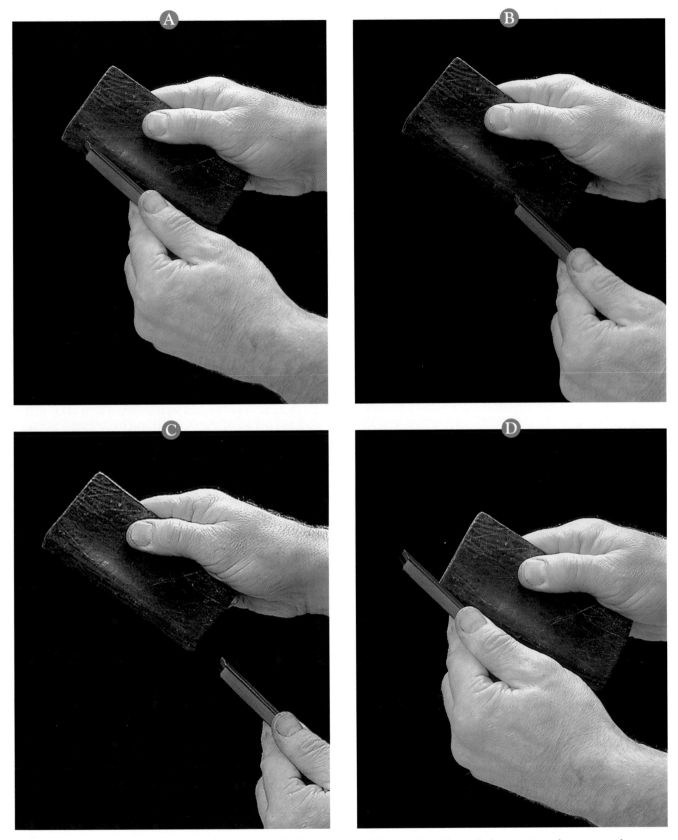

Fig 12.48 *Using the slipstrop: start firmly and push the strop out of the mouth of the tool, keeping it at the same angle. Return through the air for a second forward stroke*

U-SHAPED GOUGES

These are the veiners and fluters: deep flat-sided gouges (nos. 10 and 11). It is helpful to treat them partly as chisels and partly as gouges – a combination of approaches – while being careful to marry the effects of each (Fig 12.49).

After squaring off the end and cleaning the white line on the Arkansas stone, grind one flat side, then the other, then the curve in between. Keep the bevels flat and the edge as a straight line. Sharpen on the benchstones in the usual order, turning the stone from a chisel (end-on) to gouge (side-on) orientation. The slipstone that is used for the inside curve can be slid up and down the sides also.

Keep observing the white line of light, particularly at the juncture of the straight and curved sections, as these points can easily be over-sharpened and made to dip back.

It is quite possible to sharpen U-shaped tools entirely like gouges, rotating them fully 180° at the wrist, but be careful not to lose the corners by over-rotating from the flat sides.

LONGBENT AND SHORTBENT GOUGES

Treat these tools in the same way as the parallel-sided gouges, but use the slipstones only to remove the burr from the inside edge (Fig 12.50), not to form an inside bevel – which is not a particular advantage here. Only a small part of the slipstone can be used; otherwise it will foul on the bend in the shank (Fig 12.51).

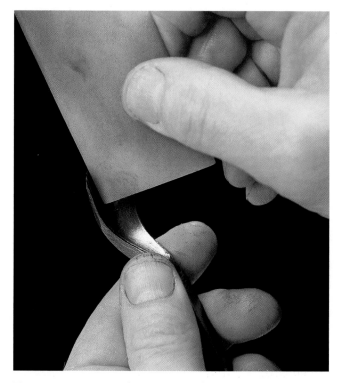

Fig 12.50 *Using a slip to remove the burr on the inside edge of a frontbent gouge*

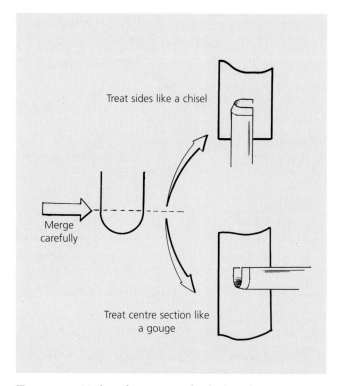

Treat sides like a chisel

Merge carefully

Treat centre section like a gouge

Fig 12.49 *U-shaped gouges can be dealt with as if they were a combination of chisel and gouge*

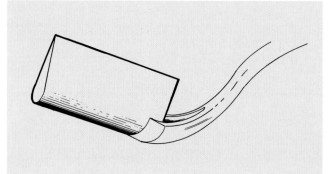

Fig 12.51 *Only the end of the slipstone can be used with a shortbent tool, as it fouls the crank*

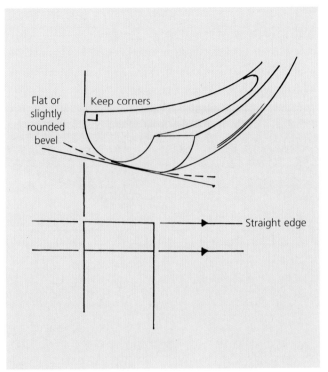

Flat or slightly rounded bevel

Keep corners

Straight edge

Fig 12.52 *Features of a correctly sharpened bent gouge – in this case a shortbent. Longbent gouges have the same requirements*

The bevel tends to be shorter and stronger on these tools, as they are subject to a lot of stress across the cutting edge, which therefore needs to be strong. The bevels tend to merge with the heel, and a slight rounding is permissible. Keep the corners (Fig 12.52).

The main problem is in holding these odd-shaped tools satisfactorily so that you can present them correctly to the grinding wheel or benchstones. Some experiment is needed to keep the bevel flat, as the handles will swing in quite a wide arc when the blade is rolling from side to side (Fig 12.53).

These tools can also be held in a vice and the flat side of a slipstone used on them, like a file.

BACKBENT GOUGES

These tools can mostly be sharpened with appropriate slipstones (Fig 12.54). Start as usual by flattening and straightening the cutting edge on the Arkansas benchstone. Place the benchstone side-on near the edge of the bench so that the handle of the gouge can hang free of the bench surface. Present the outer

Fig 12.53 *The pattern of sharpening the outside bevel of a frontbent gouge is the same as for a straight one, except that presenting the tool is a little more awkward. (For clarity the oil is not shown)*

205

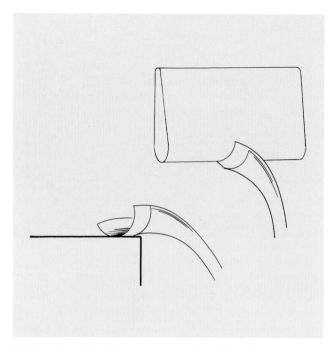

Fig 12.54 *A backbent gouge can largely be sharpened by slipstoning, cleaning the outer bevel on the benchstone*

bevel to the stone (Fig 12.55), clean up and continue to sharpen like a straight gouge. Keep the corners, and keep the outer bevel flat.

Work as much in-cannel with the slipstones (Fig 12.56) as outside with the benchstones, reducing the white line of light until it disappears. The inner surface wants to merge smoothly with the cannel, without any distinct bevel.

When stropping, only short strokes can be made, with the strop at the edge of the bench, if the outer bevel is to be kept flat. To make longer strokes you would have to lift the handle to clear the leather, which would roll the cutting edge.

Fig 12.56 *Slipstones are used with the benchstone to sharpen a backbent gouge*

Fig 12.55 *The handle of the backbent must be lower than the benchstone; bring the stone forward to the edge of the bench to allow for this*

TAPERED TOOLS

Long- and short-pod, spade, allongee or fishtail tools present no problems that are not encountered in the parallel-sided versions. As they tend to have lighter, thinner or more delicate blades, it is easier to over-grind or over-sharpen them, so a little more care is needed, especially on the corners. I would suggest you do not use the grinding wheel at all, but start with the coarse benchstone and slipstones. The bevels tend to be longer, for delicate finishing cuts, and often merge into the main shank without a noticeable bevel.

<h2 style="text-align:center">TESTING FOR SHARPNESS</h2>

There must be something of the cavalier in carvers who evaluate, or demonstrate, the sharpness of a woodcarving tool by shaving hairs from the back of their forearm, or nicking their nails. Presumably they scythe through a lot of body hair when a large number of tools need sharpening.

At the end of the day it is wood that is being carved – and very different types of wood – so it makes more sense to test the cutting quality on spare pieces of wood put aside for this purpose.

Slicing across the grain with a sharp edge will leave a clean, polished cut with no scratch marks; the tool will cut at a low presentation angle and move easily – it may even make a happy 'ssssp' noise.

Running a close series of grooves side by side is an excellent test (Fig 12.57). Assuming the wood is good, the ridges left between the grooves should remain clean and intact. If these ridges crumble or the edges of the cuts are torn; if the cuts contain scratch marks or ragged trails; if the cuts are dull or the cutting seems unduly hard work for the wood – some more sharpening is needed.

- Look at the line of light, with a magnifying glass if necessary, for telltale spots of white.

- Look at the profile of the bevel itself to see if it is rounded or 'rolled'.

<h2 style="text-align:center">MAINTAINING SHARPNESS</h2>

You could look at this the other way and ask: why do edges lose their sharpness? Given good-quality steel and tempering, there are several reasons:

- Most beginners wait too long before brightening the cut of their carving tools, and thereby make more work for themselves than need be.

- Tools can suffer from poor cutting technique.

- They may be stored badly.

- There is also the effect of the wood being carved.

Here are some guidelines to help keep tools sharp.

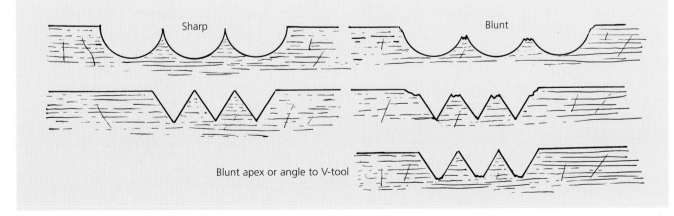

Fig 12.57 *Running grooves together in medium-density carving wood is a good way to check the sharpness of the edge*

STROPPING

- Never let woodcarving tools get into a really dull state – strop them as soon as loss of keenness is felt.

- Keep the strops on the bench, in their correct place, along with the working tools.

- Get into the habit of stropping the tools regularly. The tools become polished and bright, and this in itself eases them though the wood.

- Strop correctly, keeping the bevel flat and not rolling the edge.

Stropping a blade over a period of time gives rise to another effect which you need to be aware of. The leather of a benchstrop is only firm, not rigid like the oilstones. It 'gives' under the bevel moving along it, curling back to shape when the edge has passed. This flexing of the strop tends to roll the edge and round over the bevel (Fig 12.58). However, as the cut of the strop is very fine, the effect is only noticeable after a prolonged period of stropping. Even then, this rounding is not so easily seen, as the bevel becomes highly polished (Fig 12.59). It may escape a carver's notice

that the tool is gradually becoming harder work, or the cutting angle a little steeper – the effects of a rounded bevel. I find I notice the effect after not using a tool for a while. There is a sense of having less control of the tool; I then take a look at the flatness of the bevel.

When a gouge has been used for some time and stropped regularly to keep it keen, try setting the bevel flat on the Arkansas stone, at the original angle, and making a small, sideways movement. The

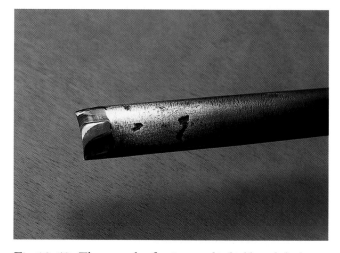

Fig 12.59 *The curved reflection on this highly polished surface is a clue that the bevel has become rounded*

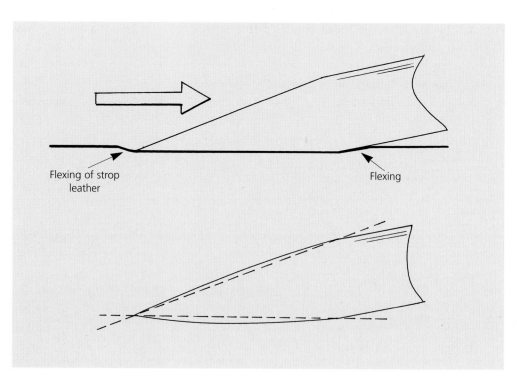

Flexing of strop leather

Flexing

Fig 12.58 *After a substantial amount of stropping, the bevel starts to become rolled, because even hard leather flexes before and after the edge is passed over it. A power honing wheel may produce a similar effect, and more quickly*

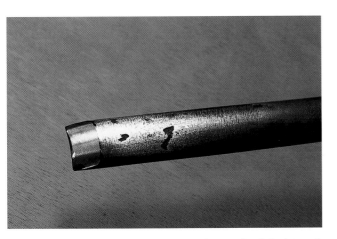

Fig 12.60 *The 'candle' effect: a final rim of polished metal towards the edge. The duller, honed surface creeps towards it as the bevel is flattened. The corners and straightness of the cutting edge will need checking over too*

appearance of a dull point of abrasion in the middle of the bevel, contrasting with the highly polished metal, indicates the bevel is rounded. A chisel can be tested similarly.

Resharpen the blade in the normal way and you will see that the initial dull point of abrasion becomes a line; it then quickly spreads over the shiny bevel towards the heel and the edge as the bevel flattens. Eventually there is only a rim of shiny metal at the very edge which has not, as yet, touched the stone. This bright margin is traditionally called the **candle** (Fig 12.60). Do not be tempted to lift the handle to get rid of it quickly, but carry on with the bevel flat. Stop when the candle is put out, but be careful not to over-sharpen. Begin the cycle of stropping again.

CARVING TECHNIQUE

Tools also become blunt and damaged as much through bad carving practice as failing to strop. Tools should be used to *cut* the wood properly – prising or levering is not cutting, and will only damage the edge of the blade.

- Do not drag the cutting edge across the wood, but enter and leave the cut cleanly.

- Do not use the blade to lever or prise wood chips away. Cut the tool in, cut it through and cut it out.

- If a gouge gets buried in the wood, try *gently* moving the tool from side to side – *along* the cutting edge, not against it. This is not a good idea with quick gouges. If such gentle persuasion does not work, another tool is needed to carefully remove wood from the sides of the embedded gouge.

- U-shaped gouges are vulnerable to cracking when they are forced too deeply into wood. Pressure on the bevels squeezes the two sides together. Never compel these veiners or fluters to cut too much, or too deeply, at once.

STORAGE AND CARE

Care is largely a matter of habit. Start with good-quality tools, then:

- Avoid damaging the edges, by using the bench discipline suggested in Chapter 7 (pages 111–13).

- Suggestions for careful storage are made in Chapter 7 (pages 107–10). Check the edges before putting the tools away in the condition you would ideally wish to find them in (Fig 12.61).

- Some carvers, when they get to the finishing stages of a carving, have a session of checking every edge for perfect sharpness and touching up

Fig 12.61 *The notch in the edge of this gouge should be dealt with before putting it away*

any scratch marks they may have let ride in the rough stages of carving. Odd scratch marks may be acceptable where a surface will be sanded or overcut to finish, but not where the naked cuts are left to be seen.

EFFECT OF THE WOOD BEING CARVED

- Some woods (such as teak and some mahoganies) contain calcium deposits that dull edges. If this is happening, there is nothing to do but carry on and have a final sharpening session before making the finishing cuts.

- Particles of abrasive remaining in a sanded surface will also take the keenness off an edge, so avoid sanding parts that will be carved later. This applies especially to carving turned work, most of which is sanded on the lathe.

- Remember that different woods require different strengths of bevel. If a cutting edge is tending to break up, it probably means the bevel is too long.

PRE-SHARPENED TOOLS

Most carving tools are bought by the increasing numbers of people wishing to carve as a leisure activity.

Understandably, they want to get into the wood straight away, without having to sharpen the tools first. Tools catering for this market are available today. At best, their bevels are set at what seems to be a good average angle, but in some cases the angle might just be what the operative felt like that Friday afternoon; 'ready sharpened' most often means the simple expedient of polishing in a secondary (micro-) bevel. They may be sharpened by an automatic process or with some degree of hand skill, but they never have inner bevels and are most often shiny and polished.

In my experience, however, there is an intrinsic problem with these ready-sharpened tools. It is not a matter of the steel, the tempering or the overall shaping of the tool – all of which may be excellent – but the strength of the edge left by the sharpening process itself.

Certainly a pre-sharpened edge looks sharp – but start carving and it will be noticed that the initial, shiny cut quickly breaks down to leave trails of scratches. When a blade is sharpened on grinding and buffing wheels which drag the metal *forwards* – away from the cutting edge – a microscopic feathering of the crystal edge is produced. This is weaker, or less supported, than when the metal has been drawn back from the edge – towards the handle – or sharpened across it (see Fig 12.1). After a short while the cut surface is left with lots of little scratches, which is entirely unsatisfactory for a finish straight from the edge.

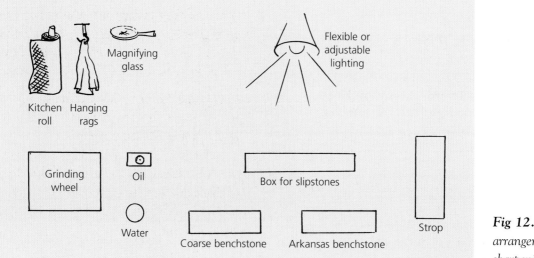

Fig 12.62 *A possible arrangement for a sharpening area*

Once these tools have been resharpened, using the normal honing methods, the problem vanishes and the quality of the tool can show itself. So this is a point to bear in mind if you are coming new to woodcarving: by all means start with a pre-sharpened edge, but make it your business to find out how to sharpen and maintain the edges properly, rather than just expediently.

THE SHARPENING AREA

Time spent on sharpening is never wasted, but contributes directly to the quality of the woodcarving as well as the enjoyment of carving itself. Ways and routines of keeping carving tools keen are worth cultivating. If there is room in the workplace, there are many benefits in setting up a permanent area near the bench specifically for sharpening woodcarving tools. The area set aside need not be very large: just enough room to work comfortably and leave important items for sharpening ready to hand. The space warrants good lighting, perhaps its own adjustable light. The grinder, with its cooling water, can be part of the arrangement, or nearby and quickly accessible. The benchstones can be laid out next to the oil; slipstones conveniently placed; and oil, stropping paste, kitchen paper and rags handy (Fig 12.62). Strops are normally kept on the carving bench next to the working tools.

Another option is a pull-out drawer or ledge – perhaps fitted to the bench – in which the sharpening stones are placed. This is not such a good arrangement, as wood chips and dust will always find their way in.

Having the sharpening and carving areas separate helps keep dust and wood chips from one, and oil and dirt from the other. Instead of getting out the benchstones each time they are needed, they are simply waiting to be turned to.

Make the sharpening area pleasant; see it as part of your whole work, and keep it clean. The idea is to make the means of sharpening woodcarving tools so easy that sharpening becomes no bother whatsoever – and carving itself benefits.

SUMMARY

- One aim of this chapter has been to instil self-reliance by providing a repertoire of techniques to deal with all shapes and states of carving tools, enabling them to be turned into exactly what you need to achieve the best work.

- In this chapter and the preceding ones we looked at some fundamental ideas about 'sharpness'; what features contribute to this end; the necessary equipment and its correct use; how to go about sharpening tools in detail; and, finally, how to retain sharpness.

- It was pointed out that sharpening is a precise skill, but well within the capabilities of someone who has the manual dexterity and the desire to carve in the first place. With the correct approach, the skills of sharpening woodcarving tools can be developed rapidly to an almost instinctual level.

- Like any skill worth acquiring, it does take practice. It often involves learning by mistakes and by trying to improve the performance of a tool every time it needs sharpening or touching up. It is not that you cannot carve until you have perfected the skill of sharpening, but by always seeking to improve, doing the best you can and trying for a little better next time, the sharpening will soon become second nature.

- The sharpening practices of individual carvers vary, with 'grey' areas where opinions differ. What matters is the experience any carver is having of the way a carving tool is cutting, and how this fits with the actual carving process. Both the final carving and the process of achieving it matter to the carver.

CHAPTER THIRTEEN

ALTERNATIVE SHARPENING STONES

AIMS

- To describe and assess the other main types of sharpening stone currently available for use instead of or in combination with traditional oilstones

There are three types of sharpening stone which are readily available and may be considered as alternatives to the Arkansas-based oilstone set-up described in the previous chapters. They are:

- waterstones

- diamond stones

- ceramic stones.

WATERSTONES

Waterstones have been steadily gaining popularity with general woodworkers as an alternative to other benchstones since the 1980s. Many such woodworkers naturally wonder whether the ones they have are suitable for a new interest in woodcarving.

Waterstones have the appearance of smooth bricks, and this is essentially what they are: bricks or blocks of quick-cutting abrasive, employed in a wash of water (Fig 13.1). Originally a natural stone from Japan was used, but the readily available waterstones of today are predominately synthetic (and still Japanese). Modern synthetic waterstones are strikingly

cheaper than natural ones, and of consistent quality. Understanding how these stones work will help you to appreciate why they are known for their remarkably fast cut but quick wear, and how they must be used and looked after.

Fig 13.1 *A basic set of waterstones: a combination stone lying on a polishing stone (mounted on a plastic base), and some water slipstones*

All sharpening stones (with the exception of ceramic stones; see pages 222–4) consist of sharp abrasive particles or crystals, which do the cutting, and another substance which bonds these particles together. In the case of waterstones, the bonding matter is soft and friable; it breaks down as the steel blade rubs over it. The outcome is twofold: firstly, new, and sharp, abrasive particles are constantly appearing at the surface as old material sloughs away; and, secondly, the surface erodes quickly.

An opposite scenario would be a very resistant bond, as in polycrystalline diamond and ceramic stones. In this case the abrasive particles would not be replaced at the surface and would eventually dull – although this might take a very long time – causing the stone to lose its cutting properties.

All stones offer a balance between these two properties of sharpness and durability. Waterstones have a soft binding and constantly present fresh abrasive particles. In effect, the sharpness of the stone never slows down because the abrasive particles never have a chance to become dull. Hence the fast, and maintained, speed of sharpening – and the need to have water sloshing around to remove the debris and expose new 'teeth'.

When you sharpen with a waterstone you see a rapid build-up of slurry; this needs washing away regularly. Indeed, these stones need so much water that some are actually kept in it.

Waterstones erode quickly: narrow or small carving tools can rapidly create grooves in the surface. This is not a small problem. A flat bevel requires a flat sharpening surface with which to work. However, as these stones are quite broad, there's a lot of surface to play with before you need to flatten them and, since the stones are soft, flattening is a much quicker process than with oilstones such as Arkansas.

TYPES OF WATERSTONE

There are several firms producing waterstones, which fall into two categories:

VITREOUS BONDED WATERSTONES

These make up the coarser grits of stone: 250–1200 grit. The particles (often silicon carbide) are first sieved and graded like sandpaper, then bonded in a clay matrix; the resulting block is open-pored and friable. Such stones are usually left in water ready for use.

- The 250 grit is a coarse stone, roughly equivalent to a medium Carborundum stone, but cutting much faster.

- The 800 grit is called a 'medium' stone, relative to the coarse 250; it is equivalent to a Washita or softer Arkansas stone.

- The 1200 grit is finer again – comparable to a white Arkansas – but not fine enough for a cutting edge which can produce a polished finish.

RESIN-BONDED WATERSTONES

These are classified as 'fine' or **polishing stones**: 4000–8000 grit. They are much harder than the vitreous bonded stones.

Extremely fine particles of aluminium oxide are separated by forced air, bonded in resin and mounted on a base. Being less porous, these stones are not usually immersed and only need a sprinkle of water to flush the debris away.

There is quite a jump in grits from 1200 to 4000. A translucent Arkansas would be somewhere in the region of 4000, so the 6000-grit waterstone is approaching the very fine black Arkansas which, to my mind, cuts too slowly to be of much use. However, grit comparison is a teacherous area: the cutting 'feel' of these stones is quite different from that of Arkansas stones. Some carvers do continue with the 6000, after which no stropping should be needed.

Some combination stones are available: 250 with 1200, for example. Waterstones tend to be full size, at least 8in (200mm) long, and they are available at an extra-wide 2½in (64mm); this size is designed for plane irons, but may be attractive to carvers for the amount of surface which can be used before the stone needs to be flattened.

WATER SLIPSTONES

At the moment, water slipstones come in limited, larger sizes and a sporadic range of grits. However, they are becoming more readily obtainable, and in a wider range of profiles, as manufacturers begin to appreciate the needs of woodcarvers. Study different tool suppliers' catalogues to see what is available. You may well need a few oil-based or other slipstones to create inside bevels on smaller tools, or you may prefer to use the waterstones just to finish off.

Water slipstones must be kept in (and used with) water in the manner of water benchstones.

Because the slips are as quick-wearing as other waterstones – and have delicate corners and edges – creating and keeping a fine angle for the inside of the V-tool is deft work. On the other hand, the softness of the waterstone material makes it readily possible to shape slipstones to suit a particular cannel, using files, wet-and-dry paper or diamond stones.

A STARTER KIT

The widest benchstone gives you plenty of surface with which to sharpen smaller carving tools before you need to flatten the stone. Synthetic stones are excellent. Probably the best for the newcomer is to try:

- 250/1000 grit combination stone to do most of the shaping (these tend to be narrower, at 2in/50mm)

- 6000 grit for finishing.

This would give you a good range of grits to play with.

If you find you like using waterstones, then move on to full-sized, single-grit stones, which can be used on *both* sides before the need to flatten becomes unavoidable.

You will also need:

- a water trough, bucket or tub, such as a plastic food container, to store the waterstones (some firms make special trough and holder combinations or 'ponds' that are well worth considering)

- non-slip carpet underlay, towelling or rubber to grip the stones, if you are not using a holder; the stone is placed on a little 'mat' of such material on a plastic tray, or partially immersed in a shallow trough

- a squeezable bottle for rinsing the stones as you use them

- a means of periodically flattening their surfaces.

CARE AND MAINTENANCE

There are two aspects of waterstones that need to be considered in detail:

STORAGE

Stones below 1200 grit should be kept immersed in water, or at least soaked for a couple of hours before you use them. Indeed, when you buy a new waterstone you should leave it soaking overnight to prime it. It is not essential to immerse the stone fully; capillary action will keep the material saturated.

It is also not necessary – and usually not recommended – to immerse the polishing stones (6000 grit and upwards) in water. You *can* leave the harder polishing stones upside down in a shallow container of water, leaving any mounting block or base clear. Being harder and far less porous than the coarser stones, just a sprinkle or squirt of water is all that is needed to remove the working slurry.

Slipstones are stored in similar fashion.

Many users just dump all their stones upright in a bucket or a lidded plastic tub, and take them out for use; but do bear in mind that these stones are brittle, so be careful not to bump them against each other: you will easily knock bits off.

If the base comes away from the harder stones, allow both parts to dry and refix with mastic or caulk.

Lastly, never allow the water in which they are stored to freeze. The freezing water will expand within the stone and crack it. And don't be tempted by antifreeze, which can dissolve the binding resins in the stone.

FLATTENING WORN STONES

This is your principal maintenance work. It is needed far more often than with oilstones, but is done in similar fashion and a lot quicker. Try to do it *before* it becomes a major problem – say, when there is a dip of no more than 1⁄16in (1.5mm).

Don't think of it as a chore. Use those moments when you leave your carving for a break, reflective thought, or to brew up. Have whatever flattening system you use readily to hand. Resurfacing is actually quite a quick operation once you get the hang of it.

You can flatten a stone either wet or dry. However, flattening dry is a dusty process.

You can buy special flattening stones with an alumina titanium coating of about 100 grit, but there are many alternative stones which will do this job very well and quite quickly: for example, diamond lapping plates or benchstones, even another waterstone. Use plenty of water to keep clearing away the slurry.

A simple alternative is to stick wet-and-dry silicon-carbide abrasive paper to a sheet of thick glass and rub the stone in a wash of water. Match the abrasive – at least for the final finishing off – to the grit of the stone: 120 grit for the coarsest stone, 220 for the middle range and 400 for the polishing stones.

You can use files, benchstones and abrasive paper to reshape water slipstones.

SETTING UP

It's a matter of minimizing the mess. Because of the amount of water needed, and the ease with which water migrates, *you had best keep the waterstone sharpening area well away from where you are carving.* So you will need a place to keep the stones – say a lidded plastic tub – and a place to do the sharpening.

The sharpening surface may be the lid of the tub itself; a tray, or similar; or a shallower plastic tub that allows the stone to sit partially immersed in water, which you then wash over with your fingers or the blade to rinse off the slurry.

You will need your plastic bottle, or similar. Include your flattening system in your layout, ready to use when needed. Keep towels, paper or otherwise, always to hand.

USING WATERSTONES

The sharpening positions and orientations are the same as you would adopt with any benchstone.

① Take whichever benchstone you need from the water where it is stored. Place the stone on the piece of non-slip rubber or carpet underlay, or in a waterstone holder that is sitting on its tray. If you don't have these, several layers of kitchen paper will do.

② Use the stone as you would an oilstone. Try to make use of the whole surface as much as possible, to minimize the creation of grooves – flat bevels need flat surfaces.

③ Rinse the slurry from the waterstone as soon as it builds up to the point where it is starting to cover the cutting edge, either with a wash from the surrounding water or with a squirt from your plastic bottle. This helps reveal the new, sharp cutting crystals.

④ When you are ready to move on to a finer stone, ease off the pressure on the blade and work more with the slurry. This means less abrasive working on the metal, which results in a smoother bevel surface and less work on the subsequent, finer-grit stone.

⑤ Return the stones to store when you have finished with them.

⑥ If you stop at the 1200 grit, then you will need an aggressive strop paste (or a power strop) to achieve that final keen edge necessary for leaving work straight from the chisel.

PROS AND CONS OF WATERSTONES

I confess to having been a little unhappy with waterstones in the past. I disliked having to keep them soaking in readiness, and preferred not to have water anywhere near the steel of my carving tools anyway (I feel that oil is actually 'good for them'). The unavailability of smaller slipstones, and intermediate grit sizes, may be an inconvenience. Also, waterstones wear quickly, and flattening them can be messy. However, if you have them already, then you will probably have come to terms with these aspects, and with the balance between fast cutting and fast wear.

On the positive side, compared with Arkansas stones, waterstones (at least the synthetic ones) are inexpensive and very consistent in structure.

The rinsing fluid is cheap, clean and easily available. Waterstones cut quickly – in fact they are famed for their speed advantage over oilstones – and you can successfully sharpen carving tools to an appropriate cutting edge using only the 1200 grit and a good strop.

As with all sharpening systems, you must find a pattern of using and maintaining them which suits both you and your carving tools.

DIAMOND STONES

Diamond is, quite simply, the hardest of all materials. It will cut any type of steel – high-carbon, tungsten, carbide, vanadium, whatever – and it will also cut any other sharpening stone for the purposes of flattening or reshaping.

A lot of poor-quality diamond, called *bort*, is produced by the mining of gemstone diamonds. For a long time bort has found industrial uses in cutting wheels, for example, but it has always been expensive. Over the last 30 years or so, two processes have been developed to create artificial diamonds, at more accessible cost:

- The Du Pont process imitates the tremendous heat and pressure of nature to create a **polycrystalline** diamond.

- A completely different process, developed by General Electric, grows a **monocrystalline** diamond.

Poly- and monocrystalline diamonds have quite distinct properties and, thus, uses.

Both types of diamond are graded by particle size, or grit, in a similar way to other abrasives. These abrasive particles must be held together in a matrix with another bonding substance to make benchstones or plates. Different manufacturers supply different ranges of grit; some specialize in one type of diamond or the other. Although monocrystalline diamond is generally seen as the best option, *both* types of diamond are used, in a bonded form, for sharpening stones.

TYPES OF DIAMOND STONE

MONOCRYSTALLINE DIAMONDS ('MONO-DIAMOND')

This type of diamond crystal is more like a natural diamond than the polycrystalline: single and uniform in structure, it does not break or fracture easily. Monocrystalline diamonds are more expensive, and are the commonest type for sharpening stones.

Monocrystalline diamonds of a uniform size (grit) are permanently bonded into perforations in a nickel plate, leaving about one third of the abrasive exposed (Fig 13.2). In turn this nickel plate is backed

Fig 13.2 A *monocrystalline diamond benchstone mounted on its stand*

216

by a steel one, and finally moulded to a glass-fibre polycarbonate. The result is very strong; the whole unit is virtually unbreakable.

Benchstones are conventionally shaped, but with the diamond abrasive residing in a pattern of 'islands' which you can easily feel if you run your fingers over the surface (Fig 13.3). The debris from sharpening ends up in the spaces between these projecting islands, which eliminates the possibility of clogging. The downside is that the sharpening of small or narrow tools is difficult and, in some instances, may be impossible: the narrow edges snag and bump over the islands.

The principal manufacturer is DMT (Diamond Machining Technology), who offer 4 grits, with a colour coding:

- *Extra-coarse* (black): 220 grit, roughly equivalent to a medium-grit oilstone

- *Coarse* (blue): 325 grit, similar to a fine oilstone

- *Fine* (red): 600 grit, similar to a coarse Washita or soft white Arkansas stone

- *Extra-fine* (green): 1200 grit, similar to hard white Arkansas or the equivalent Japanese waterstone.

In general, diamonds are much quicker-cutting than the equivalent oilstone; but the finest grit does not approach my benchmark of the translucent Arkansas stone (around 4000 grit).

Benchstone sizes tend to be larger than common oilstones, and they are used dry or with a wash of water.

POLYCRYSTALLINE DIAMONDS ('POLY-DIAMOND')

The diamond crystal in this case is multifaceted – more like fused clusters of tiny diamonds – and tends to fracture easily into finer abrasive particles. In fracturing, new cutting facets are revealed. As the bonding agent is hard (unlike waterstones), these crystals do develop a less aggressive cut with time.

Polycrystalline diamonds are mostly used in lapping compounds, and are made into **lapping plates** used for flattening other stones. However, these lapping plates are also marketed as sharpening aids for woodworkers, and are sometimes described as 'honing stones'. I intend to use the term **benchplates** to differentiate the flat, uniform, plate-like shape in which these polycrystalline diamonds are set (Fig 13.4) from the deeper, more conventional-looking benchstone, with its islands of monocrystalline diamond, just described.

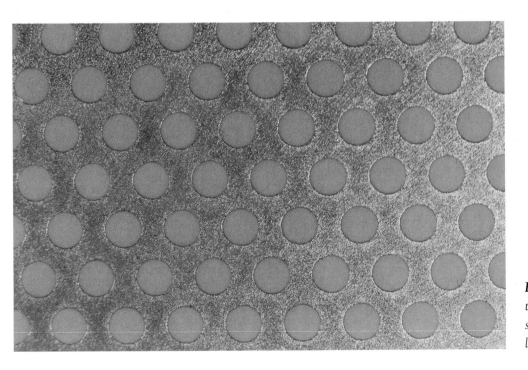

Fig 13.3 *A close-up of the diamond benchstone shows the diamonds in the little islands*

217

Fig 13.4 *Polycrystalline diamond benchplates with their protective leather pouches*

Benchplates or lapping plates are generally wider and longer than benchstones. In them, polycrystalline diamonds are nickel-bonded to a precision-ground steel backing plate (Fig 13.5). There are a lot more diamonds per square inch than in the monocrystalline type, and the working 'feel' and properties are different. For one thing, polycrystalline diamonds

Fig 13.5 *Close-up of a polycrystalline diamond surface showing the tiny cutting crystals*

break down to reveal new cutting facets. A new plate will wear in ('run in') from an initial forceful cut to a working level that remains more or less steady through its useful life. Eventually the cutting action dulls as the diamonds are worn away and the backing plate is reached. They cannot, of course, be 'freshened' by lapping. Nevertheless, given careful use, these diamond plates will still last a long time.

Eze-Lap is the principal manufacturer, offering three grits:

- *Medium*: 270 grit, similar to a fine oilstone

- *Fine*: 600 grit, similar to a coarse Washita or soft white Arkansas stone

- *Extra-fine*: 1200 grit, similar to a medium-grit oilstone.

Again, the 1200 is not good enough, to my mind, for sharpening a carving tool to an edge that will leave polished facets straight from the cut. Further work will be needed, and this can be done with a good strop.

Fig 13.6 *A set of conical diamond slipstones*

DIAMOND SLIPSTONES

The 'island' style of monocrystalline diamond setting does not suit curved surfaces or sharp angles such as are found on slipstones, so the appearance of all diamond slipstones is smooth, more like that of the benchplate or lapping plate.

Instead of the usual parallel-sided profiles, diamond slipstones are made in conical shapes. Although called 'cones', they are really half-cones, split longitudinally; I'll use the terms synonymously here. Small holes at each end allow the half-cones to be pinned to a board. A set of three fine (600-grit) cones is available (Fig 13.6) If you intend to use diamond stones alone, then you will need this collection to deal with a wide range of carving tools. Some narrow cones sold as 'knife sharpeners' come in coarse, fine and extra-fine grits; small 'files' are also available.

WHICH STONES TO USE

Whether benchstones or plates, the broadest and longest will be the most useful option in the long run.

The 1200 is the finest grit available, so this must be your finishing stone; but, really, if you want to leave surfaces straight from the chisel, it is not fine enough (the translucent Arkansas is around 4000), so further work is needed. The best plan I have found is to couple this stone with a strop and aggressive paste, or a power hone (power strop), which will produce the edge you need quite quickly (the same applies to ceramic stones). But do remember to keep the bevel flat and bear in mind all the other general points about sharpening.

Coarser stones will be suitable for the preliminary shaping of bevels. Fine (600-grit) conical slipstones are quick-cutting, and the set is worth having if you intend working with diamond.

Remember, one of the additional and valuable uses you have from these stones is the rapid flattening, dressing or freshening of other stones. Indeed, some carvers have diamond stones in their kits just for this purpose.

CARE AND MAINTENANCE

The construction of diamond benchstones and plates makes them virtually indestructible, except that the steel content, not being stainless, is subject to rust. As water may be used to lay the dust, there is the risk of rust spotting with prolonged contact. This does not really affect their sharpening properties, but one consequence is that any guarantee you have with the manufacturers will be invalidated if rust is present, as the stones or plates will be deemed to have been misused. So, when you have finished with a diamond benchstone or plate:

- Rinse (scrub out) the debris under a tap.

- Dry it well.

- Store it in a dry place.

You can freshen the appearance of diamond benchstones by rubbing with a plastic eraser (one you don't mind having a little shorter).

The surface plate around the diamond in the monocrystalline diamond 'islands' is nickel. This will be softer than the steel of the carving tool you want to sharpen. Take care that small tools, or those with sharp points, do not cut the nickel. This is an added reason why sharpening small tools is tricky.

To help minimize the wear on a polycrystalline benchplate:

- Don't use them for heavy metal removal, or drag the edge along with the tool vertical to square it off. Use the grinder instead.

- Don't press down too hard, particularly with narrow blades.

- Spread the work around the plate; keep the centre for wider blades and the outer areas for narrow ones.

SETTING UP

Diamond benchstones and plates take their place in your sharpening routine as any other benchstone. Tack the conical slipstones in a row to a board. Pinched-off panel pins beneath this board, as before, allow you to turn it around to approach the cones from either direction.

If you choose to use the stones wet – and I do recommend this – then you will need a squeezable bottle of water to hand; and keep some paper towels for mopping and cleaning up.

USING DIAMOND STONES

If you sharpen with the diamond stones *dry*, the debris collects around the pores of plates or between the 'islands' in benchstones. This fine dust from sharpening tends to get on your hands and migrate to your carving. Wipe it off regularly and *never blow the dust away* – it might get in your eyes. I prefer using these stones with water, from a plastic bottle or flower mister. This eliminates migrating dust and gives a slightly sharper cut.

Not everyone likes the bumpy feeling as the blade passes over the little islands in the monocrystalline benchstones, but this is a matter of experience and you can get used to it. Polycrystalline benchplates feel more like a normal oilstone of the equivalent grit, but somewhat sharper.

WORKING WITH THE CONICAL SLIPSTONES

A conical shape – and you can find this shape in oil slipstones as well – will deal with quite a range of cannels. The trick is to select that section of the cone that is suitable for a particular inside bevel. If you concentrate on a part of the cone that is too narrow, you run the risk of creating a groove or thin spot in the cutting edge. On the other hand, pick a part of the cone that is too wide and you are in danger of losing the corners of the edge. Getting the right balance takes a little practice, and the method I use with these half-cones is somewhat different from the conventional slipstones:

❶ Have the half-cones fixed to a sharpening board – it is important they don't move. Keep a little pot of water next to it.

❷ Orientate the cones end-on. I prefer the narrow end towards me, but try both ways.

❸ Dip the tip of your gouge in the water.

❹ Place the inside curve of the gouge (the cannel) on that part of the cone's surface which you estimate is *halfway* between the point where the width of the stone is too wide and the point where it is too narrow.

5 Rub the gouge back and forth a little. You will see a black line of water on the cone; this is metal debris from the cutting action of the diamonds (Fig 13.7).

6 Look at the gouge and you will see scratch marks where metal has been abraded. You may need to adjust the angle at which you are offering the blade to the cone to get the right degree of inside bevel.

7 Dip the blade again and, back at the cone, extend your black line both ways along the

Fig 13.7 *Start in the middle of the sweep, gauging where you are from the trail of black metal debris in the water on the cone surface*

Fig 13.8 *Go no further than the width of the edge, or you will lose the corners*

cone. It will also broaden. At some point you will see the sides of the black line approaching the tool corners; you have now reached the widest point and should go no further (Fig 13.8).

8 Keep looking at the black water on the cone and checking the scratch marks in-cannel. You will see that the cone produces a beautifully smooth inner bevel quite quickly.

9 With flatter gouges, work across the blade as well as backwards and forwards. If you skew the angle of presentation to the cone, you will cover a broader surface.

These diamond cones are excellent for getting a good, uniform amount of inside bevel to a gouge, whatever other stones you go on to sharpen the gouge with.

STROPPING

To get the final edge with either type of diamond stone, more work with a finer abrasive is needed. The best way I have found is either to use conventional stropping with an aggressive dressing, or a hard buffing wheel (see page 229).

PROS AND CONS OF DIAMOND STONES

All diamond stones are fast-cutting – faster than oilstones of the same grit – because of the aggressive arrangement of the crystals. However, the grits that in my opinion are needed to give a final cutting edge to woodcarving tools are missing. This is not a problem for normal woodworking, where the cut surfaces will be sanded or concealed inside joints; but for carving you need to hone (polish) the inside and outside bevels, and the cutting edge, further with a good strop or honing wheel to get that keenest quality.

Diamond stones are long-lasting but *will* wear out. The average individual carver (as opposed to a class, say) should get many years of good service. Of course diamonds are the one kind that cannot be re-dressed, or refreshed, by lapping.

However, one good use for any diamond benchstone or plate is this very process of lapping: flattening another stone by rubbing it to and fro on the diamond surface. If this is all you want your diamond stone for, then a coarse stone is best; the finer ones will still do the job well, albeit slower.

Diamond stones are well over twice the cost of coarse oilstones and ceramic stones, but still a lot less than the translucent Arkansas.

The bumpy surface caused by the 'islands' in the benchstones does put some people off, and makes it very difficult to sharpen small gouges. In fact, my impression is that these stones are more suitable for carvers using large gouges, perhaps for sculpture and larger, less detailed work.

CERAMIC STONES

Ceramic stones are, in effect, made in high-tech volcanoes. Alumina particles (synthetic sapphires) are mixed with a ceramic bonding agent and vitrified in kilns under high pressure at around 1,650°C (2,672°F), the firing taking as long as three days. The result is a uniform, monolithic structure (Fig 13.9), differing from the majority of artificial stones in which sieved abrasive particles and their bonding material form a matrix that breaks down with use.

The ceramic grit particles cannot be broken away to reveal fresh, sharp cutting surfaces; they can only round over and lose cutting power with time. However, since ceramic stones are only slightly less hard than diamond (around 92% of diamond hardness), they wear very slowly: the harder ones are said not to wear noticeably in the course of a 'normal lifetime'. In this respect they represent the opposite of Japanese waterstones, where the friable bonding compound continually reveals new, sharp grit. They can only be resurfaced (lapped to freshen or flatten them) with a diamond stone.

TYPES OF CERAMIC STONE

Since they have no 'grit' as such, ceramic stones are not easy to compare with other stones, and the feel when you use them is markedly different. A major manufacturer of ceramic stones is Spyderco (USA), who offer three versions in colour-coded boxes:

- *Medium* grit (dark blue box) is roughly equivalent to an 800-grit stone, such as a Washita or soft white Arkansas stone.

- *Fine* ceramic stone (light blue box) is somewhere around 1200 grit, about the same as hard white Arkansas or the equivalent Japanese waterstone.

Fig 13.9 Ceramic benchstones and slipstones. The colour of the box indicates the grit

- *Ultra-fine* ceramic stone (black box) is around 10,000 grit, very slow-cutting and producing a mirror finish on the bevel.

Benchstones are of the standard 8 x 2in size (200 x 50mm), and the commonest type comes in its own protective plastic box with non-slip rubber feet.

CERAMIC SLIPSTONES

The number of available slipstones is limited, and these tend to be small in size, presumably because of the high manufacturing cost.

Because ceramic stones are so hard, it is virtually impossible to shape pieces into slipstones for a particular cannel. This means that it is likely you will have to mix and match with oil-based or other slipstones.

WHICH STONES TO USE

There is a very big jump in grit size from fine to ultra-fine, and the grade equivalent to the translucent Arkansas stone (around 4000 grit) is missing. The fine stone does not give what I consider to be the acceptable level of honing for a final cutting edge, for wood surfaces left straight from the chisel. The finest is too fine, removing so little metal that it is hardly a replacement for a strop, and this seems to me to be the best option: finish off with an aggressive strop paste or a hard honing wheel to polish.

So, the two most useful to carvers are the medium and fine stones, followed by further work with a strop and a good abrasive compound.

As slipstones are limited in their shape, obtain the few you can.

CARE AND MAINTENANCE

Ceramic stones are brittle. Use and keep the benchstones in their boxes; be careful not to drop or knock the slipstones.

Because ceramic stones are used dry – without oil or water to wash away debris – the surfaces become covered with a black dust. This is normal but, after some use, the surface of a ceramic benchstone tends to clog and glaze over. As you pass the bevel over the stone you feel small bumps and an irregular amount of friction. The remedy is quick:

1. Turn the stone over for the moment and finish your work on the clean side.

2. Scrub the stone with a scouring household cleaner or detergent and water, using a brush or a nylon scouring pad.

3. Rinse thoroughly in water.

4. Allow the stone to dry before re-using; drying is fast because the stone is non-porous.

You might also do this if the cutting surface becomes contaminated (slippery) with oil.

Otherwise, ceramic stones are so hard that they will not wear or dish like other stones. They will, however, eventually dull as the cutting particles round over and are not regenerated with the loss of bonding matrix. You notice one day that the stone is cutting less sharply, more slowly, and it needs freshening. This is a job for a diamond benchstone or lapping plate—nothing else is hard enough. Just rub the ceramic stone on the flat diamond stone for a few minutes to reveal a new abrasive surface, and test with a carving tool.

It can be difficult to keep your ceramic stones well away from sharpening oil, especially if you are mixing the use of ceramics with that of oilstones. Once oil contaminates the cutting surface, the steel tends to skid along it and the only remedy is washing as above.

USING CERAMIC STONES

All ceramic bench- and slipstones *must be used dry*. Apart from this difference, the use of ceramic stones is straightforward and follows the normal pattern (Figs 13.10 and 13.11). Since there are no pores between grit particles, liquid is not needed to flush away debris. Any moisture will act as a lubricant, inhibiting the friction needed to cut the steel.

This dust from the sharpening does have a tendency to move or get blown around. Do make a point of keeping your hands clean for the carving. *Never blow the dust away*; if you are not prepared to wash the

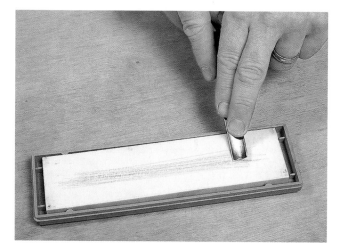

Fig 13.10 *Sharpening on the ceramic benchstone is done dry, but otherwise in the normal manner*

stone, wipe off the dust with a very slightly damp paper towel when it builds up. Glazing, where the tool skids and doesn't actually cut on the stone, *will* still happen; the stone must then be washed as described above.

Of the two, lubricating oil will create more of a problem than water and must be kept away entirely. This can be tricky if you are mixing conventional oil-based slipstones with ceramic benchstones; it is easy to transfer oil from your fingers or the blade. Do be scrupulous.

PROS AND CONS OF CERAMIC STONES

Ceramic stones lie at the space-age end of sharpening technology, and I do hope we see more developments, especially some filling-in of the big gap (1200–10,000) in the grit range.

Ceramic stones are very consistent and extremely hard-wearing; they are clean to use, and thus suitable for in-home, travelling, or similar situations where cleanliness is important. They are also quite a lot cheaper than Arkansas stones.

There is a particular 'feel' when the blade passes over the ceramic surface, and a user accustomed to benchstones with porous grit may find that this takes some getting used to.

Although hard-wearing, their cutting ability does fall off as the surface wears, a situation which is easily remedied but does need a (harder) diamond stone or lapping plate.

The manufacturer fixes the shape of ceramic stones; they cannot be ground to a different shape, so carvers are dependent on a limited range of slipstones. What is missing is a wider range for larger, broader tools. However, with strops to finish and oil slipstones for extra shapes, a carver can readily sharpen a lot of tools well within the range available.

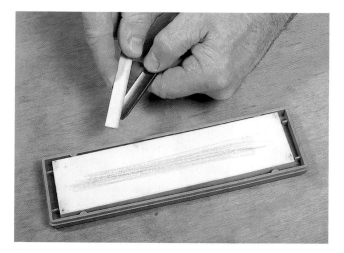

Fig 13.11 *Using a ceramic slipstone*

CHAPTER FOURTEEN

ELECTRICAL SHARPENING METHODS

AIMS

- To survey the available equipment for power sharpening

- To assess how this equipment can best be used to produce sharp, well-maintained tools

Electrical means of sharpening woodcarving tools are being pushed more and more in the direction of the carver, marketed with the promise of 'ultra-sharp' edges in the wink of an eye. When you power-sharpen, you are involved in a very different process from bench sharpening. Without any doubt, the finished product is achieved much more quickly, but – as I have pointed out many times in this book – *there is more to correctly sharpening a carving tool than simple speed and a sharp cutting edge.* Putting aside marketing claims, the fact is that power sharpening may suit some carvers, but not others. Sharpening machines perform some operations very well, but others not at all. In short, they have advantages and disadvantages.

To be clear about my view on electrical sharpening methods: there is nothing 'holy' about sharpening by hand; nothing intrinsically better in hand over electrical methods; nor anything 'wrong' about buying pre-sharpened tools. Who would willingly go back to converting timber by hand in a saw pit? The issue really is about what you want, and whether these machines enable you to achieve it.

I sharpen my tools on sharpening machines about 95% of the time. I am all for them; they have gained me many hours of carving time. However, I never encourage beginners to start with power sharpeners; I teach benchstone sharpening. 'Why?' you might ask, if I use sharpening machines myself so much? My experience is simply that this approach gives beginners the maximum understanding of what is needed in woodcarving tools, and the best level of skill in the long run. And teaching skill is what this book is about.

A careful beginning with bench- and slipstones will ensure that carving tools are sharpened correctly, and cut well and efficiently. Then, when you do eventually introduce electrical help, you will find it easy to maintain this professional level, and you will be able to deal with any carving tool that machines can't reach. My advice is always:

- Learn to sharpen all types of carving tools well by hand with bench- and slipstones.

- *Only then* introduce sharpening or honing wheels.

- Monitor your tools in the light of your previous understanding and alter your approach, or means of sharpening, to maintain your high standards.

The ceramic and diamond benchstones discussed in the previous chapter are only available in comparatively coarse grits, leaving an edge which is less than ideally sharp for work straight from the chisels. In this case a quick, precise polish on a hard honing wheel will soon bring the edge up to keenness, saving the time needed to strop by hand.

After an overview of sharpening machines and wheels, I will discuss approaches to using them so as to include or maintain the factors that I have proposed as making for an efficient, well-sharpened carving tool. With this knowledge, you can assess how useful such machines are and how they may suit your particular needs as a carver.

SHARPENING MACHINES

Effectively, electrical sharpening machines are exalted bench grinders, with wheels (or belts) in various combinations of hardness and abrasive power (Fig 14.1). In fact, they commonly *are* grinders, and may still have a grinding wheel at one end for shaping, as well as a finer 'buffing' or 'polishing' wheel at the other, which the user impregnates with a very fine abrasive. Other machines have buffing-type wheels at both ends.

We have covered the grinding wheel before (Chapter 10); it is used for preliminary shaping of the blade. A belt helps a lot in keeping a flat bevel, but the only ones which seem to be available are intended for the equivalent of grinding – that is, major metal removal – and are not suitable as honing aids.

Fig 14.1 *A typical electric sharpening machine with grinding belt; there are assorted buffing wheels and a take-off chuck on the right which can be used for other abrasive wheels or a flexible shaft*

As an alternative to a grinder-like honing machine, honing wheels and **mops** (polishing wheels made of fabric) are sold for mounting independently, either in a drill chuck or in the chuck of your own motor or lathe. Those made by Koch (Fig 14.2) would be a typical example: one wheel is a harder felt for straight edges and outside bevels, the other softer, to conform to interior curves.

When you buy separate wheels, do make sure they run true and at the optimum recommended speed. The Koch wheels, for example, have an optimum running speed of between 1,200 and 2,000rpm, slower than many sharpening machines and grinders. It is not clear what would result from a higher running speed, since the action of honing is always to compress the fibres, but you may find particles disengaging from the wheel and, at the least, its life expectancy (in terms of sharpening cycles) will be less. So, follow recommendations.

The 'buffing' or 'polishing' wheel will be of a fibrous material, such as felt or paper; there are varying degrees of hardness or softness. From now on I will call all such wheels **honing wheels** for the sake of simplicity, regardless of what they are made of, to differentiate them from the hard abrasive grinding (shaping) wheels.

Wheels are normally driven directly by the motor and rotate at a high speed, up to 3,000rpm. More sophisticated and expensive machines will have a belt drive from the motor to the wheels, and will usually feature an abrasive belt in place of one of the wheels.

Power sharpeners are quite simple to use:

❶ When the wheel is up to speed, push the block of proprietary abrasive 'soap' against the spinning surface (Fig 14.3); the block will melt into it (except in the case of a rubberized abrasive wheel).

❷ Apply the blade; a sludge of melted abrasive builds up in front of the edge.

❸ Move the blade as needed so the abrasive-impregnated wheel polishes the bevel and creates the fine cutting edge.

Now, if you know exactly what shape or profile of carving tool you want, and if there is a quick, accurate and safe electrical method of achieving it, then this is a sensible option and there is no question but that you should take advantage of it. Used in circumstances where this is possible, sharpening machines are invaluable to the busy carver. However, you must bear in mind that power machines are limited in what they can do. They may be able to achieve enough to satisfy a particular carver, but only a part of what another may want. And there is no doubt that in inexperienced hands they are capable of producing very undesirable results.

Fig 14.2 *The Koch sharpening wheel with its arbor ready for the chuck of a drill or other power source; the abrasive compound used with it is also shown*

Fig 14.3 *The buffing wheels must be dressed regularly with an abrasive compound, which is normally supplied by the makers*

SAFETY NOTE

Most importantly: all soft wheels must spin *away* from the user to prevent the cutting edge digging in and kicking back. This means that, if you make up your own power sharpener by using a grinder (you can buy buffing wheels separately), then you must either:

- Find a qualified electrician to reverse the direction of the motor. This is your best option; it is usually a simple job, but this may depend on how the motor is made.

  or:

- Turn the grinder itself around so the wheel rotates away from you, and switch or adjust the wheel guards and toolrests accordingly. The problem with this is that the on–off switch often ends up on the wrong side.

If you don't modify the machine in one of these ways, then, although *you* may remember in which direction to offer your carving tools, the machine is quite dangerous for anyone else who doesn't. The same principle applies if you are mounting a honing wheel in a power drill with an arbor.

PRINCIPLES OF POWER HONING

SPEED AND ITS HAZARDS

Most wheels are about 6in (150mm) in diameter and turn at around 3,000rpm. It follows that, in one second, nearly 80ft (about 24m) of surface have passed beneath the bevel as it is offered to the wheel. No wonder it abrades and polishes fast! Tools certainly get hand-hot on the honing wheels, if not actually hot enough to risk blueing.

The speed is a particular hazard for beginners who don't yet understand what shape is required of a particular tool. There is no doubt that the cutting edge can be polished to a high level of keenness in a very short time. However, the speed of honing wheels tends to make events happen quickly: over-shaping or plain bad shaping can easily result. At this speed it is all too easy to remove corners, or to end up with a cutting edge that is nosed, winged or undulating.

If you keep to a regime of maintaining sharpness, following the methods described in the previous chapters, little more than regular, brief touching up is necessary – any more and you are in danger of reshaping. The trick of 'sneaking up' on the edge by placing the heel of the tool on the wheel first, then slowly lifting the handle, will also help to avoid mistakes.

WHEEL SHAPE AND SIZE

Honing wheels are the same shape and size as a normal grinding wheel. If the wheel is hard, it will be too big – and the wrong shape – for creating a proper inside bevel in anything other than a large, flat gouge. On the other hand, if the wheel is soft, then you can push the inside of a gouge into it to 'de-burr' or polish the inside bevel; but this is not the same as creating a proper inner bevel, and you also run the risk of losing corners. The only satisfactory way to create inside bevels is to use smaller, specially shaped wheels, and to alter the profiles of larger ones to suit.

DIRECTION OF ROTATION

As I suggested before (see page 178 and Fig 12.1), it is my feeling that with the wheels turning *away* from the operator, the edge is weaker than one sharpened across or into it. This opinion is based entirely on my experience and not on any scientific trial.

When metal is drawn *forwards* it produces more of a wire edge; even though the effect is microscopic, metal is abraded forward by the buffing wheels. The resulting edge tends to crumble and leave fine scratch trails in the cut. Metal drawn *back*, *across* or *away from* the cutting edge to sharpen it leaves a tougher, smoother structure. This has greater resistance and lasts longer.

So it seems to me that tools sharpened on abrasive wheels need touching up far more often than hand-sharpened ones to keep the same quality of cut. Against this must be set the speed at which edges can be rejuvenated.

Additionally, because the honing wheel moves away from the user to prevent digging in, I counter this effect by offering the tool mostly, if not fully, across the wheel, as described below.

HARD AND SOFT WHEELS

The softer the wheel, the more difficult it is to produce a flat bevel. That's why it is better to produce and polish the bevel on hard wheels, and use soft ones only for polishing the inner bevel to a finished edge. At a honing speed of 80ft (24m) per second across the bevel, it is as if the tool has been rapidly stropped many thousands of times. The effect of prolonged stropping on a soft surface – even a leather benchstrop – is to round or roll the bevel, as we have already seen (page 208); and soft wheels are much softer than hard leather benchstrops. A rounded bevel means a higher cutting angle, which in turn means less control and more effort.

You really have to work against this effect. The firm, curved surface of a hard honing wheel counters the problem to some extent, compared with the more flexible surface of a flat benchstrop; and the harder the wheel, the less this effect will occur. The two hardest honing wheels are those made of dense paper (such as supplied by Rod Naylor), and rubber abrasive wheels (as made by Cratex). These mostly eliminate the problem.

TYPES OF HONING WHEEL

There are three main types of wheel used in sharpening machines, and there should be little problem in swapping or changing to the alternatives you prefer. Being soft, all these wheels must rotate *away* from the user. Some shaping of these materials is possible, allowing them to be adapted for inside bevels and for small tools, for example.

FELT WHEELS

These are synthetically stiffened, and vary in firmness and hardness. Choose the hardest, and one that will keep a smooth surface without 'fluffing'. These wheels can be shaped to some extent. Use with abrasive soap. Soft, loose-leaf, sisal and cotton mops are not suitable.

Fig 14.4 *Shaping an inside bevel on a Cratex rubberized abrasive wheel. Note the dust-extraction hood*

RUBBERIZED ABRASIVE WHEELS
Made by Cratex in the USA from a hard chemical rubber impregnated with silicon carbide particles, these come in different sizes, up to grinding-wheel size. Various grades are available, of which the fine or extra-fine are suitable for us. Rubberized abrasive wheels can be shaped to suit the hollow forms of internal bevels – in fact creating inner bevels quickly is a major benefit (Fig 14.4). Smaller sizes are available on their own to be mounted on a motor shaft or a driven spindle. I always advise dust protection when using these wheels.

I use this wheel as an intermediary between the fine grinding wheel and the abrasive-coated honing wheel. It is too coarse to give the fine edge you need, but will readily flatten a bevel offered side-on to the direction of rotation. It is not used with abrasive paste.

PAPER WHEELS
Rod Naylor supplies these for use in his Supersharp system, or separately for use with an arbor. They are used with abrasive 'soap'.

These wheels are made by compressing paper, and have a different feel from felt wheels. The paper gives excellent results: a very hard wheel which takes abrasive well, and on which precise honing and polishing is possible. Paper wheels can be shaped, but seem to be available only in limited sizes, suitable for use on a grinder.

Fig 14.5 A collection of proprietary and other sharpening 'soaps'; there are many different kinds to be had

ABRASIVE 'SOAP' BLOCKS

The appropriate abrasive, for these sharpening machines is a fine one suitable for ferrous metals, and comes in a hard block or bar often called 'soap'. The bar melts into the felt or paper from the friction arising when it is pushed against the spinning surface of the wheel.

There are so many different types of abrasive soaps, in many wonderful colours and with so many different claims, that it is impossible to list them all (Fig 14.5). Suffice it to say that suitable abrasives are readily available and, since they are inexpensive, it is worth experimenting and exchanging notes with fellow carvers. Some are coarser – have a more aggressive cut – than others.

OTHER CONSIDERATIONS

Before making or buying a honing machine, bear in mind the following points:

NOISE

Try to hear the machine you are thinking of buying. Many carvers enjoy the quiet of carving, as well as that of hand-sharpening their tools. Sharpening can be a moment for reflection before returning to the carving with increased vigour. Depending on the make and the location, sharpening machines *can* be quite noisy; this may be intrusive for carvers with a temperament that prefers quiet.

COST

Whether a machine is worth buying depends on the balance between the outlay and the amount of use you expect from it. For example, such machines would probably be of more benefit to a wood sculptor with large gouges than an instrument maker with a few small ones.

SAFETY

Do assess safety factors carefully. All sorts of particles are flung out from these fast-turning wheels: bits of felt, abrasive paste – even grit, in the case of a rubberized abrasive wheel. Suppose you spend only 5 minutes a day on these machines, that's still just a little short of standing for 24 hours in front of the fast-spinning wheel over the course of a year – plenty of chance for a particle to get in your eye, or for you to breathe in damaging dust.

I strongly suggest keeping at least a good paper dust mask next to the machine. Get into the habit of slipping it over your nose and mouth even as you switch the power sharpener on.

Fig 14.6 In this machine there is no means of supporting the tool on the flat section of the belt, which means that the blade has to be held in the air. Besides limiting the control over shaping, hovering the hand like this over the fast-moving belt is potentially hazardous

Some machines have limited wheel guards and no toolrests; the tool is supported by the hand hovering in the air (Fig 14.6). This applies especially to those 'systems' that are sold with an arbor to mount on a free motor. Take the time to make some simple wooden toolrests at least.

Long hair, loose clothing and such must be kept well out of the way, particularly if you are using a drill-mounted wheel without guards.

I have already mentioned the importance of wheel direction if you choose to make your own machine.

HOW TO USE A POWER SHARPENER

Most machines have only two wheels, one at either end. I find I need several, in a range of widths and profiles, and including smaller wheels on chucks, to cover the wide range of tools that I use. Even so, there are some tools that are difficult to power-sharpen correctly: in particular small or tight-mouthed ones, and those with sharp bends.

Try to make your set-up cover as wide a range of tool sweeps as possible. Remember that you may need more than just the two wheels on offer. At all times

bear in mind the end result which you are after: the correctly shaped cutting edge.

Obviously individual arrangements will vary, but here are some considerations:

- Have the grinder as a separate machine from the sharpener. Grinding is major metal removal; use the sharpener only for the last stages of sharpening. If you find you have a lot of metal to remove, then you should be on a grinder with coarse and fine wheels.

- Sharpening machines tend to be dirty. Site them away from your carving area; wipe the carving tool afterwards; and check your hands for grime that can be transferred to the wood.

- Have one wheel as hard as possible (paper) for outer bevels.

- Have the second wheel slightly softer, so it can deform for inner bevels and/or be split with a knife blade to give several width options (Fig 14.7).

- A chuck on the end of the sharpener shaft will allow you to use a variety of small wheels for different purposes.

You can use a machine for just polishing (stropping) a bench-sharpened tool, using a light, minimal touch; or for heavier sharpening, equivalent to what you might do on the bench.

Fig 14.7 With a split wheel it is possible to hone the inside of a gouge without damaging the corners

ACHIEVING THE CORRECT SHAPE

Recall some ideas from previous chapters: there are three factors to consider when discussing whether a carving tool cuts properly or not. It is not just a matter of a slick cutting edge: a tool can be very sharp yet still cut badly. All these factors are important:

The *bevel* must be:

- flat

- at the correct cutting angle.

An *inner bevel* is useful for:

- using the gouge upside down

- increasing the overall bevel angle

- helping to release the shaving.

The actual *cutting edge* must be:

- keen

- with corners

- straight across

- at 90° to the axis of the blade.

Unless you have sound reasons otherwise, this is what I propose as your model for a correctly sharpened tool; and I mean this to be the result of *whatever* method you choose to sharpen them. So, bearing these points in mind, let us turn to power honing wheels to see how the operation of an electric sharpener can contribute to or detract from these qualities.

KEEPING THE OUTER BEVEL FLAT AND AT THE CORRECT ANGLE

- The hard (fine) grinder or the benchstone is best to get your flat bevel to start with – this is part of the primary shaping – and you should come to the power sharpener with a flat bevel at the correct cutting angle. A rubberized abrasive wheel is a good intermediary between the fine grinding wheel and the abrasive-coated honing wheel.

Fig 14.8 *Present the heel first, then lift the handle far enough to arrive at the edge, and no further*

- Keep exactly the same angle of presentation on the honing wheel, using the toolrest (or, as I prefer, supporting the tool with a finger placed on the toolrest).

- Keeping a correctly shaped bevel is a really important point: don't just think 'sharp edge'. Start by placing the heel on the rotating wheel, and then slowly lift the handle until the sludge of the polishing compound shows you that you are at the edge (Fig 14.8). In other words, work from the bevel forwards.

- To repeat: the harder the wheel, the easier it is to keep the bevel flat.

- The best approach I have found is to offer the bevel almost side-on to the direction of rotation, first to a rubberized abrasive wheel (Fig 14.9) and then, to finish, the very hard paper one. You can present the bevel at up to 90° to the wheel (but no more, or you risk a dig-in), as for grinding (see page 179).

- Don't press too hard; this will sink the metal into the softer wheels.

MAINTAINING CORNERS

Losing a corner, or waving the edge, is a very simple thing to do on what is, effectively, a power strop. The user either over-rotates the tool, or concentrates on the centre of the blade.

Fig 14.9 *Presenting the bevel* across *the wheel is another option, and helps to keep the bevel flat*

- Use the minimum amount of 'soap'. It is not always easy to keep an eye on the corners, particularly if large amounts of sludge-building abrasive obscure the edge. It is not obligatory to prime the wheel each time you use it – perhaps once every three times is all that is required.

- Again, the harder the wheel, the easier it is to see the work.

- Be precise in your work.

- Pressure builds friction, which increases abrasion speed: take it lightly. If you need a lot of sharpening, then perhaps you should be using the grinder, or at least a hard rubber abrasive wheel.

- A good way to lose the corners of a gouge is to push the sweep – and thus the corners – into a soft wheel while attempting to polish the inside bevel.

INSIDE BEVELS

Only if the hard honing wheel is the same radius as the sweep of the gouge, or smaller, can you get into the cannel for shaping or stropping the inside bevel. What many users of power sharpeners do instead is to push the mouth (cannel) of the gouge into a softer wheel, which deforms to fit. This can be fine for the larger gouges, but with smaller ones there is a danger of losing the tool corners, which you must try to protect. So, for normal, grinder-sized wheels, some changes are needed:

- Rubberized abrasive wheels, paper and hard felt wheels can all be shaped with files or scrapers. Do protect yourself from the dust when you do this.

- You may choose to split a wheel, using a strong knife, to give you several options for smaller tools or, say, the apex of the V-tool.

- On a large wheel you can radius one corner and create a hollow in the middle, giving you quite a few options.

- Small wheels can be mounted in a chuck, which is either part of your power sharpener (see Fig 14.4), or in a separate unit such as a power drill.

SUMMARY

- Sharpening is part of the whole carving package, but it need not be a big deal, with benchstones or otherwise.

- Newcomers buying power-sharpening machines can quickly and easily produce badly or inappropriately sharpened carving tools, in which case they are really not doing themselves much of a favour.

- The fact is that beginners usually, and understandably, have no way of knowing what a 'correct', or even satisfactorily sharp, woodcarving tool should look and feel like. I believe this is best learned in a slower, more careful way first; this is priceless, but basic, knowledge and skill on which a woodcarver can build.

- So, having acquired a foundation of quite subtle knowledge, largely lodged in the hands, bring in sharpening machines where you can to speed up the process. More machines and different designs are becoming available. Incorporate them into a well-founded sharpening strategy that always has in mind the correct shape and cutting qualities of your carving tools.

PHOTOGRAPHIC CREDITS

Photographs in this book are by Chris Skarbon, © GMC Publications Ltd, with the following exceptions:

Chris Pye: pages 1 and 3; Figs 1.1, 1.3, 1.5, 1.6, 2.9, 3.2, 3.28, 3. 29, 3.30, 5.1, 5.2, 5.3, 8.3, 8.8, 9.35, 13.3, 13.5, 13.7, 13.8, 14.4, 14.5, 14.7, 14.8, 14.9

Tony Masero: page v

Ashley Iles (Edge Tools) Ltd: Figs 2.3 and 2.4

GMC Publications/Anthony Bailey: Fig 10.2

Craft Supplies Ltd: Fig 10.3

The author and publishers wish to thank the above individuals and companies for their kind assistance.

METRIC CONVERSION TABLE

INCHES TO MILLIMETRES					
inches	mm	inches	mm	inches	mm
⅛	3	9	229	30	762
¼	6	10	254	31	787
⅜	10	11	279	32	813
½	13	12	305	33	838
⅝	16	13	330	34	864
¾	19	14	356	35	889
⅞	22	15	381	36	914
1	25	16	406	37	940
1¼	32	17	432	38	965
1½	38	18	457	39	991
1¾	44	19	483	40	1016
2	51	20	508	41	1041
2½	64	21	533	42	1067
3	76	22	559	43	1092
3½	89	23	584	44	1118
4	102	24	610	45	1143
4½	114	25	635	46	1168
5	127	26	660	47	1194
6	152	27	686	48	1219
7	178	28	711	49	1245
8	203	29	737	50	1270

ABOUT THE AUTHOR

Chris Pye has been carving professionally for over 25 years, and owes his formative start to the master carver Gino Masero. His work is done mainly to commission, with clients including HRH the Prince of Wales, and ranges from architectural mouldings to figure carving, furniture to lettering, bedheads to fireplaces. Individual pieces include his own expressionist carving and abstract sculpture.

He has taught local and residential woodcarving classes in England for many years, and is also a member of the faculty at the Center for Furniture Craftsmanship (http://www.woodschool.org) in Maine, USA, where he runs carving courses each year.

He is the author of *Woodcarving Tools, Materials & Equipment* (1994), of which the present book is a revised edition; *Carving on Turning* (1995); *Lettercarving in Wood: A Practical Course* (1997); *Relief Carving in Wood: A Practical Introduction* (1998); and *Elements of Woodcarving* (2000). All of these are published by GMC Publications. He has also written extensively about woodcarving for several magazines.

Chris Pye has written and runs a website (http://www.chrispye-woodcarving.com) dedicated to the teaching, learning and love of woodcarving, from which he edits the interactive journal *Slipstones*.

He lives in rural Herefordshire with his wife Karin Vogel, a psychotherapist, and son Finian. His older son Daniel has a degree in art and plays guitar in the rock band Manchild. When not carving, teaching or writing, Chris Pye's other interests include painting, biking and tae kwon do. A Buddhist for many years, he was ordained into the Western Buddhist Order in 1990. This approach to being deeply affects his outlook and attitudes to life and work.

Chris Pye
The Poplars
Ewyas Harold
Hereford HR2 0HU

Email: chrispye@woodcarver.f9.co.uk

INDEX